STRUCTURAL REFORMS AND AGRICULTURE

STRUCTURAL REFORMS AND AGRICULTURE

Edited by .

ANIL KUMAR THAKUR

and

MITHILESH KUMAR SINHA

Published on behalf of
THE INDIAN ECONOMIC ASSOCIATION

DEEP & DEEP PUBLICATIONS PVT. LTD.
F-159, RAJOURI GARDEN, NEW DELHI-110027

STRUCTURAL REFORMS AND AGRICULTURE

ISBN 978-81-8450-358-6

Typeset by S.S. COMPOSERS
3190, Mohindra Park, Shakur Basti, Delhi-110034.

Printed in India at MAYUR ENTERPRISES
WZ Plot No. 3, Gujjar Market, Tihar Village, New Delhi-110018.

Published by DEEP & DEEP PUBLICATIONS PVT. LTD.
F-159, Rajouri Garden, New Delhi-110027.
Phones: 25435369, 25440916
E-mail: ddpbooks@yahoo.co.in • ddpubs@gmail.com
Showroom:
2/13, Ansari Road, Daryaganj, New Delhi-110002 • Telefax: 23245122

Contents

PART III

STRUCTURAL REFORMS, LIVESTOCK AND AGRICULTURE IN INDIA

Preface

Agriculture is the backbone of our country and economy. It accounts for nearly one-fourth of India's GDP and more importantly about two-third of the country's population is dependent on agriculture and allied activities for their livelihood. Indian agriculture depends on monsoon and as a result there have been fluctuations in food production over the years. The average size of cultivable landholding is only 1.84 ha and it constitutes nearly 74.5% of total holdings in the country posing a great challenge in enhancing productivity, production with sustainability. Indian agriculture will need to produce 265 million tonnes of foodgrains (as against the present production of 214 million tonnes) to feed an estimated population of 1.4 billion in 2025 A.D.

India today is not only self-sufficient in grain production but also has substantial reserves. Dependence of India on agricultural imports and the crises of food shortage encountered in 1960s convince planners that India's growing population, as well as concerns about national independence, security and political stability, required self-sufficiency in food production. This perception led to a programme of agricultural improvement called the Green Revolution. It involved bringing additional area under cultivation, extension of irrigation facilities, the use of improved high-yielding variety of seeds, better techniques evolved through agricultural research, water management, and plant protection through judicious use of fertilizers, pesticides and cropping practices. All these measures had a salutary effect and the production of wheat and rice witnessed quantum leap.

But during reform era agricultural sector witnessed stagnant trend in food production. Instead of benefiting the farmers, the process of economic liberalization and globalization is compounding their apprehensions and insecurity. Rural unemployment is increasing making the rural youth desperate. So, there is an urgent need for second Green Revolution in Indian agriculture and taking it to a higher trajectory of 4 per cent annual growth.

With the objective of bringing and discussing various issues of agricultural sector of India so far, the Indian Economic Association declared, "Structural Reforms and Agriculture" as one of the themes for deliberations during its 92nd Annual Conference, held at School of Management, KIIT University, Bhubaneswar, Orissa under the presidentship of Prof. C.H. Hanumantha Rao during December 27-29, 2009. Out of several scholarly papers submitted and presented on this theme during the conference 18 papers have been selected for inclusion in this book. There is an introduction added for the convenience of the readers, which outlines main issues, and the central tenet of the book along with a brief summary of each paper.

The editors would like to place on record their thanks and gratitude to Indian Economic Association as well as Conference President Prof. C.H. Hanumantha Rao for providing this excellent opportunity. Each one of the contributors of this book deserves appreciation for their brilliant piece of work and the editors would like to thank each one of them. Editors alone would be responsible for any mistake that has remained in the book.

ANIL KUMAR THAKUR
MITHILESH KUMAR SINHA

List of Contributors

Ajay Singh, Assistant Professor, Department of Business and Management Studies, Meerut Institute of Engineeering and Technology, Meerut.

Bipul Malakar, Professor, Department of Economics, Jadavpur University, Kolkata.

Ejaz Anwer, Research Fellow, Department of Economics, A.M.U., Aligarh

Fakhre Alam, Research Fellow, Department of Economics, A.M.U., Aligarh.

Indu Upadhyay, Lecturer, Department of Economics, Vasant Kanya Mahavidyalaya, B.H.U., Varanasi.

K. Elumalai, Associate Professor, Institute for Social and Economic Change (ISEC), Nagarabhavi, Bangalore.

Kiran Singh, Sr. Lecturer, Department of Economics, University of Allahabad, Allahabad.

Lopamudra Mishra, P.G. Department of Economics, Sambalpur University, Jyoti Vihar, Sambalpur, Orissa.

M.A. Salam, Reader, Department of Economics, AMU, Aligarh.

Md. Imdadul Haque, Assistant Professor, King Saud University, Kingdom of Saudi Arabia.

Md. Izhar Ahmad, Professor, Department of Economics, AMU, Aligarh.

Md. Shabbir Alam, Research Scholars, Department of Economics, AMU, Aligarh.

Mohd. Sharif, Research Scholars, Department of Economics, AMU, Aligarh

P. Narasimha Rao, Professor of Economics, Acharya Nagarjuna University, Guntur, A.P.

P.S. Tripathi, Department of Economics, DBS College, Kanpur.

Poonam Singh, ICSSR Doctoral Fellow, GIDS, Lucknow and Sr. Lecturer, SRS Girls PG College, Bareilly.

Rais Ahmad, Research Fellow, Department of Economics, A.M.U., Aligarh.

Rajender Kumar, Professor, Department of Humanities and Social Sciences, National Institute of Technology, Kurukshetra.

Rajesh Nigam, Department of Economics, DBS College, Kanpur.

Ravi Ranjan, Lecturer, Department of L.S.W. Allama Iqball College, Bihar Sharif, NALANDA.

Roli Mishra, Department of Economics, DBS College, Kanpur.

S. Erappa, Associate Professor, Agricultural Development and Rural Transformation (ADRT) Centre, Institute for Social and Economic Change, Nagarabhavi-PO, Bangalore.

S. Mahendra Dev, Chairman, CACP, New Delhi.

S.M. Jawed Akhtar, Reader, Department of Economics, AMU, Aligarh

S.S. Kalamkar, Gokhale Institute of Politics and Economics (Deemed University) Pune, Maharashtra.

Sanatan Nayak, Reader, Department of Economics, B.B. Ambedkar Central University, Lucknow.

Sanjeev Kumar, Assistant Professor, Dyal Singh College, Delhi University, Lodhi Road, New Delhi.

Sudip Jana, Ph.D. Scholar, Department of Economics, Jadavpur University, Kolkata.

Tariq Masood, Research Scholor, Department of Economics, AMU, Aligarh.

Tushar Kanti Das, Department of Business Administration, Sambalpur University, Jyoti Vihar, Sambalpur, Orissa.

Introduction

Agriculture is the mainstay of 52 per cent of India's population and the performance of agricultural sector influences the growth of the Indian economy. Agriculture (including allied activities like fishing and forestry) accounted for 17.8 per cent of the country's Gross Domestic Product (GDP) in 2007-08 as compared to 21.7 per cent in 2003-04.

Notwithstanding the fact that the contribution of this sector in GDP has been declining over the years, its role remains critical as it accounts for about 52 per cent of the employment in the country. The prosperity of the rural economy is also closely linked to agriculture and allied activities. Agricultural sector contributed 12.2 per cent of national exports in 2007-08. The rural sector (including agriculture) is being increasingly seen as a potential source of domestic demand and this recognition is shaping the marketing strategies of entrepreneurs in sectors like FMCG, two-wheelers, steel and cement. With an average growth of over 4.9 per cent over three years (2005-08) the agriculture sector lent credible support to the overall growth in GDP. Gross capital formation in agriculture as a proportion to the total GDP, however, has shown a decline from 2.9 per cent in 2001-02 to 2.5 per cent in 2007-08.

The post-Independence history of Indian agriculture can be broadly grouped into four periods. During the colonial era famines were frequent and famine commissions were abundant. The growth rate in food production during the 1940-47 periods was hardly 0.1 per cent. Most of the important institutional developments in agriculture emanated from the recommendations of famine commissions. The great Bengal Famine of 1942-43 proved the backdrop to India's Independence. It is to the credit of Independent India that famines of this kind have not been allowed to occur, although our population has grown from 350 million in 1947 to 1,100 million now.

Phase I: 1947-64

In this phase, the major emphasis was on the development of infrastructure for scientific agriculture. The steps taken included the establishment of fertilizer and pesticide factories, construction of large multi-purpose irrigation-*cum*-power projects, organization of community development and national extension programmes and, above all, the starting of agricultural universities, beginning with the Pant Nagar University established in 1958, as well as new agricultural research institutions, as for example the Central Rice Research Institute, Cuttack, and the Central Potato Research Institute, Shimla.

During this period, the population started increasing by over 3 per cent a year as a result of both the steps taken to strengthen public health care systems and advances in preventive and curative medicine.

The growth in food production was inadequate to meet the consumption needs of the growing population, and food imports became essential. Such food imports, largely under the PL-480 programme of the United States, touched a peak of 10 million tonnes in 1966.

Phase II: 1965-85

The emphasis was on maximizing the benefits of infrastructure created during Phase I, particularly in the areas of irrigation and technology transfer. Major gaps in the strategies adopted during Phase I were filled, as for example the introduction of semi-dwarf high-yielding varieties of wheat and rice, which could utilize sunlight, water, and nutrients more efficiently and yield two to three times more than the strains included in the Intensive Agriculture District Programme (IADP) of the early 1960s. This period also saw the reorganization and strengthening of agricultural research, education and extension, and the creation of institutions to provide farmers assured marketing opportunities and remunerative prices for their produce. The National Bank for Agriculture and Rural Development (NABARD) was set-up. All these steps led to a quantum jump in the productivity and production of crops such as wheat and rice, a phenomenon christened in 1968 as the Green Revolution. C. Subramaniam (1964-67) and Jagjivan Ram provided the necessary public policy guidance and support.

The Green Revolution generated a mood of self-confidence in our agricultural capability. The gains were consolidated during the Sixth Five Year Plan period (1980-85) when for the first time agricultural growth rate exceeded the general economic growth rate. Also, the growth rate in food production exceeded that of the population. The Sixth Plan achievement illustrates the benefits arising from farmer-centred priorities in investment and in the overall agricultural production strategy.

Phase III: 1985-2000

This phase was characterized by greater emphasis on the production of pulses and oilseeds as well as of vegetables, fruits, and milk. Rajiv Gandhi introduced organizational innovations like Technology Missions, which resulted in a rapid rise in oilseeds production. The Mission approach involves concurrent attention to conservation, cultivation, consumption, and commerce. Rain-fed areas and wastelands received greater attention and a Wasteland Development Board was set-up. Wherever an end-to-end approach was introduced involving attention to all links in the production-consumption chain, progress was steady and sometimes striking as in the case of milk and egg production. This period ended with large grain reserves with the government, with the media highlighting the coexistence of "Grain Mountains and hungry millions." This period also saw a gradual decline in public investment in irrigation and infrastructure essential for agricultural progress as well as a gradual collapse of cooperative credit system.

Phase IV: 2001 to the Present Day

This phase is best described as one characterized by policy fatigue, resulting in technology extension and production fatigues. No wonder that the farmers, who keep others alive, are now forced to take their own lives and 40 per cent of them want to quit farming, if there is an alternative option.

The agricultural decline is taking place at a time when international prices of major foodgrains are going up steeply, partly owing to the use of grain for ethanol production. Land for food *verses* fuel is becoming a major issue. For example, the export price of wheat has raised from $197 a tonne in 2005 to $263 a tone in 2007. Maize price has gone up from about $100 a tone in 2005 to $166 a tonne now. International trade is also becoming free but not fair. Compounding these problems is the possibility of adverse changes in rainfall, temperature, and the sea level as a result of global warming. Melting of Himalyan ice and glaciers will result in floods of unprecedented dimensions in north India. If agricultural production does not remain above the population growth rate and if the public distribution system is starved of grain, there is every likelihood of our going back to the pre-Independence situation of recurrent famines. The grain mountains have disappeared and we are today in the era of diminishing grain reserves, escalating prices, and persistence of widespread under-nutrition.

Agrarian reform that alters class relations in favour of the working people, frees demand constraints, opens up home markets in the countryside, and provides a basis for broad-based productive investment has been jettisoned by official policy. Legislation is being considered (and in some cases has been passed) that would raise ceilings to levels that undermine the objectives of land ceiling laws and make absentee farming by large owners and corporations a certainty. Such policies would thus reduce the extent of land for redistribution, accelerate the loss of land by poor peasants and worsen inequalities in the distribution of land.

Public investment in agriculture and rural infrastructure (and particularly irrigation and roads) has slowed down significantly, as has rural development expenditure. Economists are familiar with the concept of complementarities between public and private expenditure; when the state withdraws from investment in public works, infrastructure and programmes of mass employment; it robs the countryside of the foundations for growth and poverty-alleviation.

With respect to rural credit, the policy of social and development banking has been abandoned, the rural banking system undermined, and the distribution of credit shifted further in favour of large landholders. Village-level data show that the exploitation of the poor in the informal credit market—by usurers, mainly—has intensified as a result of financial liberalization.

The rise in production costs and fall in output prices, the new trade regime (and, in particular, the removal of quantitative restrictions on the import of agricultural products), and the emphasis on export-oriented production all serve to intensify the struggle of large sections of the peasantry for their very survival. The new policy also has very serious implications for land-use, cropping patterns, and the future of self-sufficiency in food.

Employment growth in agriculture collapsed in the 1990s. Unless the collapse in public investment is made good, and planning for farm and non-farm employment made a reality, the prospects for substantial gains with respect to employment are bleak (although the National Rural Employment Guarantee Act, whose enactment was spearheaded by the Left, is an important means of bringing some temporary relief to unemployed rural families).

Another aspect of fiscal contraction is the reduction of food subsidies and the exclusion of a large majority of nutritionally deprived and vulnerable people from access to subsidized food.

The new trade and patent regime leaves the field of agricultural research open for multinational corporations, weakening public-sector national agricultural research systems as well as open-access international research institutions. Further, this regime infringes on the rights of farmers and indigenous plant breeders and threatens to lead, in the words of India's leading agricultural scientist, "from biodiversity to genetic slavery."

It can undoubtedly be said that there is hard evidence to indicate that the initial gains of the Green Revolution are now petering out. Foodgrain production is slackening. Its rate of growth is much slower than that of population. Pulses and edible oils have been regularly imported, while wheat and sugar too are at times sourced from abroad. So, even the self-sufficiency in food production seems to be in jeopardy. Natural resource-base of agriculture is crumbling. Use of land for urbanization and industrialization is constricting the availability of cultivable land, which was 0.36 hectare per capita at the time of Independence, but has come down to around 0.12 currently, and is likely to shrink to 0.09 by 2025. Soils are experiencing serious fatigue. Yields have started showing declining trends in terms of input-output response, as several soil nutrients and organic matters have depleted drastically. Area under irrigation, instead of expanding, is contracting.

Approximately, 60% of our agriculture still remains rain-dependent. Groundwater is depleting at an alarming rate. The frequency and severity of natural disasters is increasing on account of climatic changes. Costs of cultivation have been rising at a faster pace than the prices of agricultural produce. The law of diminishing returns has already set in squeezing farmers' profits progressively. Fragmentation of landholdings has rendered about 80% of them as economically unviable. Mono-cropping patterns are causing severe imbalances in the soils and endangering biodiversity.

India although has become the world's largest milk producer, the livestock economy is in distress. The process of economic liberalization and globalization, instead of benefiting the farmers, is compounding their apprehensions and insecurity. Rural unemployment is increasing making the rural youth desperate.

The situation obviously calls for inventing a new approach and strategy. The broad contours of such a strategy could be the following:

First of all, investment in agriculture, which sustains 62% of India's population, has remained stuck up at round 1.3% of GDP since the Fifth Five Year Plan. Irrigation though the most critical input for agriculture is the most neglected sector. We should immediately formulate a Ten Year Water Plan to harness the total irrigational potential through major, medium and minor modes which includes rain water harvesting and water shed management. The investment required for this is estimated to be around Rs. 400,000 crores. States alone, however, are not in a position to mobilize such resources. The central government should share it equally with them. Secondly, there has to be a land-use policy strictly prohibiting conversion of fertile land for non-agricultural purposes, except in rare cases. Thirdly, thoroughly researched models of integrated nutrient and pest management based on use of organic matters and biological controls have to be promoted throughout the country. Fourthly, a comprehensive livestock and biodiversity policy aiming at conservation and improvement of native breeds and varieties through selective breeding must be put in place and form part of the integrated farming systems. Fifthly, the price policy, which has so far been favouring only a few crops such as wheat, rice, sugarcane and cotton, and neglected the coarse grains, that are more nutritious and can be grown with lesser water, needs to be redesigned to make their cultivation equally profitable, if not more. Terms of trade for agriculture too warrant a correction. Sixthly, all restrictions on trading, stocking, financing, movement and processing of agricultural products must be removed forthwith to make India as one integrated market. Seventhly, the numbers dependent on agriculture have to be reduced by creating alternative job opportunities in rural areas and establishing facilities for technical and vocational education for enhancing skills and employability of rural youth. And lastly, the multiplicity of Indian agriculture must be protected at all costs. We must be self-sufficient in almost every item. Food security has to be an integral component of national security. Use of food as a weapon in international politics is not an unknown phenomenon. Our own experience tells that whenever we have deficit, prices in international markets go up. On the international trade front, we must remain firm that unless the rich countries remove subsidies of all types to their agriculture, we shall continue to insulate our farmers against unfair foreign competition.

Present volume brings together various issues of agriculture sector both at macro and micro-levels. Problems of Indian agriculture sector have been discussed on theoretical plan which indicates both the potentiality and problems of Indian economic growth in contemporary phase of planning. Scholars assessed the potentiality of the agriculture sector and its challenges to cope with certain problems of Indian agriculture for achieving sustainability in agriculture. The volume is divided in three parts.

However the fall out of growth rate in agriculture raised some important issues for consideration. Impact of structural reforms on the agriculture is not heartening. It is ironical that Indian economic growth, basically neglected agriculture. The manufacture and service sector-led growth has not only produced imbalance and inflation in the economy, this has also brought misery to the farmers. With low productivity, low price of farm products and growing burden of debt, farmers in several states (even in Green Revolution belt) are committing suicides.

In order to achieving 4% growth in agriculture and raise incomes by increasing productivity (land, labour), diversification to high value agriculture and rural farm by maintaining food security; sharing growth (equity) by focusing on small and marginal farmers, lagging regions, women, etc.; maintaining sustainability of agriculture by focusing on environmental concerns various factors are needed focused reforms in the short- and medium-terms. **S. Mahendra Dev** points out that there are basically seven factors—price policy, subsidies and investments, land issues, irrigation and water management, research and extension, credit, domestic market reforms and diversification—which need focused reforms in the short- and medium-terms. He suggests that reforms will have to reduce six agricultural deficits relating to investment, credit and infrastructure; land and water management; research and extension (technology); market; diversification; institutions in order to achieve the goals of agriculture. **Fakhre Alam** and *et. al.* analyses the agricultural growth and different factors which affect the growth of Indian agriculture. Finding out the constraints to sustainable growth of agriculture in India **Tushar Kanti Das** and **Lopamudra Mishra** suggest that institutional innovations can be major sources of productivity growth. Focusing on agricultural deceleration and factor responsible for it in Uttar Pradesh **Sanatan Nayak** highlights the status of ecological, technological, economic and institutional factors determining the agricultural growth *vis-à-vis* overall development of the regions of the state. Emphasizing the urgent necessity of implementing effective measures to counter structural changes in agriculture **Kiran Singh** and **Ajay Singh** address that the biotech interventions can help break the shackles of a trend line agriculture growth of 1.5 to 2% in the last decade and with inherent advantages in biotechnology, energy input-output ratio and labour costs, Indian agriculture has tremendous potential that can be unlocked through new opportunities thrown up by the current global food crisis which is again shifting the terms of trade in favour of agriculture. Dealing with the analysis of trends in investment in Indian agriculture with specific emphasis on the period of economic reforms **Poonam Singh** points out that deceleration in public investment both at national and state level has been taking place over the period of economic reform, agricultural growth rates slowed down significantly.

Estimating the trends in capital formation, private and public and its composition in agriculture and the determinants of capital formation **P. Narasimha Rao** finds out that the rate of return on private investment which in turn depends upon terms of trade is found to be the most important determinant of private capital formation. The public sector investments mainly depend upon fiscal resources. The increase in farm subsidies and decrease in revenue receipts from agriculture caused an adverse impact on public sector capital formation.

Making an inventory of firms involved in promoting gherkin crop under contract farming in Karnataka, the structure of agreement between the primary producer and the firm, the type of crop promotion under contract farming, and assessing the impact on income and employment generation for contract farmers **S. Erappa** concludes that under contract farming income of farmers have witnessed upward trend and farmers are getting job opportunities. Analysing the trends and pattern of institutional credit for agricultural sector during pre- and post-reforms period and estimating the productions function in order to determine the impact of institutional credit on agricultural production separately during the same period **Md. Izhar Ahmad** and **Tariq Masood** concludes that during post-reform period institutional credit does not affects agricultural production. Establish the effects of terms of trade on rural poverty and assessing the combined effect of the net barter and income terms of trade on rural poverty **Roli Mishra** and *et al.* suggest that government should not allow agricultural production to fall, particularly the foodgrains production otherwise substantial increase in agricultural prices will trigger the poverty level.

The need for food security arises primarily due to the fluctuations in food production and non-availability of sufficient food from domestic sources. The growth in foodgrain production has stagnated during recent past while the consumption need of the growing population is increasing. That is why in India millions of people suffer from hunger and malnutrition. The structural imbalance between the foodgrains producing sector and the rest of the economy would generate inflation and would increase inequality in the distribution of income. Examining population and foodgrains projection for India and Indian policies for agricultural subsidies under WTO regime **Ravi Ranjan** points out that under the WTO regime the agricultural policy has been shaped by the Central Government for execution of a new development strategy which is detrimental to the peasant and the strategy is of contract agriculture by allowing multinational to agricultural sector and providing the sector and export-oriented sector. It would endanger the food security of India and dependence on imperialist nations for foodgrains means compromising on our sovereignty.

Examining the emerging trends, nature and speed of agricultural diversification in India **Sanjeev Kumar** assesses the implications of agricultural diversification on food security, employment and export. Examining various issues relating to food security such as gap between demand and supply of foodgrains, functioning of Public Distribution System, etc. (PDS) **S.S. Kalamkar** suggests that efforts must be made to help the poor farmers by developing drought resistant seeds, cost-effective dry land farming techniques. Analyzing the area, production and yield of Bt. Cotton, both state-wise and for India as a whole **S.M. Jawed Akhtar** and *et al.* propound that the challenge before the agricultural scientists today is to 'produce more from less', i.e. more nutritious food from less land, water and other resources and remove disparity of Bt. Cotton's production among states. Deliberating on the various issues - trend in food production and food security; food economy and food policy; food per capita availability **Bipul Malakar** and **Sudip Jana** suggest that suitable measures have to be undertaken immediately to influence land productivity. **Indu Upadhyay** makes an attempt to look into the effects of 'New Economic Reforms' on agriculture.

The production and productivity of the available cattle and buffalo breeds is very low in India. There is need to develop cost effective new technologies in the area of animal breeding, fodder and feed resources and animal disease control. Making a modest attempt to analyze the trends in public spending in livestock sector since the beginning of economic reforms in India

K. Elumalai suggests that declining public investment is the cause of the concern among the policy-makers and development planners as it has implications for accelerating growth in livestock production and capacity of the sector to meet to the future demand emanating from domestic and global markets.

Comparing the production and performance of livestock and livestock product industry in the pre- and post-WTO agreement period and assessing the competitiveness of Indian livestock and livestock products in a global framework, **Rajender Kumar** concludes that the livestock industry is showing structural changes in the trade pattern. This development at the domestic and global level indicates that Indian livestock industry has to compete and face the world market.

ANIL KUMAR THAKUR
MITHILESH KUMAR SINHA

1

Structural Reforms and Agriculture: Issues and Policies

S. MAHENDRA DEV

I. INTRODUCTION

The performance of Agriculture in India is important as the sector not only contributes to overall growth of the economy but also provides employment and food security to majority of the population in the country. The 11th Five Year Plan also indicates that agricultural development is an important component of inclusive growth approach. Structural reforms were introduced in India in a big way in 1991. These reforms were followed by India becoming founder member of WTO in 1994. The structural reforms and obligations of WTO have positive and negative effects on Indian agriculture[2]. The negative effects can be reduced and benefits from overall reforms can be realized by following pro-agriculture macro policies and easing of supply side constraints in agriculture. In this context, this paper provides an overview of issues and policies on two aspects: (a) Impact of structural macro policy reforms on agriculture, and (b) reforms needed in agriculture in order to benefit from overall economic reforms and cope with the emerging challenges in the post-reform era.

2. STRUCTURAL MACRO POLICY REFORMS AND AGRICULTURE

The structural reforms and stabilization policies introduced in India in 1991 initially focused on industry, tax reforms, foreign trade and investment, banking and capital markets. The economic reforms did not include any specific package specifically designed for agriculture. It was viewed that freeing agricultural markets and liberalising external trade in agricultural commodities would provide price incentives leading to enhanced investment and output in that sector, while broader trade liberalisation would shift inter-sectoral terms of trade in favour of agriculture (Balakrishnan, 2000).

On the positive side, the reforms have improved terms of trade for agriculture and opened up new opportunities such as benefits from trade and specialization, widening choices in new technology including bio-technology, increase in private investment in irrigation and marketing infrastructure like storage and transport. It is viewed that protection to industry in the form of import substitution policies like tight import controls and high import duties have hurt the agriculture till 1991. Disprotection to industry since 1991 are supposed to correct this bias and increase terms of trade for agriculture. "This would create a potentially more profitable agriculture, which would be able to bear the economic costs of technological modernization and expansion" (Manmohan Singh, 1995, p. 2).

A look at terms of trade (TOT) in post-reform period shows that it was favourable to agriculture with fluctuations (Table 1). Agricultural growth was 3.7% per annum in the first six years of the reform period (1991-97). The terms of trade in agriculture improved during this period due to dis-protection to industry, devaluation of rupee and increase in minimum support prices. Then the growth rate started declining since mid-1990s. The TOT deteriorated during this period. Agricultural growth has picked up again and growth was more than 4% during the period 2004-08. There seems to be a revival in TOT again during this period. Thus, the favourable TOT in agriculture has some impact on agriculture in the post-reform period. Similarly, private investment in agriculture improved in the post-reform period although there has been stagnancy in

TABLE 1

Index of Terms of Trade between Agriculture and Non-agricultural Sector

Year	*Combined Index of Prices paid*	*Index of Prices Received*	*Agriculture's terms of trade*
1981-82	61.9	54.9	88.7
1982-83	66.0	60.3	91.4
1983-84	70.1	64.2	91.6
1984-85	72.4	68.0	93.9
1985-86	75.2	70.4	93.6
1986-87	80.2	76.7	95.7
1987-88	88.3	86.0	97.4
1988-89	91.8	90.3	98.3
1989-90	98.1	97.5	99.4
1990-91	110.2	112.3	101.9
1991-92	123.8	130.8	105.6
1992-93	133.5	138.7	103.9
1993-94	146.1	151.4	103.6
1994-95	160.5	171.1	106.6
1995-96	173.7	182.9	105.3
1996-97	184.8	190.6	103.1
1997-98	194.9	205.9	105.6
1998-99	209.9	220.8	105.2
1999-00	214.0	219.8	102.7
2000-01	223.0	225.0	100.9
2001-02	229.0	235.3	102.8
2002-03	239.3	247.9	103.6
2003-04	248.7	251.2	101.0
2004-05	257.5	258.2	100.3
2005-06	270.6	275.8	101.9
2006-07*	285.4	291.1	102.0

*provisional.

Note: Index of terms of trade are based on the triennium ending 1990-91.

Source: Directorate of Economics and Statistics, Ministry of Agriculture.

recent years. Terms of trade for agriculture based on GDP implicit price deflators indicate the TOT increased significantly since 2004-05. Particularly, the TOT for agriculture increased significantly in 2007-08 and 2008-09 and they are the highest in the last two decades (Table 2).

TABLE 2

Agriculture Terms of Trade-based GDP Implicit Price Deflators (1999-00=100)

Year	*Term of Trade for Agriculture*
1989-90	88.9
1990-91	89.8
1991-92	96.4
1992-93	93.3
1993-94	93.9
1994-95	95.8
1995-96	96.2
1996-97	97.6
1997-98	101.1
1998-99	101.0
1999-00	100.0
2000-01	97.1
2001-02	96.3
2002-03	97.3
2003-04	95.7
2004-05	93.4
2005-06	96.8
2006-07	97.7
2007-08	101.4
2008-09	103.4

Note: GDP implicit price deflators for agriculture and non-agriculture are used to derive agricultural terms of trade.

Source: Estimated based on National Accounts Statistics, CSO.

Trade reforms are expected to have positive impact on agriculture. There has been significant increase in agricultural exports after economic reforms were initiated. Agricultural exports rose from $3.2 billion in 1991-92 to $6.86 billion in 1996-97 but thereafter it declined. Increase in exports initially was due to significant reduction in the import duties and devaluation of Indian rupee. The economy-wide reforms seem to have benefited agriculture because of increasing business transactions between agriculture and rest of the economy over time (Mishra and Rao, 2003). Sharp reduction in global commodity prices and East Asian crisis could be the principal reasons for decline in

FIGURE 1

Terms of Trade for Agriculture Based on GDP Implicit Price Deflators

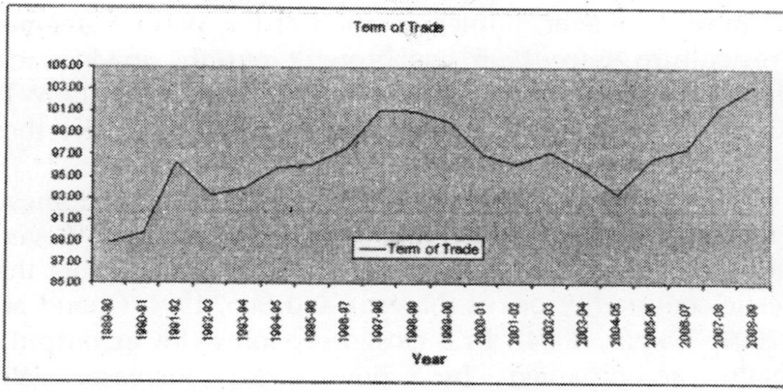

Source: Estimated from National Accounts Statistics, CSO.

agricultural exports in the late 1990s. They picked up again from 2004-05 and continued till the financial crisis in 2008.

Trade liberalization in agriculture has been faster towards the end of 1990s in tune with WTO agreements. The impact of trade liberalisation on agriculture works through various channels such as volatile prices, problems in imports and exports, impact on livelihood and other employment opportunities. For farmers, perhaps the single most adverse effect has been the combination of low prices and output volatility for cash crops. Some prices such as those of cotton and oilseeds declined for long periods. Plantation crops like tea, coffee and rubber were also affected. This reflected not only domestic demand conditions but also the growing role played by international prices consequent upon greater integration with world markets in this sector.

But, monitoring of the imports for 300 sensitive products has indicated that such imports constitute only a small proportion of total agricultural imports in the country (GoI, 2003). Thus, the concern of significant imports due to trade liberalization has not been proved. India has considerable flexibility to counter-flooding of the Indian market by cheap agricultural imports through imposition of tariffs (bound rates) under WTO. The major food and agricultural policies initiated in

India are those of: Procurement policy, buffer stocking, public distribution system, public investment, input subsidies, and government support to research. Clearly, India does not have to change any of these policies because of Agreement on Agriculture. However, implementation of the WTO Agreement on Agriculture since 1995 has brought out the inadequacies inherent in the agreement. The ongoing negotiations in the WTO on the AOA provide an opportunity for India to rectify these inadequacies and inequalities.

One problem with trade is that volatility in domestic agricultural prices will increase with globalization. Several studies have shown that volatility in global prices is higher than domestic commodity prices (Nayyar and Sen, 1994; Chand and Jha, 2001; Sekhar, 2004). In a closed economy, lower output is normally accompanied by some price increase. With liberalization, we had a situation of lower production with lower prices. This pattern reflected the effect of the growing integration of Indian agriculture with world markets, resulting from trade liberalisation. There is a need for extreme vigilance so as to be able to take timely measures, within the existing tariff bindings to arrest heavy import of certain commodities (Rao, 2005).

India has done well in recent global food price crisis. The country almost insulated from this increase as compared to soaring global food prices during 2005-08. For example, global cereal prices increased by 150% as compared to 20% rise in India during 2005-08. There were food riots in many other countries. Although somewhat protectionist, India's trade policies and food management policies (support prices, buffer stock and PDS) were responsible for insulating India from global volatility.

The negative effects of structural reforms have been also due to fiscal and financial policies. In terms of fiscal policies, the reduced spending of central and state governments was the most significant feature in the 1990s. Due to tax reforms, the tax/GDP ratio declined at central level. Central transfers to state governments also declined. In the late 1990s, most state governments were in fiscal crisis and did not have funds for capital expenditures. This has been especially important since state governments are responsible for areas critical for agriculture such as rural infrastructure, power, water supply, health and education. At the central government level, capital expenditure declined as a share of national income, and all public expenditure directed towards the rural areas fell both as a per cent of GDP and in real per capita terms.

Financial liberalisation measures, including reduced emphasis on priority sector lending by banks, which effectively reduced the availability of rural credit, and thus made farm investment more expensive and more difficult, especially for small farmers. In addition to declining credit-deposit ratios in rural areas, the reduction in the number of rural bank branches and less manpower for rural service provision all meant that the formal sector was unable to meet the requirements of farmers, who were forced to turn to private moneylenders (who were often also input dealers and traders) in more exploitative relationships.

However, as shown below, the situation on public investment and credit has improved in the second half of this decade.

To conclude, slowing of agriculture growth occurred at a time when the economic reforms were undertaken in the country. It has been concluded by some that this slowing is linked directly to structural macro reforms in the country and globalization. This view is limited and the slowing in agriculture is not due to industrial and trade reforms including joining of WTO. Slowing down of agriculture growth could be attributed to the structural factors on the supply side such as decline in public investment, credit, technology, etc. rather than trade and industrial reforms. The adverse effects of structural reforms were more to do with the manner in which reforms were undertaken in the country rather than intrinsic to structural reforms. Also, there have been positive effects on agriculture in terms of improvements in terms of trade, private investments, technology and specialization in agriculture. The negative effects can be reduced with a focus on supply side factors in agriculture.

3. ISSUES AND POLICIES RELATING TO REFORMS ON SUPPLY SIDE FACTORS IN AGRICULTURE

Before going to these reforms, few words on the performance of agriculture are in order.

Agriculture sector has many problems. Growth

decelerated from 3.5% during 1981-97 to 2% during 1997-2005. Further scope for increase in net sown area is limited. Land degradation in the form of depletion of soil fertility, erosion and, water logging has increased. There has been decline in the surface irrigation expansion rate and reduction in ground water table. Risk and vulnerability increased. Disparities in productivity across regions and crops persisted. Long-term factors like steeper decline in per capita land availability and shrinking of farm size are also responsible for the slow performance of agriculture.

The Steering Committee report on agriculture for 11th Plan (GoI, 2007) has identified the possible reasons for deceleration in agriculture since mid-1990s. According to the report, the major sources of agricultural growth are: public and private investment in agriculture and rural infrastructure including irrigation, technological change, diversification of agriculture and fertilizers. The progress on all these sources slowed down in the 1990s particularly since mid-1990s (Table 3). Expansion was noticed in the case of agricultural credit.

There has been some revival in agriculture in recent years. Agricultural growth was more than 4% during 2003-04 to 2007-08. The total foodgrains production for the year 2008-09 was 233.88 million tonnes and stands out as record production. There were significant exports in cotton, rice and sugar. Cotton crop experienced a revolution due to adoption of BT cotton. Production of cotton increased from 99.97 lakh bales in 2000-01 to 258.84 lakh bales in 2007-08. There has been some increase in high value agriculture. Some of the lagging regions like Bihar showed relatively high growth in recent years. Similarly, Gujarat recorded high growth of 9% per annum during 2001-02 to 2007-08 (Gulati, 2009).

There has been demand problem in the economy due to financial crisis since 2008. However, rural demand and purchasing power were higher due to several factors: increase in minimum support prices, National Rural Employment Guarantee Scheme (NREGS), loan waiver scheme and higher agricultural growth in recent years. In the year 2008-09, however, agricultural growth was only 1.6%. There is a concern in 2009-10 due to drought conditions in several parts of the country.

There are three goals of agricultural development. These

TABLE 3

Trend Growth Rate in Area, Input Use, Credit and Capital Stock in Agriculture during 1980-81 to 2005-06

	1980-81 to 1990-91	*1990-91 to 1996-97*	*1996-97 to 2005-06*
Technology	3.3	2.8	0.0
Public Investment	3.9	1.9	1.4
Private Investment	0.6	2.2	1.2
Irrigated Area	2.3	2.6	0.6
Area under Fruits and Vegetable	5.6	5.6	2.7
NPK Use	8.2	2.5	2.3
Credit	3.7	7.5	14.4

Source: GoI, 2007

are: (a) achieve 4% growth in agriculture and raise incomes by increasing productivity (land, labour), diversification to high value agriculture and rural non-farm by maintaining food security; (b) sharing growth (equity) by focusing on small and marginal farmers, lagging regions, women, etc.; (c) third is to maintain sustainability of agriculture by focusing on environmental concerns.

What are the policy reforms needed to achieve the above goals? There are basically seven factors which need focused reforms in the short and medium terms. These are: (a) price policy; (b) subisidies and investments; (c) land issues; (d) irrigation and water management; (e) research and extension; (f) credit; (g) domestic market reforms and diversification. Institutions have to be developed in all these aspects. *The reforms needed in supply factors are well known. But, it is important to keep repeating for better policies and implementation.*

(a) Price Policy

The major underlying objective of the Indian government's price policy is to protect both producers and consumers. Currently, food security system and price policy basically consists of three instruments: procurement prices/ minimum support prices, buffer stocks and public distribution system (PDS). There is a need to provide remunerative prices for farmers in order to maintain food security and increase incomes of farmers. There has been a debate on price *vs.* non-price factors in the literature. In our view both price and non-price factors are important in raising agricultural production.

One criticism of procurement policy is that it is limited to few crops and few states. Our field visits to different states reveal the following farmers' perceptions about agricultural prices. The cost of cultivation is increasing due to increase in input prices. Particularly agricultural wages have increased due to National Rural Employment Guarantee Scheme (NREGS) in several states. They want to resort to mechanization due to labour shortages in peak season. Farmers respond to prices as shown by increase in yields of wheat in Punjab and other states with significant increase in MSP. Farmers have to undergo distress sales due to lack of procurement in states like Bihar, parts of UP, M.P. and Orissa. If rice production is to be shifted to Eastern region, rural infrastructure including procurement centres has to be improved. Pulses production can be enhanced in several states with higher MSP and procurement. Provision of electricity has to be raised in order to exploit ground water in Eastern region.

In the context of globalization, tariff policy becomes important for agricultural commodities. In other words, it is important to monitor exports, imports, global supply and demand and fix tariffs accordingly. There is a need to balance between producer prices and consumer prices by careful calibration of minimum support prices and tariff policy (import duties).

There is a need for reforms in buffer stock operations and targeted public distribution system (TPDS). Buffer stock operations are becoming expensive. As FCI gets full reimbursement for its procurement, handling and storage costs, the scope for its efficiency improvement through reduction in operating costs need to be examined. Similarly, there are significant leakages in PDS. There can be better ways of more efficient food management practices in procurement, buffer stock and PDS. Policy reforms are needed here. Private sector can be involved in storage and some other activities with regulations.

(b) Subsidies and Investments in Agriculture

One major reform needed in agriculture sector relates to reduction in subsidies and increase in investments. Agricultural subsidies are fiscally unsustainable and encourage misuse of resources, leading to environmentally malignant developments. There is trade-off between subsidies and investments. Public investment declined from 3.4% of agricultural GDP in the early 1980s to 1.9% in 2001-03. At the same time subsidies increased from 2.9% to 7.4% of agricultural GDP (GoI, 2007). Rise in public and private investment is crucial for enhancing agricultural growth. Fortunately, gross capital formation in agriculture has increased from 12% of agricultural GDP in 2004-05 to 14.2% of GDP in 2007-08 (Table 4). Public sector investment has increased significantly during this period. However, we need 16% agricultural GDP as investment in order to get 4% growth in agriculture. In this context, the announcement of *Bharat Nirman* programme in 2005 by the Government of India in order to improve agriculture and rural infrastructure is in the right direction. However, the pace of this programme has to be improved.

TABLE 4

Gross Capital Formation in Agriculture and Allied as Percentage of GDP in Agriculture and Allied

Year	*Public Investment (%)*	*Private Investment (%)*	*Total Investment (%)*
1999-2000	1.94	9.29	11.23
2000-01	1.81	8.40	10.21
2001-02	2.05	9.99	12.04
2002-03	1.99	10.69	12.68
2003-04	2.24	8.85	11.09
2004-05	2.70	9.28	11.98
2005-06	3.12	9.81	12.93
2006-07	3.53	10.26	13.79
2007-08	3.97	10.27	14.24

Source: Ministry of Agriculture, Government of India.

(c) Land Issues

Some argue that small size of farm is responsible for low profitability of agriculture. Chinese and the experience of other East Asian countries show that it is not a constraint. On land market, the Report of the Steering Committee recommended the following. "Small farmers should be assisted to buy land through the provision of institutional credit, on a long-term basis, at a low rate of interest and by reducing stamp duty. At the same time, they should be enabled to enlarge their operational holdings by liberalizing the land lease market. The two major elements of such a reform are: security of tenure for tenants during the period of contract; and the right of the land owner to resume land after the period of contract is over" (GoI, 2007). Basically, we have to ensure land leasing, create conditions including credit, whereby the poor can access land from those who wish to leave agriculture. There are some emerging land issues such as increase in demand for land for non-agricultural purposes including special economic zones, displacement of farmers, tribals and others due to development projects. There is a need for careful land acquisition. Land alienation is a serious problem in tribal areas.

(d) Irrigation and Water Management

Water is the leading input in agriculture. Development of irrigation and water management are crucial for raising levels of living in rural areas. Major areas of concern in irrigation are: decline in real investment, thin spread of investment, low recovery of costs, decline in water table, wastages and inefficiencies in water use and, non-involvement of users Both investment and efficiency in use of water are needed. Major areas of reforms needed in irrigation are: stepping up and prioritizing public investment, raising profitability of groundwater exploitation and augmenting ground water resources, rational pricing of irrigation water and electricity, involvement of user farmers in the management of irrigation systems and, making groundwater markets equitable (Rao, 2005). In a recent study, Shah *et al.* (2009) indicate that the impact of the drought of 2009 is expected be less severe than the drought of 2002 due to ground water recharge in the last few years. Ground water can be exploited in a big way in Eastern region. Watershed development and, water conservation by the community are needed under water management. New watershed guidelines based on Parthasarathy Committee's recommendations were accepted by the Central Cabinet in March 2009. The implementation has to be stepped up in order to obtain benefits in rainfed areas. National Rainfed Area Authority has big responsibility in matters relating to water conservation and watershed development. Assets created under NREGS can help in improving land and water management.

(e) Research, Extension and Technology Fatigue

The yield growth for many crops has declined in the 1990s. Technology plays an important role in improving the yields. The National Commission on Farmers indicates that there is a large knowledge gap between the yields in research stations and actual yields in farmers' fields. The yield gaps given by the Planning Commission (GoI, 2007 a) range from 5% to 300% depending on the crop and State.

National Food Security Mission (NFSM) has been launched in 2007 to increase 20 million tonnes of foodgrains (10 m.t. for rice, 8 m.t. for wheat and 2 m.t. for pulses) during the 11th Plan period. It has already shown some results by increasing yields in different regions. There is a need to strengthen this mission to increase productivity.

The issue of technology fatigue in agriculture is well known now. There is a need to shift away from individual crop-oriented research focused essentially on irrigated areas towards research on crops and cropping systems in the dry lands, hills, tribal and other marginal areas (Swaminathan, 2007). In view of high variability in agro-climatic conditions in such unfavourable areas, research has to become increasingly location-specific with greater participation or interaction with farmers. Private sector participation in agricultural research, extension and marketing is becoming increasingly important especially with the advent of biotechnology and protection being given to intellectual property. However, private sector participation tends to be limited to profitable crops and enterprises undertaken by resource rich farmers in well endowed regions. Therefore, the public sector research has to increasingly address the problems facing the resource-poor farmers in the less endowed regions.

The new agricultural technologies in the horizon are largely biotechnologies. There has been a revolution in cotton production due to success of BT cotton in this decade. Similarly, there is a need to strengthen extension. The ATMA (Agricultural Technology Management Agency) scheme was launched in 2005 to support state governments' efforts to revitalize the extension. This scheme gives an opportunity to improve extension system. The returns to investment on research and extension will be much higher on agricultural growth as compared to other investments.

(f) Credit

According to the expert group on Financial Inclusion (GoI, 2008) only 27% of farmers have access to institutional credit. It is true that there have been some improvements in flow of farm credit in recent years (Table 5). However, the Government has to be sensitive to the four distributional aspects of agricultural credit. These are: (a) not much improvement in the share of small and marginal farmers; (b) decline in credit-deposit (CD) ratios of rural and semi-urban branches; (c) increase in the share of indirect credit in total agricultural credit; and (d) significant regional inequalities in credit.

TABLE 5

Credit Flow to Agriculture

(Rs. in crores)

Year	*Target*	*Achievement*	*% Achievement*	*% Growth*
2004-05	105000	125309	119.34	44.06
2005-06	141000	180486	128.00	44.03
2006-07	175000	229400	131.09	27.10
2007-08	225000	243569	108.25	6.17
2008-09	280000	287149	102.55	4.87
2009-10	325000	92070 (upto July 2009)	28.33	—

Source: NABARD, 2009 quoted by Ministry of agriculture, Government of India, 2009.

(g) Diversification to High Value Agriculture and Marketing

There has been diversification of Indian diets away from foodgrains to high value products like milk and meat products and vegetables and fruits. Since risk is high for diversification, necessary support in infrastructure and marketing are needed. Price policy should also encourage diversification. The Government wants to have second 'green revolution' by diversifying agriculture in crop sector and allied activities. To promote holistic growth of the horticulture sector through area based regionally differentiated strategies, the National Horticulture Mission (NHM) was launched in the country during 10th Plan. The impact has to be strengthened further to improve productivity in horticulture sector.

The true benefit of diversification will come if more emphasis is given to allied activities like animal husbandry and fisheries. The livestock sector contributes 5.4% to GDP and 22.7% to total output from agriculture sector. Ownership of livestock is more equitable than that of land and women play significant role in animal husbandry.

For small and marginal farmers, marketing of their products is main problem apart from credit and extension. In recent years , there has been some form of contract arrangements in several agricultural crops such as tomatoes, potatoes, chillies, gherkin, baby corn, rose, onions, cotton, wheat, basmati rice, groundnut, flowers, and medicinal plants. There is a silent revolution in institutions regarding non-cereal foods. New production-market linkages in the food supply chain are: spot or open market transactions, agricultural co-operatives and contract farming (Joshi and Gulati, 2003). Contract farming in India is neither backed up by law nor by an efficient legal system. This has to be strengthened as legal system is the single most constraint to widespread use of contract farming in India.

There is a need to revamp some of the legal hurdles for agro processing and APMC Act. Several State Governments have already amended their APMC Acts allowing varying degrees of flexibility. However several States are yet to notify the relevant rules that would make the amendment fully operational. These steps should be speedily completed to provide a boost to promotion of direct marketing, contract farming, and setting up of markets in private and co-operative sectors.

Most important problem for the farmers is output price fluctuations. There is a big gap between producer prices and consumer prices. There are different models for marketing collectively by the small and marginal farmers. These are: *self-help* group model, co-operative model, small producer co-operatives and contract farming. *Apni Mandi* in Punjab, *Rytu Bazars* in Andhra Pradesh, dairy co-operatives are some of the successful cases in marketing. The real challenge lies in organising the small and marginal farmers for marketing and linking them to high value agriculture. Thus, group approach is needed for getting benefits from marketing.

4. FEW OTHER ISSUES

Emerging Challenge: Climate Change

Climate change is a reality. India has reasons to be concerned about climate change. Vast majority of population depends on climatic sensitive sectors like agriculture, forestry and fishery for livelihood in the country. The adverse impact of climate change in the form of declining rainfall and rising temperatures and thus the increased severity of drought and flooding, would threaten food security and livelihood in the economy. For example, rise in temperature would affect wheat yields.

India has prepared a document namely the National Action Plan on Climate Change. It provides a direction for changes at the national level in policy, planning and public-private partnerships and lays out a global vision for modifying longer time trends for sustainable development. Successful adaptation coupled with mitigation holds the key to food security and livelihoods for the 21st century and beyond in India.

Equity in Agriculture

Regional Disparities: Growth rates in agriculture SDP were high for many states during the period 1984/85 to 1995/96. However, growth decelerated in all the states except Bihar during the period 1995/96 to 2004/05 (GoI, 2007). The deceleration is the highest in the states with greater proportion of rain-fed areas (Gujarat, Rajasthan, M.P., Karnataka and Maharashtra). Recent experience, however, shows that Gujarat recorded the highest growth of around 9 per cent during 2000/01 to 2007/08 (Gulati, 2009). During this period, six states viz., Gujarat, Rajasthan, Himachal Pradesh, Andhra Pradesh, Chhattisgarh and Bihar recoded more than 4% growth per annum. Public investment in infrastructure like irrigation, power, roads, watersheds, check dams, technology like BT cotton and diversification in agriculture played crucial roles in raising agricultural growth in Gujarat. Other states can learn from the experience of Gujarat. There is a need to shift rice cultivation to Eastern region from Punjab and Haryana for growth, equity and environment reasons. In order to encourage the States to invest more towards agriculture and allied sectors and to achieve 4% growth in agriculture, the government launched the Rashtriya Krishi Vikas Yojana (RKVY) in 2007-08 with an outlay of Rs. 25,000 crores for the 11th Five Year Plan. The scheme requires the States to prepare District agriculture plans and provides adequate flexibility and autonomy to State governments. The States should make use of this scheme to improve the agriculture sector.

Small and Marginal Farmers: It is known that more than 80% of India's farmers belong to the categories of small and marginal farmers with an area share of more than 40%. The support systems and policy changes have to support in raising productivity and incomes of the small and marginal farmers. National Commission on Enterprises for Unorganized Sector (NCEUS, 2008) suggests special programmes for small and marginal farmers. Principal activities proposed under this include promotion of marginal-small farmers' groups, enabling greater access to institutional credit, training and capacity building, support for strengthening and non-farm activities, gender-focussed activities and planning for development of marginal and small farmers.

5. CONCLUSION

This paper provides an overview of the issues and policies on (a) the impact of structural macro policy reforms on agriculture, and (b) reforms relating to supply side factors in agriculture sectors. There are two major conclusions as given below.

(1) Structural reforms on agriculture have positive and negative effects. Agriculture benefited indirectly due to disprotection given to industry in the post-reform period. The terms of trade, private investment, opportunities for technology and specialization have increased for agriculture. On the negative side, trade reforms might have affected some crops and increased dependence on global prices which are volatile. Fiscal and financial liberalization also had some adverse impact on investments and credit. It has been concluded by some that the slow down in agriculture growth is linked directly to structural macro reforms in the country and globalization including joining of WTO. It may be noted that the slow down is more to do with domestic policies. Some of the adverse effects due to structural reforms can be reversed if macro pro-agricultural policies are followed as happened since 2004-05. Higher GDP growth due to domestic reform policies and global boom helped in having higher tax/GDP ratio and better allocations to agriculture in the form of public investment and credit.

(2) It may be noted that the slowing in agriculture growth could be attributed to the structural factors on the supply side such as public investment, credit, technology, land and water management, etc. rather than globalization and trade reforms *per se*. There are six deficits in Indian agriculture. These are: (a) investment, credit and Infrastructure deficit; (b) land and water management deficit; (c) research and extension (technology) deficit; (d) market deficit; (e) diversification deficit; (f) institutions deficit. Reforms are needed to reduce these deficits in order to achieve the goals of agriculture: (i) Achieving 4% growth in agriculture; (ii) equity in terms of higher growth in lagging regions, small and marginal farmers and women; and (iii) sustainability.

Apart from high growth, efficiency (cost reduction) is also needed in globalized world. Group approach among farmers should be encouraged in order to get inputs at cheaper rates and marketing of output at higher prices.

The four central government's special programmes viz., National Food Security Mission (NFSM), Rastriya Krishi Vikas Yojana (RKVY), National Horticulture Mission (NHM) and Agricultural Technology Management Agency (ATMA) would be useful, if implemented properly, in improving growth and equity in agriculture.

The medium and long-term measures relating to supply side can also improve drought-proofing and de-risking agriculture. Similarly, rural non-farm sector has to be developed. Inspite of these measures, agriculture would always be subjected to shocks in the form of volatility in global agricultural prices and natural calamities like droughts, floods and temperature changes. Therefore, there is a need to put in place social protection programmes and drought or flood management practices including crop insurance to take care of risks or shocks in agriculture. For example, social protection programmes like PDS and rural public works programmes helped in a big way the drought effects in Gujarat and Rajasthan in 1987-88.

'Business as usual approach' may not help revival of agriculture. The government is thinking of big push to education in 11th Five Year Plan. Such a big push is needed for reforms in supply side for agriculture. Similarly, demand factors also have to be addressed. Given the short-run and structural long-term problems in agriculture, the government should give large push to core issues to make cultivation viable and profitable. There is a need to concentrate on delivery systems also. India's large numbers of farmers can benefit if there are right policies and effective implementation.

References

Acharya, S.S. (1997), "Agricultural Price Policy and Development: Some Facts and Emerging Issues", *Indian Journal of Agricultural Economics*, Vol. 52, No. 1.

Ahluwalia, M.S. (1996), "New Economic Policy and Agriculture: Some Reflections", *Indian Journal of Agricultural Economics*, Volume 51, No. 3.

Alagh, Y.K. (2006), "Indian Economic Strategies After Doha" in Radhakrishna, R, S.K. Rao, S. Mahendra Dev and K. Subbarao (2006 eds.), India in a Globalising World: Some Aspects of Macroeconomy, Agriculture and

Poverty, Essays in honour of C.H. Hanumantha Rao, Academic Foundation.

Balakrishnan, P. (2000), "Agriculture and Economic Reforms: Growth and Welfare", *Economic and Political Weekly*, March 4-10.

Bhalla, G.S. (1995), "Globalization and Agricultural Policy in India", *Indian Journal of Agricultural Economics*, Vol. 50, No. 1.

Bhalla, G.S. (2006), "Agricultural Growth and Regional Variations", in R. Radhakrishna, S.K. Rao, S. Mahendra Dev and K. Subbarao (eds.), India in a Globalising World: Some aspects of Macro economy, Agriculture and Poverty, Essays in honour of Prof. C.H. Hanumantha Rao, Academic Foundation, New Delhi.

Bhattacharya, B.B. (2003), "Trade Liberalization and Agricultural Price Policy in India Since Reforms", *Indian Journal of Agricultural Economics*, Vol. 58, No. 3.

Chadha, G.K. (2009), "Agriculture and Rural Industrialization in India: Recent Developments and Future Concerns" in Rao, N.C. and S. Mahendra Dev (eds. 2009) India: Perspectives on Equitable Development, Academic Foundation.

Chand, Ramesh and Dayanath Jha (2001), "Trade Liberalization: Agricultural Prices and Net Social Welfare", in S.S. Acharya and D.P. Chaudhari (eds.), Indian Agricultural Policy at the Cross Roads, Rawat Publishers, New Delhi

Deshpande, R.S. (2004), "Liberalization, Domestic Price Policy and Agricultural Growth", Summaries of Group Discussion, *Indian Journal of Agricultural Economics*, Vol. 89, No. 1.

Dev, S. Mahendra (2008), Inclusive Growth in India, Agriculture: Poverty and Human Development, Oxford University Press, New Delhi

GoI (2007), Report of the Steering Committee on Agriculture for 11th Five Year Plan, Yojana Bhavan, New Delhi.

GoI (2007a), Agricultural Strategy for the Eleventh Plan: Concerns and Way ahead, Yojana Bhavan, New Delhi

GoI (2008), Expert Group on Financial Inclusion, Chaired by Dr. C. Rangarajan, Government of India.

Gulati, Ashok (2009), "Emerging Trends in Indian Agriculture: What can we learn from these?" 2nd Prof. Dayanath Jha Memorial Lecture, National Centre for Agricultural Economics and Policy Research, New Delhi.

Joshi, P.K. and A. Gulati (2003), 'From Plate to Plough: Agricultural Diversification in India', Paper presented at the 'Dragon and Elephant: A Comparative Study of Economic and Agricultural Reforms in China and India', New Delhi, India, March 25-26.

Mishra, V.N. and Govinda Rao (2003), Trade Policy, Agricultural Growth and Rural Poor: Indian Experience, 1978-79 to 1999-00, *Economic and Political Weekly*, October 25, 2003.

Nayyar, Deepak and Abhijit Sen (1994), "International Trade and Agricultural Sector in India", in G.S. Bhalla (ed.), Economic Liberalization and Indian Agriculture, Indian Studies for Industrial Development, New Delhi.

Rangarajan, C. (2005), "Agricultural Credit: Reaching the Marginalised Farmers", Lecture delivered at the Bankers' Conference (BANCON) 2005, Kolkata, November 12, 2005.

Rao, C.H. Hanumantha (2003), "Reform Agenda for Agriculture", *Economic and Political Weekly*, Feb. 15.

Rao, C.H. Hanumantha (2005), Agriculture, Food security, Poverty and Environmen, Oxford University Press, New Delhi.

Rao, N.C., and S. Mahendra Dev (forthcoming), Biotechnology in Indian Agriculture-Potential," Performance and Concerns, Academic Foundation, New Delhi.

Sekhar, C.S.C. (2004), "Agricultural Price Volatility in International and Indian Markets", *Economic and Political Weekly*, October 23, 2004.

Sen, Abhijit (1999), "Agricultural Price Policy: Achievements and the Emerging Problems", in Krishna Rao, Y.V. (ed., 1999), New Challenges Facing Indian Agriculture, Vishalandra Publishing House.

Shah, Tushar, Avinash Kishore, P.Hemant, (2009), Will the Impact of the 2009 Drought be Different from 2002, *Economic and Political Weekly*, Vol. 44, No. 37.

Singh, Manmohan (1995), "Inaugural Address", *Indian Journal of Agricultural Economics*, Vol. 50, No. 1.

Swaminathan, M.S. (2007), Agriculture cannot Wait: New Horizons in Indian Agriculture, Academic Foundation, National Academy of Agricultural Sciences.

Vaidyanathan, A. (2006), India's Water Resources: Contemporary Issues on Irrigation, Oxford University Press, New Delhi.

Vyas, V.S. (2007), "Market Reforms in Indian Agriculture: One Step Forward, Two Steps Back", in Gulati, A. and S. Fan (eds., 2007), The Dragon and the Elephant: Agriculture and Rural Reforms in India and China, Oxford University Press, New Delhi.

2

Economic Reforms and Growth of Agriculture in India: A Review

Fakhre Alam, Rais Ahmad, Ejaz Anwer and M.A. Salam

INTRODUCTION

Agriculture is the mainstay of Indian economy because of its high share in employment and livelihood creation notwithstanding its reduced contribution to the nation's GDP. The share of agriculture in the gross domestic product has registered a steady decline from 36.4 per cent in 1982-83 to 18.5 per cent in 2006-07 (Figure 1), yet this sector continues to support more than half a billion people providing employment to 52 per cent of the workforce.

It is also an important source of raw material and demand for many industrial products, particularly fertilizers, pesticides, agricultural implements and a variety of consumer goods. Growth of agriculture over a period of time remained lower than the growth of non-agriculture sectors and this decelerating trend is cause for concern. The gap between the growth of agriculture and non-agriculture sector began to widen since 1981-82, and more particularly since 1996-97, because of an acceleration in the growth of industry and service sectors. There has been a

FIGURE I

Share of Agriculture in Total GDP in Relation to other Sectors in Different Time Periods (in per cent)

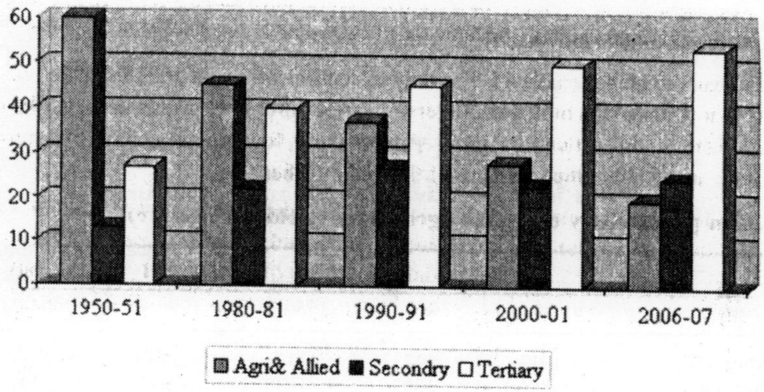

consistent decline in the growth of agriculture since 1990 onwards as compared to 1980s. It was 4 per cent during 1980 is on an average which came down to 3.2 per cents during the 1990s and 2 per cent after 2000. There are wide fluctuations in the annual average growth rate of agriculture (at constant prices) during different plan periods and there is definite downward

TABLE I

Agricultural Growth Rate during Different Plan Periods

Five Year Plan	*Overall GDP growth rate (at constant price)*	*Agriculture and Allied Sectors*
Seventh Plan (198k5-1990)	6	3.2
Annual Plan (1990-92)	3.4	1.3
Eighth Plan (1992-97)	6.7	4.7
Ninth Plan (1997-2002)	5.5	2.1
Tenth Plan (2002-07)		
2002-03	3.8	-6.9
2003-04	8.5	10
2004-05	7.5	0.7
2005-06	8.1	2.3

Source: Central Statistical Organization, 2007.

trend overall including some negative patches (Table 1). The only exception we see is 2003-04 which is due to good monsoon in that year. Due to rich biological diversity various crops are grown in India like foodgrains, oilseeds, plantation crops and horticultural crops. Among these, foodgrains occupy 75% of the cultivated area of India. Paddy is the most important crop followed by wheat.

TABLE 2

Trends in Productivity of Indian Agriculture

(yield per hectare)

Crops	*1960-61*	*1970-71*	*1980-81*	*1990-91*	*2003-04*
Wheat (kg)	1013	1123	1336	1740	2051
Rice (kg)	851	1307	1630	2281	2707
Sugarcane (tonne)	46	48	58	65	59
Cotton (kg)	125	106	152	225	307

Source: Govt. of India, Economic Survey, 2004-05, p. s-18, Table 1.14.

Ever since the launching of the first five year plan, the farm productivity has increased in terms of foodgrains and raw materials for agro-based industries. This trend can be observed from the Table 2 and Figure 2.

FIGURE 2

Trends in Productivity of Indian Agriculture (yield per hectare) over Different Time Period

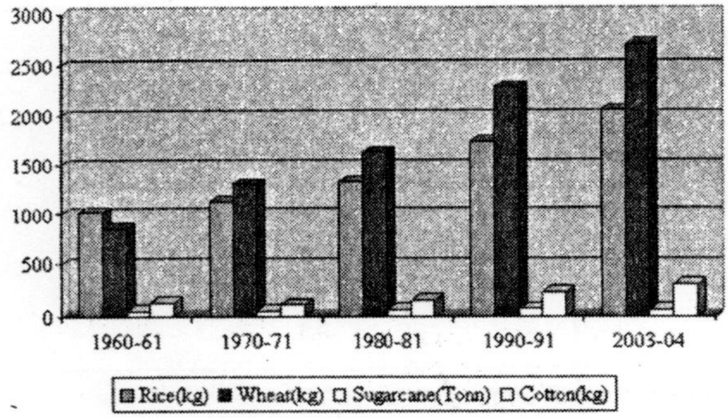

Although per hectare yield of major crops has increased over the last four decades yet it is far below the international level.

The bulk of our population continues to get their livelihood from agriculture and allied sectors but their contribution to GDP is diminishing over the decades as shown earlier in Figure 1. In industrialized countries, the declination of agricultural's contribution to GDP was accompanied by transfer of people from agriculture to other sectors. Today percentage of population in agriculture in these countries varies from 9 per cent to 11 per cent. In India, the proportion of population dependent on agriculture declined in a modest way—from 73.9% in 1972-73 to 60.2% in 2000. The relative productivity of agriculture is less than one-fourth of that in non-agricultural occupations.

In this paper, the analysis of agricultural growth has been done by using the time series data of different crop's productivity and also the data of quantitative magnitudes of different factors which affect the growth of Indian agriculture. In what follows, we explain first the background of this study, methodological framework and then present the empirical results of our analysis .The paper is organized as follows; section two presents the background of this study and the problems and prospects linked with the growth of agriculture. Section 3 describes the data set-sources and methodology used. The empirical results are presented in section 4. Finally, in section 5, some concluding observations have been drawn.

BACKGROUND OF THE STUDY

The present growth rate in agriculture is only 2.6 per cent as against the target growth rate of 4 per cent put up by the Government in the budget 2006-07. This low agricultural growth rate is due to many problems surrounding the agriculture. C.H.H. Rao (2005) analyzed the agricultural growth from the first decade of the plan period and suggested the continued need for provision of irrigation facilities, strengthening of extension services, developing biotechnologically improved seeds along with adequate supply of institutional credit to raise farm productivity and profitability. Bhatia (1999) established a strong relationship between rural infrastructural development and level of per hectare yield of foodgrain as also of the value of out put from agriculture. According to Bhattarai and Naraynamoorthy (2003), improvement in irrigation and rural literacy are the two most important factors for agricultural growth in India. Mahendra Dev (2002) argued that there is a greater need for public investment in agriculture, irrigation, credit availability, better marketing of agricultural products, research and development (R and D) along with adequate pricing and other incentives for private investment that would help reviving the agricultural growth. Sahu and Rajasekhar (2005) emphasized the importance of administered allocation of credit to the priority sector at concessional rates for agriculture. Dhar and Kallumal (2004) suggested that throughout the 1990's, the share of agriculture in gross capital formation has remained a single digits which explains the slackness of its growth momentum during the past decade . Gulati and Bathla (2001) observed that there has been an increasing role played by private sector investment in this sector. Public sector investment along with terms of trade has an inducement effect on private sector capital formation. Desai (2002) suggested that government expenditure should be focused on agricultural R and D, education and extension services, rural electricity and marketing, irrigation and watershed development, etc. Reddy and Reddy (2005) emphasized that there is a need for devolution of powers to water user associations for important functions like assessment, collection of water charges, sanctioning of works, etc. Rao and Gulati (2005) showed that public sector capital formation in agriculture as a proportion of total capital formation in agriculture declined in the recent past as compared to the 1980s. The authors emphasize the need to reverse this trend and increase public investment in agriculture so as to be able to increase the growth in the sector. According to Shariff and Mallik (1999), the Indian food basket has changed drastically since 1973-74. Both the share of cereals in the food basket has decreased in rural and urban areas, while the share of other items has increased. This also has reduced the incentives to growth of cereal production. Bhalla and Hazell (2003) observed that there is a secular decline in the employment elasticity in agriculture over time. One more incentive to the growth of agricultural production is that, despite output per worker increasing in the non-agricultural sector, this increased income causes the demand to increase only for white and luxury goods-imported or otherwise and not for agricultural products because the increased income accrue mostly to managerial profits and salaries of the upper classes whose demand for wage goods is relatively satiated, as observed by Chandrasekhar (2006).

THE DATA AND METHODOLOGY

In the present exercise, we have used the secondary data's of productivity of different types such as foodgrains, commercial crops and oilseeds. We have also used the secondary data of magnitudes of different factors and their growth rates in different time periods. The sources of these data's have been the "Handbook of statistics on the Indian economy, 2004-05, Reserve bank of India", Agricultural statistics at a glance (2006), Ministry of Agriculture, and Economic Survey, 2006, Ministry of Finance GoI, New Delhi. The dataset have been analysed in two groups, one for pre-reform period (before 1991) and another for post-reform period (after 1991).

The empirical exercise has been done separately for each of the crop in the pre-reform period, and the post-reform period and also for the whole period. The mean, standard deviation and coefficients of variation have been calculated for each crop's productivity. The formula used for determining mean, standard deviation and coefficient of variation are;

(1) $$\overline{x} = \frac{\Sigma xi}{N}$$

(2) $$\sigma = \sqrt{\Sigma(Xi\text{-}\overline{X})^2/N}$$

(3) $$C.V. = (\sigma / \overline{X})^* 100$$

where "x" is the mean measured in kilogram per hectare , "ó" is the standard of deviation and "C.V." the coefficient of variation expressed in percentage. Similarly, "Xi" is the productivity (yield per hectare) of crop in each year and "N" is the number of years in specific time-period. Apart from this, the effect of other factors on the agricultural growth has also been analyzed by their quantitative magnitudes over the years.

RESULTS

The analysis of dataset of the productivity of various crops gives the findings that the average productivity of all types of foodgrains has increased in the post-reform period when compared with that in the pre-reform period. Apart from this, the deviation of the value of productivity from their average value, i.e. fluctuation, of all foodgrain excepts the coarse cereals is high in the pre-reform period than in the post-reform period (Table 3). This trend has been illustrated with the help of Figures 3, 4, 5 and 6.

TABLE 3

Trends in per hectare Yields of Different Types of Foodgrains in India

(kg per hectare)

Year	*Rice*	*Wheat*	*Coarse cereals*	*Pulses*
1	2	3	4	5
967-68	1032	1103	608	534
1968-69	1076	1169	545	490
1969-70	1073	1208	578	531
1970-71	1123	1307	665	524
1971-72	1141	1380	564	501
1972-73	1070	1271	548	484
1973-74	1151	1172	623	427
1974-75	1045	1338	606	455
1975-76	1235	1410	694	533
1976-77	1089	1387	689	494
1977-78	1308	1480	710	510
1978-79	1328	1568	721	515
1979-80	1074	1436	652	385
1980-81	1336	1630	695	473
1981-82	1308	1691	733	483
1982-83	1231	1816	685	519
1983-84	1457	1843	813	548
1984-85	1417	1870	795	526
1985-86	1552	2046	664	547
1986-87	1471	1916	675	506

(Contd.)

1	2	3	4	5
1987-88	1465	2002	721	515
1988-89	1689	2241	814	598
1989-90	1745	2121	922	549
1990-91	1740	2281	900	578
1991-92	1751	2394	778	533
1992-93	1744	2327	1063	573
1993-94	1888	2380	939	598
1994-95	1911	2559	929	610
1995-96	1797	2483	940	552
1996-97	1882	2689	1072	635
1997-98	1900	2485	986	567
1998-99	1921	2590	1068	634
1999-2000	1986	2778	1034	635
2000-01	1901	2708	1027	544
2001-02	2079	2764	1131	607
2002-03	1804	2619	962	556
2003 -04	2051	2707	1228	623

Pre-reform Period (1967-1991)

Rice	*Wheat*	*Coarse cereals*	*Pulses*	
Mean (kg/hec)	1649	1649	769.33	524.7
σ	145	352.4	129.04	72.7
C.V.(%)	10.9	21.4	16.8	13.7
Post-reform period (1991-2004)				
Mean (kg/hec)	1893.5	2574	1012	589.77
σ	98	147.4	151.1	35.7
C.V. (%)	5.17	5.7	14.8	5.9
Combined (1967- 2004)				
Mean (kg/hec)	1510.5	1974.3	800.5	547.5
σ	175.2	609.7	187.4	98.9
C.V. (%)	11.5	30.8	23.2	18.1

Source: R.B.I., Handbook of Statistics on the Indian Economy, 2004-05, Table 21.

FIGURE 3

All India Yield of Rice (in kg/hectare) 2006-07= Advance Estimate

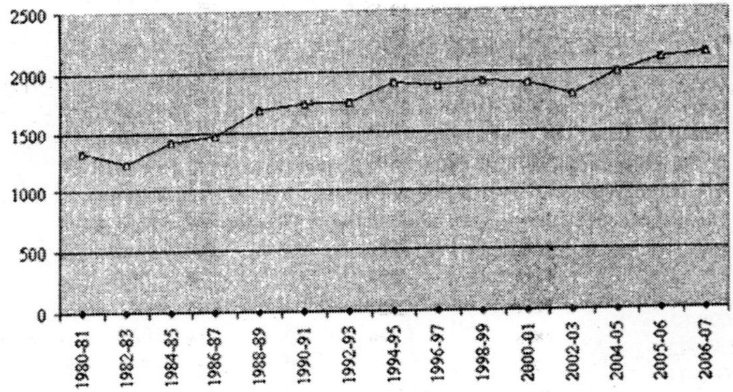

2006-07= Advance Estimate

Source: Economic Survey, 2008.

FIGURE 4

All India yield of Wheat (in kg/hectare)

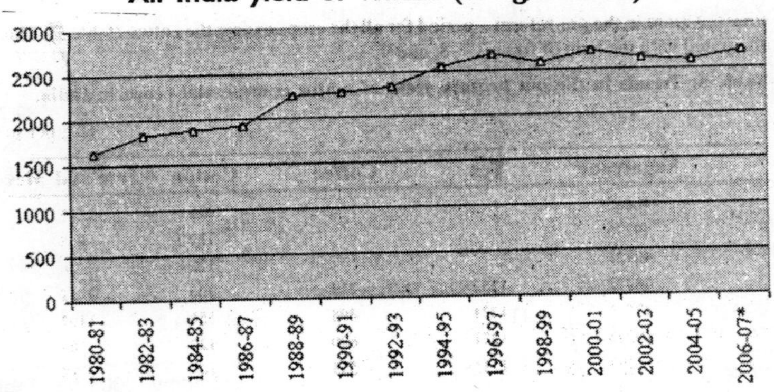

*AE.

Source: Economic Survey, 2008.

FIGURE 5

All India Yields of Pulses (in kg/hectare)

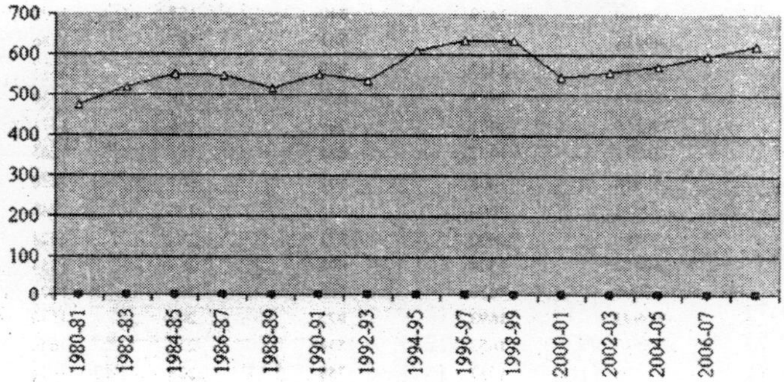

* 2006-07= AE.
Source: Economic Survey.

FIGURE 6

All India Yields of Coarse Cereals

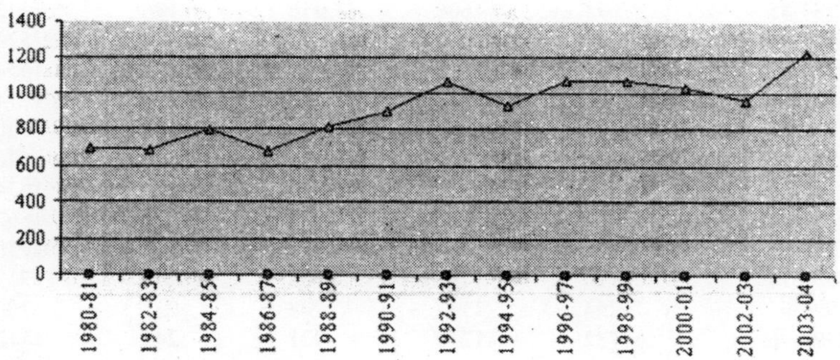

The average productivity of major commercial crops has slightly increased in the post-reform period as compared to the pre-reform era. The fluctuation, i.e. deviation from the average value, in the productivity is witnessed more in the pre-reform period for all the crops except the cotton (Table 4). This trend has been illustrated with the help of Figures 7, 8, and 9.

TABLE 4

Trends in the per hectare Yield of Major Commercial Crops in India

(Kg per hectare)

Year	*Sugarcane*	*Tea*	*Coffee*	*Cotton*	*Jute and Mesta*
1967-68	40665	.	.	123	1137
1968-69	49236	.	.	122	855
1969-70	49121	.	.	122	1120
1970-71	48332	1182	814	106	1032
1971-72	47511	1221	498	151	1107
1972-73	50933	1271	620	127	1104
1973-74	51163	1311	555	142	1188
1974-75	49855	1353	592	161	1068
1975-76	50903	1341	490	138	1164
1976-77	53383	1407	712	144	1173
1977-78	56160	1519	840	157	1108
1978-79	49114	1528	741	167	1186
1979-80	49358	1455	889	160	1177
1980-81	57844	1491	624	152	1130
1981-82	58359	1461	789	166	1311
1982-83	56411	1422	624	163	1265
1983-84	55978	1468	507	141	1320
1984-85	57673	1606	936	196	1242
1985-86	59889	1600	571	197	1524
1986-87	60444	1508	891	169	1454
1987-88	60006	1628	563	158	1274
1988-89	60992	1693	972	202	1540
1989-90	65912	1652	534	252	1646
1990-91	65395	1727	759	225	1634
1991-92	66069	1800	805	216	1662
1992-93	63843	1664	758	257	1658
1993-94	67120	1796	732	249	1713
1994-95	71254	1767	708	257	1760
1995-96	67782	1739	921	242	1712
1996-97	66476	1821	816	265	1818
1997-98	71134	1865	797	208	1792
1998-99	71203	1844	877	224	1722
1999-2000	70935	1685	947	225	1836
2000-01	68577	1679	959	190	1867
2001-02	67370	1675	937	186	2008
2002-03	64562	1679	939	193	1968
2003-04	59119	1656		307	1923

Pre-reform Period (1967-1991)

Statistics	*Sugarcane*	*Tea*	*Coffee*	*Cotton*	*Jute and Mesta*
Mean (kg/hect)	54311.2	1380	604.4	160.4	1239.9
σ	6140.6	345.5	177.09	36.3	197.2
C.V. (%)	11.3	25.2	29.3	22.3	15.9
Post-reform period (1991-2004)					
Mean (kg/hect)	67343.7	1613.8	871.8	232.3	180.3
σ	3385.2	155.2	78.2	34.6	110.7
C.V. (%)	5.02	9.5	8.9	14.6	6.2
Combined (1967-2004)					
Mean (kg/hect)	58889.6	1355.2	756.6	185.7	1437.8
σ	8231.2	634.4	234.7	44.8	228.2
C.V. (%)	13.9	46.8	30.9	26.6	16.6

Source: R.B.I. Handbook of Statistics on the Indian Economy, 2004-05, Table 22.

FIGURE 7

All India Yield of Sugarcane (kg per hectare)

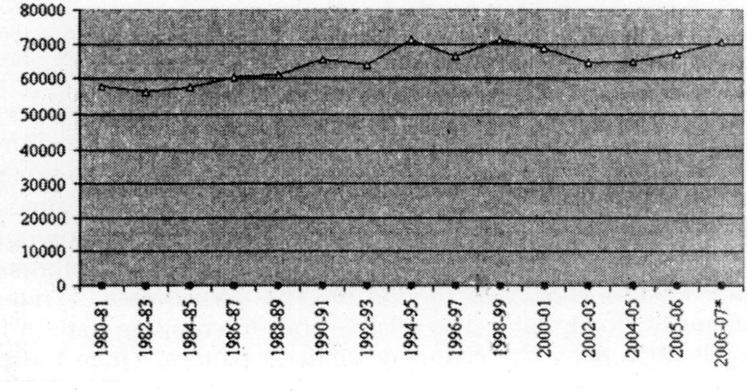

FIGURE 8

All India Yield of Cotton (kg per hectare)

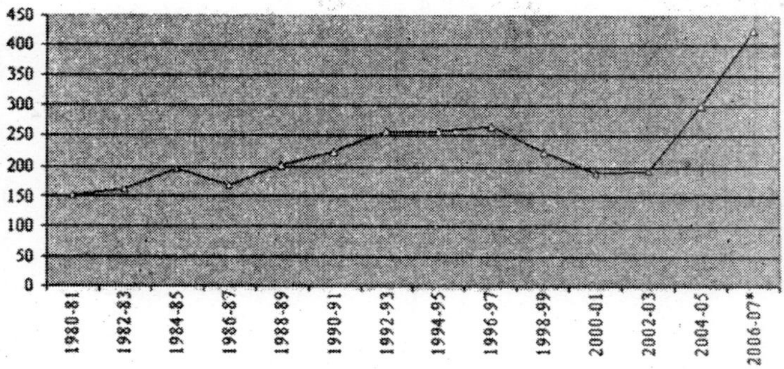

FIGURE 9

All India Yields of Oilseeds (kg per hectare)

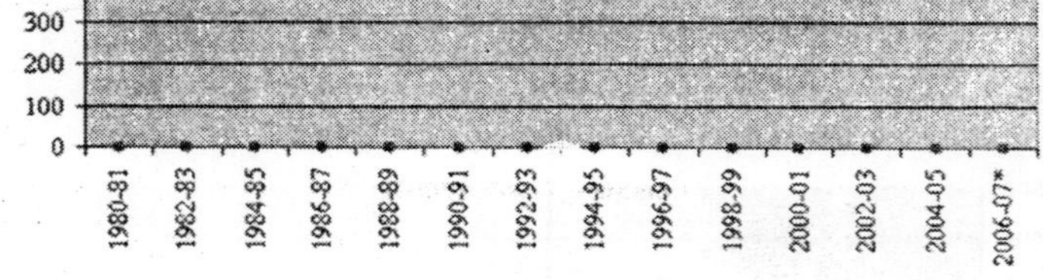

The total area under principal crops has changed very little in recent decades, though area allocation within agriculture has changed from foodgrain crops in favour of non-foodgrain crops. Foodgrain output growth in recent decades is almost entirely due to increase in yield per hectare. The deceleration in agricultural production for both foodgrains and non-foodgrains since 1990 is shown in Figure 10. The deceleration is more evident for foodgrains. The relative shift in cropping pattern is largely driven by the changing demand pattern. Huge buffer stocks of cereals built up by the government—reaching above 60 million tonnes for several months in 2002—points to the limited future consumption growth potential for cereals and the need for further agricultural diversification. Gross production of foodgrains has increased from 130 million tonnes in 1980-81 to 209 million tonnes in 2006-07. The rate of growth of foodgrain production, however, decelerated to 1.2 per cent during 1990-2007, lower than annual rate of growth of population, averaging 1.9 per cent which has caused the decline in the per capita availability of foodgrains in the recent years.

FIGURE 10

Percentage Growth in Yields of Food, Non-food and Total Crops: (1980-81 to 2004-05)

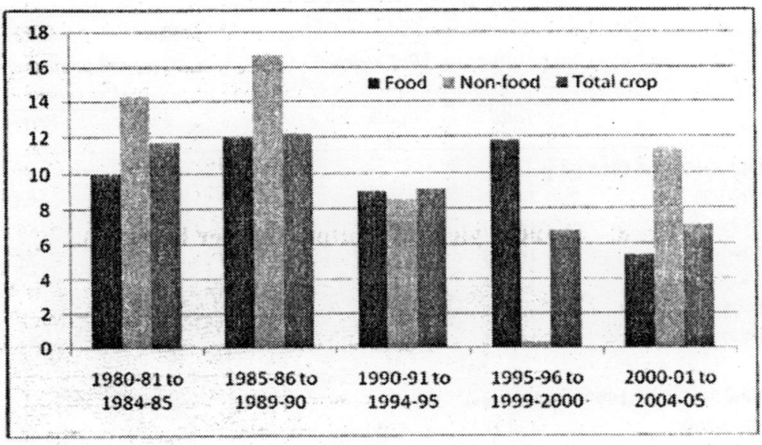

Source: Handbook of Statistics, 2004-05, RBI.

The fall in public investment in agriculture during the 1980s and subsequent near stagnation in the post-reform period has been a matter of concern. The public sector accounted for 54% of agricultural total gross capital formation in 1980-81, but this share fell to about 30% in 1990-91 and further to a quarter by the end of 1990s. This has led to the net irrigated area remaining stagnant at around 53-55 million hectare since mid-1990s. Agricultural public investment in the National Account

Statistics (NAS) mostly covers expenditure on medium and major irrigation systems. The increase in capital formation over the years has been shown in the Table 5.

However the capital formation in recent years (Figure 11), which is primarily due to the private investment component. Despite this investment increase, agriculture growth has stagnated; this reflects rising capital intensity of agricultural production due to factors such as rising cost of land development and depletion of water table in areas dependent on ground water.

TABLE 5

Gross Capital Formation in Agriculture

(in Rupees Crore)

Year	*Investment in Agriculture (Rs Crore)*			*Share in Agricultural gross investment (Per cent)*	
	Total	*Public*	*Private*	*Public*	*Private*
Old Series (at 1993-94 prices)					
1990-91	14836	4395	10441	29.6	70.4
1995-96	15690	4849	10841	30.9	69.1
1996-97	16176	4668	11508	28.9	71.1
1997-98	15942	3979	11963	25	75
1998-99	14895	3870	11025	26	74
1999-2000	17304	4221	13083	24.4	75.6
New Series (at 1999-2000 prices)					
1999-2000	43473	7754	35719	17.8	82.2
2000-01	38176	7018	31158	18.4	81.6
2001-02	46744	8529	38215	18.2	81.8
2002-03	45867	7849	38018	17.1	82.9
2003-04	47833	12809	35024	26.8	73.2
2004-05 (quick estimate)	43123	12951	30532	29.2	70.8

Source: CSO, various issues.

The declining trend in public investment in agriculture since 1980s is attributes to several factors: rising subsidies, growing opposition to big dams and so on.

FIGURE 11

Gross Capital Formation (GCF) in Agriculture (at constant prices)

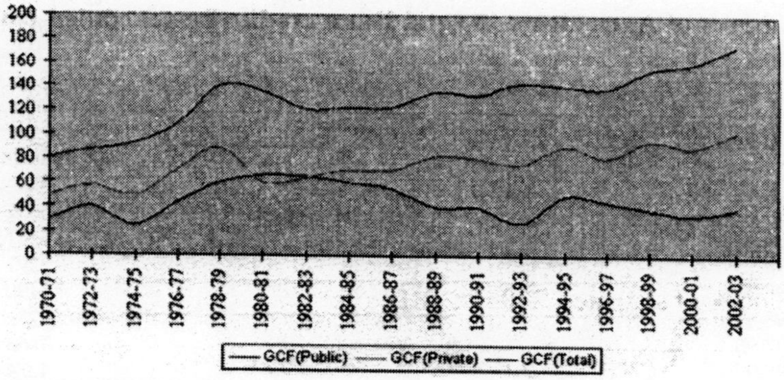

Note: Figures are in Rs. Trillion.
Source: Based on National Accounts Statistics.

The official statistics on the lending of bank credit to Agriculture reveal a steady deterioration since the early 1990s. This is shown in Table 6 and Figure 12. The share of bank credit for agriculture in total bank credit was at its peak level of 17.7 per cent, around the end of the 1980s or early 1990s; they have fallen steadily since then and reached their lowest levels of 10.0 per cent of total bank credit around 2000-01. One evidence of the growing gap in the supply of bank credit for the agriculture lies in the drastic decline in the number of small borrowers' accounts level, as shown in Table 6 and Figure 13.

The number of borrower accounts had touched the peak of 27.74 million at the end of March 1992 and this steadily declined to the lowest level of 19.84 million at the end of March 2001 – a loss of about 29 per cent. But with renewed emphasis given on institutional and structural features in credit policy formulation, the number of loan accounts in agriculture rose by 25 per cent from 21.3 million at the end of March 2004 to 26.66 million at the end of March 2005.

The progress and changes in various factors which affects the agricultural growth and output are presented in Table 7. The table shows that as compared to 1980s there was a sharp increase

TABLE 6

Trends in Lending to Agriculture and Small Borrowal Accounts

Year	*Share of Agriculture as a proportion of total bank credit (in per cent)*	*No. of small borrowers account below Rs. 25,000 (in Thousands)*
1990-91	15.00	5878
1991-92	15.10	6254
1992-93	13.60	5852
1993-94	13.00	5581
1994-95	11.90	5391
1995-96	11.40	5190
1996-97	11.40	4732
1997-98	11.40	4683
1998-99	11.00	4274
1999-2000	9.90	3927
2000-01	9.60	3725
2001-02	9.80	3732
2002-03	10.00	3687
2003-04	10.90	3676
2004-05	10.79	3873

Source: Basic Statistical Returns, various issues.

FIGURE 12

Percentage Shares of Agriculture in Total Bank Credit (By Scheduled Commercial Banks)

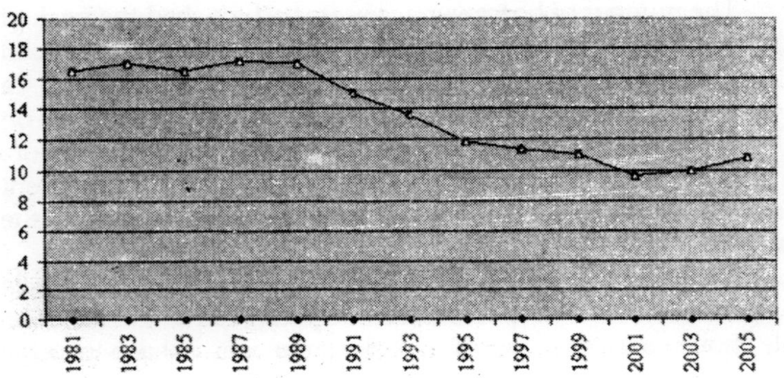

TABLE 7

Growth Rate in Area, Input Use, and Credit and Capital Formation in Agriculture before and after Reforms

(per cent/year)

Variable	*1980-81 to 1990-91*	*1990-91 to 1996-97*	*1996-97 to 2004-05*
Gross cropped area	0.430	0.43	-0.48
Net sown aria	-0.080	0.04	-0.55
Gross irrigated	2.280	2.62	0.51
NPK use/hectare	8.255	2.401	2.044
Electricity consumed in agriculture per hectare	14.162	9.39	-0.159
Area witnessed crop shift (per cent)	5.6	5.6	4.8
Terms of trade	0.189	0.947	-1.63
Public sector net fixed capital stock per hectare	3.939	1.872	1.976
Private sector net fixed capital stock per hectare	0.642	2.134	1.721
Total net fixed capital stock per hectare	2.085	2.01	1.838
Credit supply per hectare	3.810	7.466	15.336

Source: (1) National Accounts Statistics, various issues.
(2) Agricultural Statistics at a Glance (2006), Ministry of Finance, GoI, New Delhi.
(3) Economic Survey, 2006, Ministry of Finance, GoI, New Delhi.

FIGURE 13

Number of Small Burrower Accounts with Credit Limits of Rs. 25,000 or Below (for SCBs)

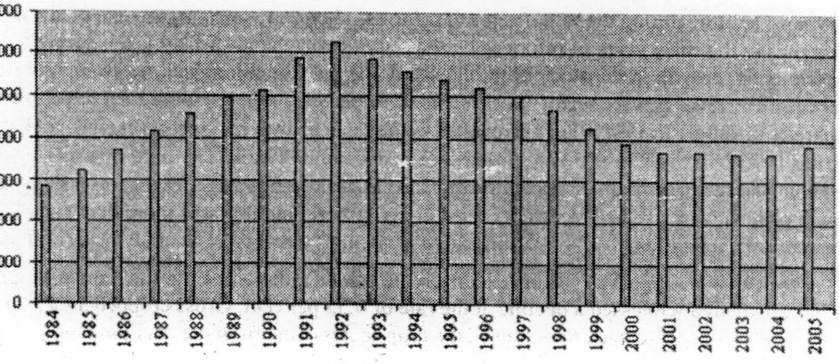

in the terms of trade for agriculture during the initial years of reforms. There was some improvement in the growth of irrigation during the early years of reforms; Public sector investments did not grow during these years, and consequently, growth in the stock of public sector capital formation declined from 3.94 per cent to 1.87 per cent. However, private sector investments in these years showed more than three times growth as compared to 1980-81 to 1990-91. This resulted in the same growth rate in total capital stock in agriculture during 1990-091 to 1996-97, as seen during the decade of 1980s. The pace of expansion in gross cropped area and the pace of diversification were also as strong as 1980s. There was a sharp decline in the growth of fertilizers use and electricity used in agriculture, but this was more than compensated by expansion in area, irrigation, diversification and movement of terms of trade in favour of agriculture.

After 1996-97, almost all factors except credit, turned unfavourable for the growth of agricultural output. Net sown area witnessed a decline at the rate of 0.55 per cent. Gross cropped area also declined on the trend. The biggest setback to output of the crop sector came from the declining terms of trade for agriculture and slowdown in expansion of irrigation.

CONCLUSION

For the revival of agricultural growth, the simultaneous efforts would be required on several fronts. These include: (a) stepping up investment and putting in place suitable institutional mechanisms to exploit irrigation potential that exists in most of the states; (b) increasing power supply to the sector; (c) promoting fertilizer use by expanding the distribution network and improving credit facilities for farmers; (d) establishing competitive seed markets and ensuring attractive prices for seeds; (e) improvement in terms of trade for agriculture; (f) measures to mitigate risk in farming; (g) promoting grouping farming; and (h) developing appropriate micro, meso and macro level institutions for facilitating the agricultural production.

References

A Narayana Murthy (2007): "Deceleration in agricultural growth", *Economic and Political Weekly*, June 23.

Agricultural statistics at a glance, (2006): Ministry of Agriculture, GoI, New Delhi

Bhagirath Behra and Pulak Mishra (2007): "Acceleration of agricultural growth in growth in India: Suggestive policy framework", *Economic and Political Weekly*, October 20.

Bhalla, G.S. and Peter Hazell (2003): "Rural employment and poverty: Strategies to eliminate rural poverty within a generation", *Economic and Political Weekly*, August 16.

Bhatia, M.S. (1999): "Rural infrastructure and growth in agriculture", *Economic and Political Weekly*, March 27.

Central Statistical Organization, various issues.

Chandrasekar, C.P. (2006); "The agrarian constraint on industrial growth: A reassessment in the light of recent experience: Vaidyanathan Felicitation Volume, unpublished collection of papers, April, Institute of Social and Economic Change, Banglore.

Desai, B.M. (2002): "Policy framework for reorienting agricultural development", *Indian Journal of Agricultural Economics*, Vol. 57, No. 1.

Dev, S. Mahendra (2002): "Bold initiatives needed on agriculture and rural employment", *Economic and Political Weekly*, March 23.

Dev, S. Mahendra (2006): "Half- hearted attention to agriculture", *Economic and Political Weekly*, April 8.

Dhar, Biswajit and Murali Kallummal (2004): "Trade liberalization and agriculture: Challenges before India" in Economic Survey, 2006 and 2008, Ministry of Finance, GoI, New Delhi.

Gulati, Ashok and Seema Bathla (2001), "Capital formation in Indian agriculture: Revisiting the debate". *Economic and Political Weekly*, May 19.

Krishnaraj, M. (2006):"Food security agrarian crisis and rural livelihoods: Implication for women", *Economic and Political Weekly*, December 30.

Majumdar, N.A. (2006): "Centrality of agriculture to India's economic development, *Economic and Political Weekly*, January 7.

Mathur, S. Archana, Surajit Das, Subhalakshmi Sircar (2006):"Status of agriculture in India: Trends and prospects", *Economic and Political Weekly*, December 30.

Meeta, Rajivlochan (2008): "Rejuvenating agriculture with the help of the small farmers", *Economic and Political Weekly*, March 15.

Narsimha Rao, P. and K.C. Suri (2006): "Beyond demography, dialogue with people", B.R. publishing corporation, Delhi.

National Accounts Statistics, various issues.

Patil, V.B. (2008): "Agricultural indebtedness: Crisis and revival", *Economic and Political Weekly*, February 2.

R.B.I., Handbook of Statistics on the Indian Economy, 2004-05.

Raesh Chand (2007): "Demand for foodgrain", *Economic and Political Weekly*, December 29.

Ramakumar, R. and Chavan, P. (2007): "Revival of agricultural credit in the 2000s:An explanation, *Economic and Political Weekly*, December 29

Ramesh Chand, S.S. Raju, and L.M. Pandey (2007): "Growth crisis in agriculture-Severity and options at national and state levels", *Economic and Political Weekly*, June 30.

Rao, C.H. Hanumantha (2005): "Agricultural growth, farm size and rural poverty alleviation in India", Academic Foundation, New Delhi.

Rao, C.H.H. and Ashok Gulati (2005): "Indian agriculture: Emerging perspectives and policy issues", Academic Foundation, New Delhi (14) Reddy, V. Ratna, P.P. Reddy (2005): "How participatory is participatory irrigation management? Water user's associations in Andhra Pradesh", Centre for Economic and Social Studies, working paper No. 164.

Satish P. (2007): "Agricultural credit in the post-reform era-A target of systematic policy", *Economic and Political Weekly*, June 30.

Shariff, Abusaleh and Ananth C. Mallick (1999): "Dynamic of food intake and nutrition by expenditure class in India, *Economic and Political Weekly*, July 9.

3

Agriculture in Sustaining Indian Economic Growth

TUSHAR KANTI DAS AND LOPAMUDRA MISHRA

I. INTRODUCTION

Economic growth is the most powerful instrument for reducing poverty and improving the quality of life in developing countries. The goal of development is to improve human well-being in a sustainable way, with particular emphasis on less well off. Rapid and sustained economic growth, though not sufficient for eliminating poverty, is certainly a necessary condition for improving living standards.

India's economic growth has received potential attention in recent years. It is also evident that the India's growth has accelerated over the past two decades. Sweeping economic reforms that commenced in 1991 have included the delicensing of most industries, deregulation of industries earlier monopolized by the public sector, liberalization of foreign trade through a steady reduction in tariffs and freeing up of the foreign investment limits in nearly all industries. These measures have had far reaching consequences and today, India has a strong, vibrant and fast-growing economy which is rapidly integrating with the global economy (Ernst and Young, 2006). India is forecast to become the third largest economy in the world, after China and the US, by the year 2050 overtaking all other developed economies (Wilson and Purushothaman, 2003).

Now the policy challenge for India is not to raise growth from 8 to 10 percent. Rather the primary challenge is to sustain rapid growth while extending rapid growth and its benefits to more regions, sectors and people. Questions have been raised about the distribution of the benefits of growth on income groups, especially the poor. A key concern is the perception of two Indians, one shining and the other bleak, referring to the large gap in the living standard of the rich and the poor (World Bank, 2006; Kohli, 2006).

High growth rate of India can be sustained only if necessary policies are adopted for removing binding constraints like poor infrastructure, stagnant agriculture and lack of fiscal space (Kumar, Palit and Singh, 2007). India's post-independence leadership had undertaken to abolish mass poverty remains only partially fulfilled. Half the battle still lies ahead. The challenge for policy-makers today is to balance the growth momentum with inclusionary policies (Ahmed and Varshney, 2008). The eventual prospects for making India's growth process more inclusive are not encouraging. If rapid growth continues, some of this will necessarily 'trickle down' and help the poor. Beyond that the scope for hastening this trickle via deliberate redistribution is limited (Kohli, 2008).

Evidence suggests that income inequality is rising and the gap in average per capita income between the rich and poor states is growing. In the agriculture-based country like India, agriculture is essential to growth, which in turn necessary to reduce poverty and food insecurity. As the largest sector of the economy agriculture has an important role in providing resources for the development of the overall economy. The objective of the study is to find out the constraints to sustainable growth of agriculture in India and then prescribe appropriate policy measures.

The present section introduces the study. Section II presents the theory of inclusive growth. Section III outlines the measurement of inequality using the convergence principles. Analytical framework of the study is presented in section IV. In section V the empirical findings of different measures of convergence across the fourteen major states of India are presented. Analysis of the present study is presented in section VI. Finally, the concluding remarks of the study are presented in section VII.

II. THEORY OF INCLUSIVE GROWTH

The strategy of 'inclusive growth' combines empowerment with entitlement and investment. Education empowers, improved health care empowers, employment guarantee entitles, fulfilling quota obligations entitles. Through a combination of offering entitlement, ensuring empowerment and stepping up public investment the growth process can be made more inclusive. Inclusive growth also means empowering the disadvantaged. The strategy for inclusive growth is to provide access to basic facilities such as health, education, clean drinking water, etc. to the common people. In the short-run these essential services impact directly on welfare, in the long-run they determine economic opportunities for the future.

Inclusion implies not only reduction in absolute poverty but also in income inequality across income groups and geographical regions. A variety elements and dimensions are involved in determining whether growth is inclusive. The most important dimension is the improvement of the livelihood of the poor. The general consensus is that for growth to be inclusive it must be pro-poor, i.e. growth that is not pro-poor is definitely not inclusive.

Inclusive growth allows people to contribute and benefit from economic growth. Rapid pace of growth is necessary for substantial poverty reduction. For this growth to be substantial in the long-run it should be broad-based across sectors and inclusive of large part of the country's labour force. This definition of inclusive growth implies a direct link between the macro and micro determinants of growth (Ianchovichina and Lundstrom, 2009). The micro dimension captures the importance of structural transformation for economic diversification and competition. Inclusive growth refers both to the pace and pattern of growth which is considered interlinked and therefore they should be addressed together. For achieving a sustainable growth record as well as poverty reduction both the pace and pattern of growth are critical.

The Commission on Growth and Development in their report ***Growth Report: Strategies for Sustained Growth and Inclusive Development*** (2008) stated that 'inclusiveness' is an essential ingredient of any successful growth strategy. Inclusiveness is a concept that includes equity, equality of opportunity and protection in market and employment transitions. The Commission considers systematic inequality of opportunity will be toxic and it will derail the growth process through political channels or conflicts.

The extent to which growth reduces poverty depends in the degree to which the poor participate in the growth process and share in its proceeds. Thus, both the pace and patterns of growth matter for reducing poverty. India's most recent development plan has two main objectives: raising economic growth and making growth more inclusive.

Growth Diagnostics

Last 25 years has seen considerable developments in thinking on development policies. The standard policy reforms included in the Washington Consensus have the potential to be growth promoting. Many countries have adopted the Washington consensus, i.e., the enforcement of property rights, maintenance of macroeconomic stability; integration with the world economy and creation of a sound business environment. However, experiences of last 15 years have shown that impact of these reforms is heavily dependent on circumstances. Growth strategies are likely to differ according to domestic opportunities and constraints. The disappointments with the Washington Consensus led to the Barcelona consensus of 2004. The key recommendation of the Barcelona consensus is that the growth strategies require a sense of priorities. This has led to the development framework for growth diagnostics (Hausmann, Rodrik and Velasco, 2005), i.e., a strategy for figuring out the policy priorities.

Growth diagnostics require in depth knowledge of the economy that is being analyzed (Leipziger, and Zagha, 2006). The strategy is aimed at identifying the most binding constraints on economic growth such as limitations in mobilizing sufficient domestic or foreign finance, low levels of human capital and technological capabilities, weaknesses in governance structures and the poor functioning of institutions that regulate markets or provide public goods and social services. The importance and relevance of these constraints tend to vary from country to country.

The implementation of the Growth Diagnostics framework aims to give the meta-steps that a persuasive growth diagnosis should have, and elaborates on the strategies and methods that may be used (Hausmann, Klinger and Wagner, 2008). Rather than a step-by-step instruction manual or handbook it suggests how to think about the problem of identifying a country's constraints to growth. Analysing constraints does not necessarily make Growth Diagnostics an advocate of economic growth. Countries should find the trade-offs, if any, between growth and other goals through an appropriate political process.

III. INEQUALITY: CONVERGENCE THEORY

The most striking aspect of the per capita income distribution of the economies is very large and has persistent disparities. There have been "growth disasters" economies in which per capita income have fallen and "growth miracles" economies which have risen rapidly up the world income distribution. One of the first questions we might ask is whether there is a systematic tendency for poor countries to grow faster than rich ones, which would allow them to catch up.

Convergence theory dates back to the standard neo-classical growth model with exogenous technological process and a closed economy. Neo-classical growth models for closed economies are given by Solow (1956), Cass (1965) and Koopmans (1965). Their model states that the per capita growth rate tends to be inversely-related to the starting level of output or income per person in the economy. In particular, if economies are similar in respect to preferences and technologies then poor economies grow faster than rich ones.

The seminal theoretical contributions of Romer (1986) and Lucas (1988) on endogenous growth mechanisms have generated a lively empirical literature. This literature has primarily focused on the so called 'convergence hypothesis'. The hypothesis asserts that differences in contemporaneous per capita income between any pair of economies will be transitory so long as the two economies possess identical technologies, preferences and population growth rates [Bernard and Darlauf, (1996)]. By implication the effects of initial stocks of human and physical capital on per capita output differences will be transitory so long as these other factors are accounted for.

In recent years, since the appearance of the pioneering studies [Baumol (1986) Barro (1991) and Mankiew *et al.* (1992)] considerable effort have been devoted to identifying changes over time in the cross-sectional distribution of per capita income between economies. These studies have observed that economies with low initial income tend to grow faster than economies with high initial incomes with controlled savings rate and population growth. This finding has been treated as an evidence of convergence. There are many studies of the international processes of growth and convergence across countries [Baumol (1986), De Long (1988), Dowrick and Nguyen (1989) and Barro and Sala-i-Martin (1995) among others] and regional growth patterns within any given country.

A summary statistics is used to measure convergence directly employing coefficient of variation (C.V.) by Baumol and Wolff (1988), Metha, Crihfield and Gietz (1992), Izraeli and Murphy (1997) and Roberts (1997). Izraeli and Murphy (1997) have also used Bourguignon's L-statistics to measure convergence directly.

Empirical models which estimate a relationship of the form $y_{it} = f(y_{io})$, where 'y_{it}' measures the size of some economic unit 'i' at time 't', have a long tradition in the economics literature. It is known that cross sectional estimation is hazardous in the case where 'y_{it}' tends to converge towards steady state values, which differ across 'i'; or in other words, when there are heterogeneous individual effects. Islam (1995) for example, has pointed out that, since the omitted individual effects are correlated with the explanatory variable 'y_{io}', the estimated coefficient on the latter is upward biased. Recent studies like Funke and Strulik (1999) and Goddard and Wilson (2001) have used panel estimation of convergence.

IV. ANALYTICAL FRAMEWORK

State level data of India on the per capita income are taken as the source of convergence in the present analysis. Per capita incomes for the fourteen major states of India at constant prices are collected from the Central Statistical Organisation. Also the per capita agriculture income is taken for the fourteen major states and the inequality is verified using the convergence principle. The availability of data restricted the period of study from 1980 to 2006 for the fourteen major states of India. Three distinct methods have been adopted in the present study to measure convergence.

(a) Direct Measures of Convergence

Direct measures of convergence seek to measure convergence directly using a summary statistic such as the square of coefficient of variation (C.V.) or Bourguignon L-statistics (1979). Both the measures are aggregative, income zero homogeneity, obey Pigou-Dalton condition and also are additively decomposable. These statistics are not sensitive to the national rate of inflation, as both the measures are proportions (pure-numbers).

$$\text{Here,}\quad \text{C.V.} = \frac{\sigma}{\overline{X}} \times 100 \tag{1}$$

An 'σ' represents the standard deviation in the per capita income of the fourteen major states at a particular time period and $\overline{X}$ the simple arithmetic mean.

Likewise,

$$L = \log\left(\frac{1}{4}\sum_{i=1}^{n} y_i\right) - \frac{1}{n}\sum_{i=1}^{n} \log y_i, \tag{2}$$

Here 'y_i' is the per capita income of the 'i'th state.

(a) Indirect Measurement of Convergence

Indirect measurement of convergence deals with two concepts of convergence. They are: (i) b-convergence, and (ii) s-convergence. Absolute b-convergence occurs if poor economies tend to grow faster than rich ones. Let 'y_{it}' be the per capita income for a cross section of economies (of states) in time period 't'.

Also, let, $g_{i, t, t+T} = [\log (y_{i, t+T}/y_{i, t})]$ (3)

be the 'i'th economy's growth rate of per capita income between 't' and 't+T' and let $\log(y_{i,t})$ be the logarithm of economy i's income per capita at time 't'.

If, $g_{i, t, t+T} = a + b \,.\, \log (y_{i,t}) + \hat{I}_i$ (4)

or, $g_{i, t, t+T} = a + [\log (y_{i,t}) \,.\, (1-e^{-b\,T})] + \hat{I}_i$ (5)

The above equation is estimated and if $b<0$, then the data set exhibits b-convergence.

Here, $b = (1-e^{-b\,T})$, where, 'b' is the speed of convergence.

The concept of s-convergence can be defined as, a group of economies are converging in the sense of 's' if, the dispersion of per capita income tends to decrease overtime. That is, $s_t > s_{t+T}$ where 's_t' is the time 't' standard deviation of $\log (y_{i,t})$ across 'i'.

(b) Panel data estimates

One common issue that arises in panel data estimation is whether the individual effects are to be thought of as 'fixed' or 'random'. In the later case the effects are to be uncorrelated with the exogenous variables included in the model. It is clear that estimators relying on such assumptions [for example, GLS in Maddala (1971)] are not suitable because it is precisely the fact of correlation that forms the basis for panel approach. The least square with dummy variable estimator, which is based on the fixed effect assumption, is still permissible [Islam (1995)].

By exploiting a pooled time-series and cross-sectional structure, less information is lost than taking an average value for each variable for each region over the period in question. In other words, panel data estimates introduced here provide more transparent and intuitively more reasonable results [Funke and Strulik (1999)]. The growth equation as a dynamic panel data model is formulated below.

Let 'y_{it}' be the ratio of (Y_{it}/Y_t^*) where 'Y_{it}' is the 'i'th state per capita income in period't' and Y_t^* is aggregate (average) per capita income in fourteen major states of India in period 't'. Allowing for different steady states and different convergence rates across the 14 major states gives the following expression for 'y_{it}'.

The model here is

$$\ln (y_{it}) = g \cdot y_{i,o} + r_i \cdot \ln (y_{i,t-1}) \quad (6)$$

In the above equation, i = 1, 2, ...N and t = 1, 2.... T.

The model allows for initial per capita incomes to influence future growth through the parameter 'g'. The corresponding statistical model can be written as

$$\ln (y_{it}) = a_i + r_i \cdot \ln (y_{i,t-1}) + \hat{I}_{it} \quad (7)$$

Note that b_i = -ln (r_i) and '$\hat{I}_{it}$' represent independently drawings from a normal distribution with mean zero and variance $s^2\hat{I}$. The model allows the initial conditions to influence future growth through a_i. The (relative) steady state value of y_{it} is ($a_i/1-r_i$) which is a measure of efficiency and reflects total factor productivity in region 'i'.

V. AGRICULTURAL GROWTH AND STATE INCOME

In the direct measures of convergence two statistics, i.e. the square of coefficient of variation and Bourguignon L-statistics are used to measure the degree of variation in the per capita state income and per capita agricultural income. The estimates of the two statistics for the fourteen major states of India during 1980 to 2006 are presented in Table 1. Both the statistics indicate the variability among the states in the per capita income and per capita agricultural income has increased.

In the indirect measurement of convergence, the estimated value of 'b' in case of per capita income during 1980-81 to 2006-07 for the fourteen major states is 0.3493 (Table 2). Similarly for per capita agricultural income the estimated 'b' is 0.1062 (Table 3). Clearly, b>0 and hence over the period 1980-81 to 2006-07 we

TABLE I

Square of C.V. and L-Statistics of per capita State Income and per capita State Agricultural Income

Year	Per capita Income		Per capita Agriculture Income	
	Sq of C.V.	L Statistics	Sq of C.V.	L Statistics
1980	878.622523	0.016770711	1707.06863	0.027676291
1981	920.8218495	0.017246962	1753.145889	0.029196073
1982	995.595992	0.018363916	2108.489214	0.034023059
1983	798.2845766	0.015162054	1597.151838	0.028948645
1984	926.9832124	0.016846321	1799.664448	0.028117118
1985	1212.763246	0.021408088	2422.174266	0.03555224
1986	1093.476921	0.018921263	2389.419907	0.035364148
1987	1129.213356	0.019895778	2695.935741	0.039543567
1988	1017.312234	0.018707475	2217.558178	0.035128402
1989	1070.441001	0.020375998	2454.335753	0.036503924
1990	1124.854619	0.021231951	2527.490028	0.036027273
1991	1187.711591	0.022608791	2933.719373	0.04123983
1992	1230.752539	0.025495056	2617.586671	0.038671103
1993	1259.916544	0.026601056	2575.675717	0.037038578
1994	1168.712326	0.025500924	2277.799802	0.033217239
1995	1254.204029	0.029710731	2363.33646	0.03676112
1996	1244.619241	0.028225813	2322.308649	0.036316593
1997	1195.857298	0.028519807	2150.974012	0.035462745
1998	1184.109179	0.029027977	1937.479345	0.031423792
1999	1196.256173	0.029239198	2454.962127	0.038076401
2000	1239.967429	0.028961579	2637.257014	0.039634497
2001	1238.661493	0.030453317	2300.455573	0.036702893
2002	1360.929016	0.032263333	2802.538291	0.040949825
2003	1301.733384	0.032883492	2489.055513	0.042180711
2004	1344.86595	0.033530746	2328.460394	0.036238481
2005	1460.206649	0.037282301	2161.733817	0.036915119
2006	2080.95695	0.045594637	2803.045825	0.044909107

have b-divergence in both the per capita income and per capita agricultural income. Likewise there is s-divergence for both the variables.

The set of results and the steady state values obtained through the panel data estimates for the fourteen major states are presented in Table 4 and Table 5. The states are diverging in terms of the per capita income and per capita agricultural

TABLE 2

Cross-sectional Regression of per capita State Income [(dépendent variable log) (y_{2006}/y_{1980})]

Parameters	*Ordinary Least Square*
Constant	-1.0049
(-1.1752)	
log (y_{1980})	0.3493**
(1.6063)	
R^2	0.1769
σ-convergence in the per capita state income	
σ_{1980}	σ_{2006}
0.1244	0.1923

** indicates significance of the t-value at 5% level of significance.

Note: Figures in the parentheses indicates the respective t-value.

TABLE 3

Cross-sectional Regression of per capita Agricultural Income [(dependent variable log) (y^a_{2006}/y^a_{1980})]

Parameters	*Ordinary Least Square*
Constant	0.4904
(0.7618)	
log (y^a_{1980})	0.1062
(0.5800)	
R^2	0.0272
σ-convergence in the per capita state agricultural income	
σ_{1980}	σ_{2006}
0.1532	0.1679

Note: Figures in the parentheses indicates the respective t-value.

income. The steady state value can be negative, implying in the steady state, these states grow at a lower rate than the average. The significant 'a_i' coefficients in some states indicate persistence of inequality, with the passage of time some rich regions tend to remain rich while other poor regions continue to lag behind.

Now the question is why has the growth rates of various

TABLE 4

Panel Data Estimates of per capita Income of Fourteen Major States

State	α	ρ	*Divergence rate*	*Steady state*
Andhra Pradesh	-0.00868 (-0.50)	0.73453* (4.64)	0.3085	-0.0327
Bihar	-0.09912 (-1.36)	0.89637* (10.38)	0.1094	-0.9565
Gujarat	0.06939* (2.64)	0.42561 (2.13)	0.8542	0.1208
Haryana	0.13591 (-0.62)	0.68371* (3.36)	0.3802	0.4297
Karnataka	-0.00123 (-0.102)	0.87634* (7.96)	0.1320	-0.0099
Kerala	0.008847 (0.58)	0.96273* (8.89)	0.0380	0.2374
M. P.	-0.05892 (-1.67)	0.84828* (7.67)	0.1645	-0.3883
Maharashtra	0.05097 (1.56)	0.83095* (7.08)	0.1852	0.3015
Orissa	-0.08779* (-2.09)	0.75066* (6.25)	0.2868	-0.3521
Punjab	0.02812 (0.61)	0.93466* (10.16)	0.0676	0.4304
Rajasthan	-0.16654* (-3.72)	0.20942 (1.04)	1.5634	-0.2107
T.N.	0.01918 (1.71)	0.89443* (8.89)	0.1116	0.1817
U.P.	-0.01862 (-0.93)	0.98635* (21.05)	0.0137	-1.3641
W.B.	-0.01294 (-1.04)	0.80986* (6.10)	0.2109	-0.0681

Note: * indicates significance of the t-value at 1% level of significance.

states diverged so much in the period 1980-2006: First it is well known that greater reliance on market forces tends to generate inequalities to begin with. States better endowed with infrastructure benefit more when markets are freed up. This was

TABLE 5

Panel Data Estimates of per capita Agricultural Income of Fourteen Major States

State	α	ρ	*Divergence rate*	*Steady state*
Andhra Pradesh	0.00905	0.48784*	0.7178	0.0177
	(0.56)	(2.62)		
Bihar	-0.23079*	0.63105*	0.4604	-0.6255
	(-2.46)	(4.20)		
Gujarat	-0.08718	0.145918	1.9247	-0.1021
	(-1.68)	(0.69)		
Haryana	0.40776*	0.30320	1.1934	0.5852
	(3.44)	(1.52)		
Karnataka	-0.0906*	0.28608	1.2515	-0.1269
	(-2.78)	(1.43)		
Kerala	-0.07858	0.7494*	0.2885	-0.3136
	(-1.54)	(5.14)		
M. P.	-0.23299*	0.0978	2.3248	-0.2582
	(-4.13)	(0.46)		
Maharashtra	-0.14189*	0.46678*	0.7619	-0.2661
	(-2.52)	(2.49)		
Orissa	-0.06054	0.729597*	0.3153	-0.2239
	((-1.73)	(5.42)		
Punjab	0.45910*	0.44195*	0.8166	0.8227
	(3.50)	(2.75)		
Rajasthan	-0.00255	0.15188	0.6697	-0.0052
	(-0.09)	(-0.75)		
T.N.	-0.23842*	0.43240*	0.8384	-0.4200
	(-3.03)	(2.47)		
U.P.	-0.0682*	0.71148*	0.3404	-0.2364
	(-1.97)	(4.36)		
W.B.	-0.00861	0.81795*	0.2010	-0.0473
		(-0.40)	(7.05)	

Note: * indicates significance of the t-value at 1% level of significance.

true even when the green revolution technologies and farm price incentives were introduced in the mid-1960s. Punjab, Haryana, and western Utter Pradesh were the first to have the green revolution. The other states benefited later. By now, of course, Punjab and Uttar Pradesh have declined, showing that the initial advantages do not last forever and other states may eventually catch up. The early beneficiaries of the new reforms in India are all states with a better infrastructure.

Second, especially after 1991, India's states have been allowed to negotiate directly with foreign investors and international financial institutions. Before 1991, all state-level negotiations of this kind were routed through Delhi. Moreover, during 1950–80, central planning ensured some equity in investment and resource flows. The better endowed states are now able to attract greater investment.

VI. ANALYSIS

The liberalization policy of 1991 has allowed the states to play a larger role in determining their development paths and attracting investment. India's success in fostering economic growth has created new challenges. The question now is how India can sustain that success and expand the opportunities for all to participate in it and benefit from it. Increased growth since the mid 1980s has helped substantially to reduce the national poverty rate to 22% of the population in 2004, with the speed of poverty reduction appearing to increase between 1999 and 2004. To meet one of its Millennium Development Goals, of halving poverty by 2015, the government is aiming to achieve an even higher medium-term economic annual growth rate of 10%. In addition, growth needs to become more inclusive by increasing the prosperity of poorer states, whose economies have expanded at a slower pace than those of richer states in the past decade, and so reducing their difficulties in lowering poverty.

On the structural side there are three main constraints to sustained growth in India. They are infrastructure, shortages of skills and slow agricultural growth. The first two are exacerbated by the fast growth of the Indian economy in recent years. Agriculture which accounts for a fifth of GDP grew at only 2.5% per year over last decade. Agricultural growth was faster over the last five years (4.7%) facilitated by very good monsoons, greater production of high-value agricultural products (fruits, vegetables and dairy products), an increase in the minimum support price for grains and the sudden increase in global prices for agricultural products. Sustaining this level of performance over the longer-term will be difficult without addressing several policy and structural constraints.

Important challenges persist for agriculture. The need to accelerate growth in India's agricultural sector prompts special consideration due to the slow down on agricultural production, employment and wages. Where growth in nonagricultural sector has accelerated, the reallocation of labour out of agriculture is lagging, concentrating poverty in rural areas and widening rural-urban income disparities. More divergence of agricultural income in low income states implies the need for strategies for these regions. There should be new strategy which should rely much more on policies to liberalise agricultural inputs and outputs by reforming land administration and tenancy requirements and by supporting research and development that is tailored by specific needs. A comprehensive policy approach to stimulate agricultural growth includes four key elements: improving core public goods and a better climate for private investment, building effective institutions and ensuring sustainable use of natural resources.

As the largest sector agriculture has an important role in providing resources for the development of the overall economy. Successful countries have invested in agriculture to stimulate growth. Investments in core public goods—science, infrastructure and human capital—combined with better policies and institutions are major drivers of agricultural productivity. In additions, investments will have to come from rural savings and the private sector, with the rural investment climate an important determining factor. Investment in public goods such as infrastructure is part of a good investment climate for the private sector, but well-functioning institutions and regulations are equally important.

VII. CONCLUSION

Institutional innovations can be major sources of productivity growth. Three major groups of institutions are important for agriculture. They are: (a) Institutions to make markets work better, such as market regulation and information systems; (b) Secure property rights for land and water to motivate private investment in agriculture especially investments with a longer term pay-off, and (c) Collective action by farmers through well performing farmer organizations to reduce transactions costs connect farmers to markets and improve their bargaining position in those markets.

A look at agricultural sector strategies, results of appropriate stakeholder surveys, political analysis and micro-level sectoral diagnostics (such as investment climate assessments and public expenditure reviews) will provide an essential supplement in arriving at an informed decision in this regard.

The policy underpinning of sustained, high growth create an environment for high level of investment, job creation, competition, mobility of resources, social protections, equity and inclusiveness. An understanding of the dynamics and a focused attention on the policy foundations will significantly increase the chances of accelerating growth. Conversely, persistent inattention will harm it.

Finally, in a rapidly growing economy like India, as one constraint is lifted, another will emerge and become 'binding' for economic growth. The government of India's justifiable concern with the inclusiveness of economic growth can be addressed by focusing on expanding the regional scope of economic growth, expanding access to assets and thriving markets and expanding equity in the opportunities for the next generation of Indian citizens.

References

Acharya, S., 2007, Can India Grow without Bharat? Academic Foundation, New Delhi.

Aghion, P. and Howitt, P., 2005, 'Appropriate Growth Policy: A Unifying Framework'. Harvard University, Working Paper.

Aghion, P. and Williamson, J.G., 1998, Growth, Inequality and Globalization: Theory, History and Policy, Cambridge: Cambridge University Press.

Ahmed, S. and Varshney, A., 2008, 'Battles Half Won: The Political Economy of India's Growth and Economic Policy since Independence'. Working Paper No. 15. Commission on Growth and Development, Washington DC.

Alan Winters, L. and Yusuf, S. (Eds.), 2007, Dancing with Giants: China, India, and the Global Economy, The World Bank and The Institute of Policy Studies, Singapore.

Barro, R.J. and Sala-i-Martin, X., 1995, Economic Growth, Singapore: McGraw-Hill International Editions.

Barro, R.J. and Sala-i-Martin, X., 1992, 'Convergence', *Journal of Political Economy*, Vol. 100, May, pp. 223-52.

Baumol, W.J., 1986, 'Productivity Growth, Convergence and Welfare: What the long-run data show', *American Economic Review*, Vol. 76, No. 5, pp. 1072-85.

Baumol, W.J. and Wolff, E.N., 1988, 'Productivity Growth, Convergence and Welfare: Reply', *American Economic Review*, Vol. 78, No. 5, pp. 1155-59.

Bloom, D.E., Canning, D., Hu, L., Liu, Y., Mahal, A. and Yip, W., 2006, 'Why has Chinas Economy Taken-off Faster than India's?', Princeton University.

Bosworth, B. and Collins, S.M. and Virmani, A., 2007, 'Sources of Growth in the Indian Economy', NBER Working Paper 12901, Cambridge, MA, February.

Bosworth, B. and Collins, S.M., 2007, 'Accounting for Growth: Comparing China and India', NBER Working Paper No. 12943, Cambridge, MA, February.

Bourguignon, F., 1979, 'Decomposable Income Inequality Measures', *Econometrica*, Vol. 47, No. 4, pp. 901-20.

Broadman, H.G., 2007, Africa's Silk Road: China and India's New Economic Frontier, World Bank, Washington, DC.

Cashin, P. and Sahay, R., 1996, 'Regional Economic Growth and Convergence in India', *Finance and Development*, March, pp. 49-52.

Commission on Growth and Development, 2008, Growth Report: Strategies for Sustained Growth and Inclusive Development, the World Bank.

Das, T.K., 2000, 'Economic Growth and Convergence across Indian States', International Symposium on Development Policies for the New Millennium, Contributed Papers, IGIDR, Mumbai, 12th-14th July, pp. 89-94.

De Long, J.B., 1988, 'Productivity Growth, Convergence and Welfare: Comment', *American Economic Review*, Vol. 78, No. 5, pp. 1138-54.

Dowrick, S. and Nguyen, D.T., 1988, 'OECD Comparative Economic Growth 1950-85: Catch up and Convergence', *American Economic Review*, Vol. 79, pp. 1010-30.

Ernst and Young, 2006, Doing Business in India, Ernst and Young Private Limited, New Delhi

Funke, M. and Strulik, H., 1999, 'Regional Growth in West Germany: Convergence Divergence', *Economic Modeling*, Vol. 16, pp. 489-502.

Ghosh, B., Marjit, S. and Neogi, C., 1998, 'Economic Growth and Regional Divergence in India, 1960 to 1995', *Economic and Political Weekly*, June 27, pp. 1623-30.

Goddar, J. and Wilson, J., 2001, 'Cross Sectional and Panel Estimation of Convergence', *Economic Letters*, Vol. 70, pp. 327-33.

Gordon, J. and Gupta, P., 2003, 'Understanding India's Services Revolution', IMF-NCAER Conference, New Delhi, November 14-16.

Government of India, 2006, Towards Faster and More Inclusive Growth: An Approach to the 11th Five Year Plan (2007-12), Planning Commission, Yojana Bhavan, New Delhi, December.

Hausmann, R., Pritchett, L., and Rodri,k D., 2004, 'Growth Accelerations', Harvard University, May.

Hausmann, R., Rodrik, D. and Velasco, A., 2005, 'Growth Diagnostics', John F. Kennedy School of Government, Harvard University, Cambridge, MA, March.

Hausmann, R. Klinger, B. and Wagner, R., 2008, 'Doing Growth Diagnostics in Practice: A 'Mindbook', Working Paper No. 177, Center for International Development, Harvard University, September.

IMF, 2006, 'Understanding Growth', *Finance and Development*, Vol. 43, No. 1

IMF, 2006, Learning from Each Other: Reforms and Policies for Sustained Growth, Washington, DC.

Islam, N., 1995, 'Growth Empirics: A Panel Data Approach', *Quarterly Journal of Economics*, 60: 1127-70.

Ianchovichina, Elena and Lundstrom, Susanna, 2009, Inclusive Growth Analytics: Framework and Application, World Bank Policy Research Working Paper 4851, March.

Izraeli, O. and Murphy, K., 1997, 'Convergence in State Nominal and Real per capita Income', *Public Finance Review*, Vol. 25, No. 6, pp. 555-76.

JM Morgan Stanley, 2006, India and China: New Tigers of Asia, Part-II, Special Economic Analysis, Mumbai, June.

Khanna T., 2004, 'India's Entrepreneurial Advantage', The McKinsey Quarterly, Special Edition, *China Today*, p. 111.

Kohli, Atul, 2006, 'Politics of Economic Growth in India, 1980-2005, Part I: The 1980s', *Economic and Political Weekly*, April 1, pp 1251-1259 and 'Politics of Economic Growth in India, 1980-2005, Part II: the 1990s and Beyond', *Economic and Political Weekly*, April 8, pp. 1361-70.

Kohli, Atul, 2008, 'State and Redistributive Development in India', Working Paper, Princeton University.

Kumar, R., Palit, A. and Singh, K., 2007, 'Sustainability of Economic Growth in India', Working Paper No. 25, Center for International Governance Innovation, Ontario, May.

Lane, P.R. and Schmukler, S.L., 2007, The International Financial Integration of China and India, WPS 4132, World Bank, Policy Research Working Paper.

Leipziger D. and Zagha R., 2006, 'Getting Out of the Rut', *Finance and Development*, Vol. 43, No. 1, pp. 16-18.

Lin, J.Y., 2004, 'Development Strategies for Inclusive Growth in Developing Asia', China Center for Economic Research, Working Paper No. E2004007.

Lucas, R.E., 1988, 'On the Mechanics of Economic Development', *Journal of Monetary Economics*, Vol. 22, July, pp. 3-22.

Lucas, R.E., 1990, 'Why Does not Capital Flow from Rich to Poor Countries?', *American Economic Review*, Vol. 80, May, pp. 92-96.

Maddala, G.S., 1971, 'The use of Variance Components Model in Pooling cross-section and Time Series Data', *Econometrica*, Vol. 39, pp. 341-58.

Mankiew, N.G., Romer, D. and Weil, D.N., 1992, 'A Contribution to the Empirics of Economic Growth', *Quarterly Journal of Economics*, Vol. 107, May, pp. 407-37.

Metha, S.J., Crihfield, J.B. and Giertz, F., 1992, 'Economic Growth in American States: The End of Convergence', Working Paper No. 20, Institute of Governments and Public Affair, University of Illinois.

Poirson, H., 2007, India: Country Study, IMF Research Bulletin, June.

Purfield, C. and Schiff, J. (Eds.), 2006, India Goes Global: Its Expanding Role in the World Economy, International Monetary Fund, Washington, DC.

Roach, S., 2006, India and China: New Tigers of Asia, Part-II, JM Morgan Stanley Research, Mumbai, June.

Roberts, C.A., 1997, 'Interregional per capita Income Differences and Convergence: 1880-1950', *Journal of Economic History*, Vol. 39, No. 1, pp. 101-12.

Romer, P., 1986, 'Increasing Returns and Long-run Growth', *Journal of Political Economy*, Vol. 94, October, pp. 1002-37.

Romer, P., 1989, 'Capital Accumulation in the Theory of Long-run Growth', R.J. Barro (ed.) Modern Business Cycle Theory, Cambridge-Mass: Harvard University Press.

Solow, R.M., 1956, 'A Contribution to the Theory of Economic Growth', *Quarterly Journal of Economic*, Vol. 70, February, pp. 65-94.

United Nations, 2006, World Economic and Social Survey: Diverging Growth and Development, *Economic and Social Affairs*.

Wilson, D. and Purushothaman, R., 2003, Dreaming with BRICs: The Path to 2050, Goldman Sachs Global Economics, New York, Paper No. 99.

World Bank, 2005, Economic Growth in the 1990s: Learning from a Decade of Reforms, Washington, DC.

World Bank, 2006, Inclusive Growth and Service Delivery: Building on India's Success, *Development Policy Review*, Washington, DC

World Bank, 2009, India: Country Strategy (CAS) 2009-2012, accessed on 18/1/2009.

Zagha, R., Nankani, G. and Gill, I., 2006, 'Rethinking Growth', *Finance and Development*, Vol. 43, No. 1, pp. 7-11.

4

Agricultural Deceleration in Uttar Pradesh: An Ecological, Institutional and Technological Investigation

SANATAN NAYAK

INTRODUCTION

Agricultural crisis in India in recent years is the combination of economic, ecological, technological and institutional factors (Behera, *et al.*, 2007). It is pointed that the recent agricultural deceleration is due to combination of policy fatigue, institutional fatigue and ecological fatigue. The analysis of growth of agriculture at the all India level in recent years confirms that government expenditure in agriculture including public investment, subsidy for fertilizer and electricity consumption in agriculture are the main factors affecting agricultural production in India. Agricultural prices have a positive significant impact on its production. Exogenous variables like rainfall and population are also important. However, the recent agrarian crises have been resulted by various factors. The present crises is attributed due to technological, ecological, socio-economic and other policy-related factors (Reddy and Galab, 2006), lack of an interesting farming approach (Desai, 2002), weak agricultural and extension network, restriction on agricultural trade and processing (Rao, 2003), inadequate public expenditure on rural infrastructure (Sharma and Gulati, 2005). However, the experts called for the 43rd National Development Council in May, 2007 opined that technological fatigue is one of the important reason for the agrarian crisis started from the mid of 90's. The same reasons have been supported by the Prime Minister as "One feature that stands out is the lack of any breakthrough in agricultural production technology in recent years. There is a technological fatigue, which need to be addressed", (GoI, 2007). Moreover, the poor performance of agriculture experienced in recent years is not because of technological fatigue but mainly because of policy fatigue (Narayanamoorthy, A., 2007). In fact, the intensive cultivation of mono-crops along with heavy doses of chemical fertilizers may have affected the soil fertility, which may be causing deceleration in agriculture. Disproportionate use of chemical fertilizer may have affected the fertility of the soil (Narayanmoorthy, 1995). The stagnation in the productivity of pulses varieties and other crops, namely, cotton is not due to technological factor but definitely due to policy fatigue. There are several policy fatigues are the main reasons for the agrarian crisis and deceleration in agricultural growth. Major policy fatigue is the faulty agricultural price policy. Farmers are unable to recover even the cost of cultivation because of faulty price policy. The cost of cultivation of crops has been increasing over the years because of increase in wage rate of labour, input prices and other managerial costs. The ratio of value of crops to costs of cultivation became less than one for major crops like cotton, paddy, wheat, sugarcane and groundnut for some states as the CACP data revealed. Secondly, fixed capital formation by public sector in agriculture has been continuously declining both in absolute term as well as in relation to agricultural GDP. Thirdly, there has been significant reduction in the growth of institutional credit to agriculture during post-reformed period. Fourthly, there is no appreciable increment in the NIA since mid-1990 because of inadequate allocation of funds required for completing ongoing projects and poor monitoring of project by the state agency. This poor growth in surface irrigation has compelled farmers to rely heavily on groundwater irrigation. The increased dependence on groundwater irrigation increases the cost of cultivation. It also depletes the water level and increases the rate of well failures in many places of India.

Objectives

Considering the above issues on agricultural deceleration in recent years in India, the study would focus on agricultural deceleration and factors responsible for it in Uttar Pradesh. First, brief outline on the growth of important crops in the regions of Uttar Pradesh. Secondly, analyze the trend and dynamics of some of the economic, some of exogenous ecological factors, institutional and technological factors, which are held responsible for the deceleration of various crops in the State. Thirdly, draw some conclusions and policy prescriptions.

This study consists of four sections. Section I deals with introduction and review of some problems. Section II highlights the regional analysis of the growth of various crops in the state. Section III deals factors responsible for the crisis in the recent years. Last section deals with summery and conclusions of the study.

II. AGRICULTURAL GROWTH IN UTTAR PRADESH

The CAGR of major foodgrains such as Rice, Wheat, Jowar, Bajra, and Pulses are shown deceleration over decades since 80's. The CAGR in 90's is lower than that of in 90's in UP for major cereals as well as pulses in the State. The CAGR of foodgrains in the present decade is lower compared to the CAGR in 90's at the UP level. However, this has been true for major oil seeds in the state but become reverse for the case of sugarcane in the state. However, the CAGR of rice in Western region has come down dramatically from 4.5 percent in 90's to 0.00 percent in the present decade till 2006-07. The CAGR of Wheat in Western region has come down from 2.9 percent in 90's to -1.1 percent during the present decade. Similar decelerations are observed for major non-foodgrain crops in this region. The CAGR of rice in Bundelkhand region in 90's was higher than that of UP but declined very sharply in the present decade. The trend also took place for wheat in the region. Moreover, CAGR of foodgrains in Bundelkhand region has declined from 90's to present decade. The overall performance of major crops has been decelerated from 90's to the present decade in the region. The CAGR of major cereals such as rice, wheat, jowar, some of pulses, namely, urd, moong, arhar, foodgrains and some of the oil seeds, namely, rapeseeds, linseeds, til, sunflower and other non-foodgrains, namely potato and onion in 90's has come down drastically in the present decade in the Eastern region. Moreover, similar pictures have been observed for the major crops in the Central region of the State. Therefore, the CAGR of major crops in all the regions as well state as a whole decelerating from 90's to the present decade, as it has been showing the similar picture in the country and major states in India (Mathur, A.S., *et al*, 2006). Similarly, state-wise analysis shows that agricultural output at current prices is significantly and positively dependent on government expenditure on agriculture, fertilizer usage, rainfall and population. The agricultural price is positively-related showing that supply *vis-a-vis* demand side is the dominant factors for agricultural output.

III. FACTORS RESPONSIBLE FOR DECELERATION

I. Ecological Factors

Rainfall

Rainfall is crucial factor, which determine the production and yield of major crops of particular region. However, the variation of the annual rainfall or the variation of rainfall during a crop season plays a crucial role for the variation of the yield rate of major crops, as the surface and groundwater also directly or indirectly depend on rainfall. The average annual rainfall of Uttar Pradesh has been declined from 1042 cm in 80's to 983 cm in 90' and again drastically declined to 782 cm during 2001-06. Highest precipitation occurs in Eastern region, whereas it is lowest in Western region of the state. Highest level of productivity along with production occurred in this region is mainly due to assured irrigation practice. More than 78 percent of the rainfall is received during the period from June to October (Table 1). Rainfall during a year is highly uneven and uncertain in the in the regional level as well as state level. From June to

October, the wet crop like paddy production is possible if monsoon is favourable. As the data show, rainfall becomes very much negligible and sometimes becomes nil during the period from October to March. Therefore, irrigation (both surface and groundwater) is highly essential for increasing cropping intensity, changing cropping pattern towards high valued crops, productivity and eventually eradicating poverty.

TABLE 1

Decade-wise Mean of Annual Rainfall in various Regions of the State

Year	*Western Region*	*Central Region*	*Bundelkhand Region*	*Eastern Region*	*Uttar Pradesh Region*
1981-1990	826.16	994.15	905.42	1115.10	1042.80
1991-2000	871.43	834.19	878.70	1019.35	983.87
2001-2006	725.92	794.20	740.35	870.02	782.62

Source: Agricultural Statistics, Department of Agriculture, Government of UP.

Variation of the annual rainfall affects the pattern and productivity of the crops in the region because the level moisture, groundwater recharge and level of surface irrigation depend on level of current as well as previous year's rainfall. The trend of region-wise rainfall shows high degree of variability during 1908-81 to 2004-05 in various regions as well as state level (Figure 1). Heavy fluctuations in rainfall pattern in a particular place affect the cropping pattern, productivity, profitability and living pattern of the people. It is clearly reflected here that the amount of rainfall in a particular year or season is not at all constant, which could be conducive for particular crop.

The instability in the rainfall analyses the level of variation among years, which affects the crop production and productivity in a region. However, the variation of rainfall in the state is highest for the present decade followed by 80's and 90's. The regional analysis reveals clearly that the level of instability is highest in case of Western region followed by Central, Bundelkhand and Eastern region (Table 2). The level of instability in Western region is highest during the present

FIGURE 1

Trend of Annual Rainfall in Regions of UP

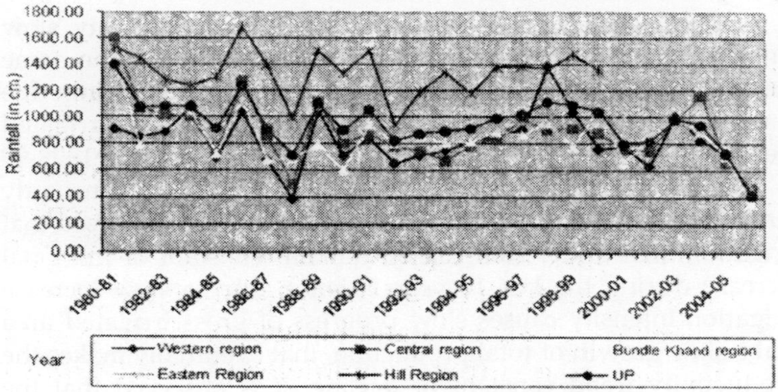

TABLE 2

Region-wise Instability of Rainfall during 1980-81 to 2005-06

Period/Region	*Western Region*	*Central Region*	*Bundelkhand Region*	*Eastern Region*	*Hill Region*	*Uttar Pradesh Region*
1980-2005	25.51	24.68	23.09	14.97	13.06	16.92
1980-1990	23.77	27.16	25.33	11.47	13.17	15.54
1990-2000	23.69	10.82	12.96	9.26	8.53	11.35
2000-2006	30.11	31.74	22.86	14.92	NA	24.66

Source: Agricultural Statistics, Department of Agriculture, Government of UP.

decade, which coincides with the lowest growth of foodgrains and other crops as well in the present decade. The degree of variability in rainfall is highest in the present decade in central regions of the state, where majority of the crops are decelerated during the last 5 recent years. The fate of Bundelkhand region also facing same situation as it has low rainfall with high variability. The Eastern region faces high level of rainfall compared to other regions with low instability, which favours better yields but other factors might have affect much more for the low productivity in the region.

2. Technological Factors

(a) Irrigation Pattern

The trend of gross irrigated areas become highly slow. nineties, as there is no clear positive trend during the same period. The declining trend of gross irrigated area is mainly due to declining trend of canal irrigated area. However, net irrigated area have been remaining constant or declining during 1998-99 to 2004-05, as the canal irrigation was declining constantly during the same period (Nayak, 2006a). It has been observed that irrigation area under zaid season remains constant or marginal increase during the last 10 years. Hence, due to slow increase irrigation intensity causes slow progress of gross irrigated area make slow growth of total production, that eventually makes the productivity trend constant or decline. It is observed that the share of canal irrigation (both major and medium irrigation) and surface minor irrigation has declined on the one hand and the share of ground water irrigation (private and public) has increased drastically on the other hand. In a broad sense, the share of public irrigation has declined on the one hand and the share of private irrigation has increased on the other. As a consequence of the use of large number of private tube-well and state tube-well, the irrigated area under tube-well has increased from 23.30 lakh hectares (32 percent of the net irrigated area) in 1970-71 to 94 lakhs hectares (72 percent of the net irrigated area) in the state during 2004-05. The slow and disproportionate growth of irrigation sector has serious ecological, institutional and policy implication, which directly or indirectly affect the agricultural sector in the state (Nayak, 2005).

Failure of Public Policy

The slow and disproportionate growth in canal irrigation is due to defective public policy. The share of pubic investments in irrigation sector compared to power and transport has declined over various five year plans (Government of UP, 2004-05). Though, total public investment in absolute terms in irrigation has increased continuously during 1980-81 to 2002-03 with the exception of few years, yet the real investment has remained constant since mid-eighties till late nineties and declined in the recent years (Nayak, 2005). Moreover, irrigation sector have an overwhelming bias towards designing and construction of projects without commensurate concerns and budgetary share on the utilization of the potential created, operation and maintenance of the project completed (Nayak, 2005). It is also observed that not only the public investment on command area development (O & M costs) to maintain the existing irrigation sector is highly low but also the allocation among sub-sectors is non-judicious. It shows that substantial part of the expenditure earmarked for O & M costs, goes to meet the expenditure on the staffs in the irrigation department leaving very little for maintenance and repairing work in the state. The diversification of fund within the O & M costs looks unfavourable and non-judicious for the sustainability of the irrigation systems (Nayak, 2006a). Thin Spread of Investment in irrigation sector is also another biggest single malady in the major and medium irrigation sector right from first plan. It has observed that continued tendency to start more and more new projects resulting proliferation of projects recklessly, which lead to thin spreading of resources and consequent time and cost overruns (Government of India, 2007). The benefit yet to realize is also quite large for these projects (Nayak, 2006a). Another important policy failure for the efficient irrigation sector in the state is the price policy. The cost recovery through water tariff is highly low, outdated and quite burdensome on the irrigation department. It has declined to the lowest up to 7 percent of O & M costs in 1999-2000 and remained at nearly 34 percent on an average basis during 1986-87 to 2002-03 (Nayak, 2007). Various reasons are important for low cost recovery ratio, such as the prices are fixed in nominal terms and are not revised for years, the pricing structure is based on crop area irrigated and not on volume of water consumed, there is hardly any link between the agency levying water charge and the agency that collects it, the cost of collection is itself high due to over-staffing (Gulati, *et al*, 2005).

Ecological Implications

There has been serious environmental degradation due to inadequate allocation of funds required for completing the on going projects, non-judicious allocation of funds for maintenance of on going projects or poor maintenance by the state agency.

Firstly, it has been observed that waterlogging and sodicity is one of the major forms of land degradation in the fertile irrigated land. The irrigated induced waterlogging (consequently converts into salinisation/alkalinisation) is mainly due to poor or mismanagement of the existing canals (Nayak, 2006a). Secondly, this poor growth in surface irrigation has compelled farmers to rely heavily on groundwater irrigation. It also depletes the water level and increases the rate of well failures in many places of India as well as Uttar Pradesh (Narayanmoorthy, 2007; Nayak, 2009). Moreover, canal irrigation plays a crucial role for recharging and provides enough strength for the groundwater irrigation. Due to heavy demand for private tube-well and other reasons, 40 percent of the villages are under semi-critical and critical level in Western region of the state. As Bundelkhand region belongs to naturally disadvantages position, 49 percent are under critical level (Nayak, 2006b). In the Central Region, 32 percent are under semi-critical and critical region. Eastern region of the state is the least affected regions, so far as ground water exploitation is concerned. However, 25 percent are under semi-critical and critical level.

(b) Disproportionate Use of Fertilisers

When fertilisers are first applied to a soil, high response is frequently obtained from nitrogen. The improved crop growth depletes the soil of other nutrients (FAO, 1994). Keeping the problems in mind, the balanced use of nitrogen (N), phosphorous (P) and potassium (K), the standard suitable mix of NPK has been estimated at all India level by keeping the soil, climatic condition, cropping pattern and other variables into consideration. Accordingly, the suitable mix of NPK in the country is 4:2:1 (Government of India, 2000-01). The use of NPK ratio in different sub-periods at aggregate level in Uttar Pradesh shows serious imbalance, viz., 18:4:1 during the green revolution period. The ratio has increased from 7:2:1 in 1970-71 to 11:3:1 in 1980-81 and reached to the highest of 24:7:1 in 2001-02. It shows the consumption of nitrogenous variety of fertilizer is quite higher than the standard mix. This excessive use of fertilizer could be a damaging factor for the environment and decline of productivity. However, the ratio of N and P with respect to K has been increasing over the study period in all the regions as well as the State level. Moreover, the NPK ratio is observed unbelievable in Bundelkhand region due to the application of negligible amount potassium in the soil. As there is no availability of specific data of fertilizer consumption in irrigated land separately, but it is understand that irrigation plays an important role for increasing total fertilizer consumption and plays a big role for disproportionate use.

The impact of excess and disproportionate consumption of fertilisers has been explained variously. The crops and plants cannot take all the fertilizers applied and significant portion is lost in the soils. It means application of more than the required quantity of fertilizers remains in the field, ultimately leads to polluting the soils. The excess or inappropriate consumption of various fertilizers than the recommended quantity or ratio leads to polluting the soil, which ultimately causes for the decline of productivity of various crops. The excess amount of nitrogen applied in the soils automatically converts into nitrate. As nitrate is not observed by most soils, it remains in solution. If it is not taken up by plant roots, it is either washed into the drainage water or biologically reduced to dinitrogen gas. Nitrate that is washed out of the soil represents an economic loss to the farmers and possible health hazard if it reaches drainage water (Wild, 2003). Rao (1994) found that the major source of environmental degradation in rural areas is the misapplication of yield increasing inputs like water, chemical fertilizers, and pesticides causing waterlogging, salinity and pollution of drinking water and loss of fish, etc. The subsidy on urea has resulted in an unbalanced use of nitrogen, phosphorous, and potassium fertilisers in the state. This has led to decline in the productivity of fertilisers apart from depleting soil nutrients. However, chemicalization of agriculture may pose a greater threat to the rural economy at much higher levels of application of chemical fertilizers and pesticides. High doses of fertilizer lead to salinity in the soil (Singh, 1997). A change towards balanced use of NPK by raising both P and K per unit of N would raise output by 2 million tonnes in India (Rao, 2005).

3. Failure of Institutional Policy in Irrigation

Uttar Pradesh is at the elementary stage in terms of participatory irrigation management both in surface and groundwater irrigation. Experience shows in Andhra Pradesh, Maharashtra, Madhya Pradesh and Gujarat that Participatory Irrigation Management (PIM) not only enables to improve the O & M of irrigation systems (increasing the efficiency of water uses), but also reduce the fiscal deficit of the government either by reducing the expenditure on irrigation or by increasing collection by bringing additional resources (cash or kind) (Oblitas, K. *et al.*, 1999). The efficiency of irrigation water has been developed two critical factors, i.e., level of water users' organization and changes in the collection of irrigation fees. The former is necessary for better way of managing water resources, O & M of the systems by the users' and the latter is essential for reduction of state's fiscal deficit either through increase in revenue collection or participation by the user in term of labour. Both can be possible by adopting participatory approach by the users. PIM has been adopted at the centre at different level since mid-seventies, while the level of success differs widely among state as water is a state subject. Though Uttar Pradesh Government has taken some encouraging steps in terms of institutional and legislative reforms at various levels to ensure the implementation of PIM in surface irrigation, yet the activities is at the elementary stages to achieve the objective (Nayak, 2005).

There has no legislation for development of institution for use of groundwater through a participatory model in UP. The natural resources have been used as private property though it is common pool resources. This has led to indiscriminate exploitation of groundwater by the medium and large farmers. As a consequence, large number of marginal and small farmers are debarred to use water for drinking and agricultural purposes. Therefore, medium and large farmers are directly involved for the depletion of the natural resources due to the inequity in the accessibility of the minor and groundwater schemes. As a result, there has been serious depletion of the natural resources in many parts of the State as well as in the country (Nayak, 2009). Moreover, the pricing of groundwater by the use of private pump sets creates different types of inequity such as number of hours of water extraction per acre, costs per hour, frequency of watering, costs of groundwater irrigation among various types of farmers, who have different extent of land base (Nayak, 2008). In the process of use, small and marginal farmers are debarred from the use of water and resource crunch took place, which affects more these categories of farmers.

4. Economic Factors

Landholding Size

Operational holding is an important economic indicator, which provides the base for a minimum living standard. Therefore for the subsistence, minimum land base is required. Average operational holding was 0.81 hectare in the state in 1995-96 and it has increased marginally to 0.83 hectare showing the number of marginal farmers has declined marginally. In addition, Eastern and Central region have lower average operation holding compared to the State level, whereas it is highest in Bundelkhand region.

Moreover, inequity in the distribution of operational land-holders and area under cultivation plays a crucial distributional factor for poverty reduction *vis-à-vis* economic development of a region. However, 77 percent of the total landholders are marginal farmers, who hold only 37 percent of the total area under operation in the state during 2000-01. On the other hand, 14 percent of the total land holders are small farmers, who hold 24 percent of the total area under operation. Similarly, semi-medium and medium farmers constitute 9 percent of the total operational holders, who holds nearly 36 percent of the total area. Importantly, large farmers constitute nearly 0.14 percent of

TABLE 3

Region-wise Inequality of Operation Holding and Area under Cultivation in Uttar Pradesh

Regions	*1995-96*	*2001*
Western	0.42	0.46
Central	0.40	0.40
Bundelkhand	0.51	0.49
Eastern	0.40	0.38
Uttar Pradesh	0.44	0.44

Source: Agricultural Census in Uttar Pradesh.

the total operational holders hold nearly 3 percent of the total area under cultivation. Similarly kind of disproportionate distribution of area under operational land among various categories of farmers is observed in Western region followed by Central, Eastern and Bundelkhand region. The estimation of Gini-coefficient also confirms the level of inequality of operational holding and area under cultivation among different category of farmers in the State (Table 3). However, highest level of inequality prevails in Bundelkhand region followed by Western, Central and Eastern region of the State.

IV. SUMMARY AND CONCLUSIONS

This study highlights the status of ecological, technological, economic and institutional factors determining the agricultural growth *vis-à-vis* overall development of the regions of the state. While analyzing the ecological factors, the study emphasizes the behavior of rainfall pattern and temperature during last 25 years at the regions and state level as a whole. The study observed that there has been drastic decline of average annual rainfall in 1980-90 to 1990-2000 and 2001-2006 in all regions of the state. This is further substantiated by very high variation in annual rainfall in all the regions of the state. The regional analysis of instability reveals clearly that the level of instability is highest in case of Western region followed by Central, Bundelkhand and Eastern region of the state. However, mean of temperature (both maximum and minimum) has not been changed much at the regions of the state. Moreover, irrigation (both surface and groundwater) plays a crucial role for stabilizing the uncertainty of rainfall for overall development of the agricultural sector in the state. But, the irrigation sector has been suffering from various setbacks such as failure of public and institutional policy, and serious environmental degradation. Moreover, some of the economic factors such as high proportion of marginal and non-workers, decline of land-man ratio, increase in the inequity of distribution of operational holder and land area affects the agricultural growth and economic development of various regions and the project districts in the study. Disproportionate use of chemical fertilsers also causes serious damage to the agricultural growth in the state. Therefore, a holistic approach is needed manage the resources by putting equal emphasis on soil and water conservation, while adopting the intensive cultivation of green revolution. The unimplemented agenda of the land reforms can be implemented to avoid the inequity issue of land distribution in the society. A comprehensive policy framework for correcting the deceleration tendency and facilitating the process of growth with greater emphasis on developing appropriate micro, meso and macro level institutions.

References

Behera, B. and P. Mishra (2007), 'Acceleration in Agricultural Growth in India: Suggestive Policy Framework', Vol. 42, No. 42, Oct. 20.

Desai, B.M. (2002), "Terms of Trade, Trade and Technical Change: Strategies for Agricultural Growth', *Economic and Political Weekly*, Vol. 37, No. 8.

Food and Agricultural Organization (1994), "Land Degradation in South Asia: Its Severity, Causes and Effects Upon the People", World Soil Resources Report, Rome.

Government of India (2007), 'Inaugural Address of Dr. Manmohan Singh, the Prime Minister of India, 53rd Meeting of the National Development Council, Government of India, New Delhi, May 29.

Government of India (2002-07). 10th Five year Plan, Vol. II, Department of Planning, New Delhi.

Gulati, A.; Ruth Meinzen-Dick; K.V. Raju (2005), 'Institutional Reforms in Indian Irrigation', Sage Publication, New Delhi.

Mathur, Archana S., Surjit Das and Subhalakshmi Sircar (2006), "Status of Agriculture in India: Trends and Prospects", *Economic and Political Weekly*, December 30.

Narayanamoorthy, A (2007), "Fertiliser Consumption after Decontrol: Myth and Realities', *Artha Vijnana*, Vol. 37, No. 4.

Nayak, Sanatan (2005), "Development of Irrigation in Uttar Pradesh: Extent and Dimensions, How Strong and How Weak?" presented at National Seminar on "Agricultural Growth in the Post-Reform Period: Regional Perspectives", at Giri Institute of Development Studies, Lucknow during 27th-29th March, 2006.

Nayak, Sanatan (2006a), "Agricultural Growth and Development of Irrigation in Uttar Pradesh: The Linkages", *UPEA Economic Journal*, Vol. 1, No. 1, Oct.

Nayak, Sanatan (2006b), "Are Groundwater irrigation Common Pool Resources? District level analysis in UP", UPEA Conference Volume, GIDS, Lucknow.

Nayak, Sanatan (2007), "Plight of Irrigation Sector in Uttar Pradesh", in D.M.Diwakar and Sanatan Nayak (eds.), Development Challenges: Afflicting Uttar Pradesh, Manak Publication, New Delhi.

Nayak, Sanatan (2008), "Does Distributional Inequality led to Degradation of

Natural Resources? An Analysis of Groundwater Irrigation in Villages of Uttar Pradesh, India", presented at the "International Conference on Water Resources Policy in South Asia", held at Colombo during December 17-20, 2008, organised by SaciWATERs, Hyderabad.

Nayak, Sanatan (2009), "Distributional Inequity and Groundwater Depletion: An Analysis across Major States in India", *'Indian Journal of Agricultural Economics'*, Vol. 64, No. 1, January-March.

Oblitas K.; J. Reymond Peter (1999), 'Transferring Irrigation Management to Farmers in Andhra Pradesh, India, The World Bank, Washington D.C.

Reddy, V.R. and S. Galab (2006), "Agrarian Crisis: Looking Beyond the Debt Trap", *Economic and Political Weekly*, Vol. 41, No. 19, May 13.

Rao, C.H. Hanumantha (1994), Agricultural Growth, Rural Poverty and Environmental Degradation, Oxford University Press, New Delhi.

Rao, C.H. Hanumatha (2005), Agriculture, Food Security, Poverty and Environment: Essays on Post-Reform India, Oxford University Press, New Delhi.

Sharma, P. and A. Gulati (2005), 'Can the Budget Boost Agricultural Performances?', *Economic and Political Weekly*, Vol. 40, No. 21.

Singh, A.K (1997), Land Use, Environment and Economic Growth in India, MD Publications Pvt. Ltd, New Delhi.

Wild, Alan (2003), Soils, Land and Food: Managing the Land during the Twenty-First Century, Cambridge University Press, Cambridge.

5

Crop Biotechnology: A Way to Sustainable Solution

KIRAN SINGH AND AJAY SINGH

Indian economy is predominantly agriculture-based, and the poor show in agriculture sector has put India in economic pressures. The performance of the agricultural sector influences the growth of the Indian economy. India can not achieve prosperity in real sense, farmers and rural population living in distress. Growth rates in agriculture have dipped and its share in national income has halved from about 36% in 1980 to 18% in 2007 (Sheel, 2008). Agriculture (including allied activities) accounted for 17.8 percent of the Gross Domestic Product (GDP at constant prices) in 2007-08 as compared to 21.7 percent in 2003-04. Notwithstanding the fact that the share of this sector in GDP has been declining over the years, its role remains critical as it accounts for about 52 percent of the employment in the country (Economic Survey, 2008-09). Global warming and climate change have become the major areas of concern. These coupled with fertilizer shortage and poor agriculture policies have further worsened the situation of agriculture sector.

I. STRUCTURAL CHANGES IN AGRICULTURE

Heading towards crisis

Over the last few years, Indian agriculture sector has gone under immense structural changes. Yield and productivity has been stagnant or lessen over the years. Some important structural changes are:

1.1. Economic Structural Changes

Table 1 presents the comparative average GDP growth rate of total economy, agriculture and allied sectors and crops and livestock.

TABLE 1

Average GDP Growth Rates—Overall and in Agriculture (% Per Year at 1999-2000 Price)

Period	*Total Economy*	*Agriculture and Allied Sectors*	*Crops and Live-stock*
1. Pre-green revolution 1951-52 to 1967-68	3.69	2.54	2.65
2. Green revolution period 1968-69 to 1980-81	3.52	2.44	2.72
3. Wider technology dissemination period 1981-82 to 1990-91	3.52	3.65	—
4. Early reforms period 1991-92 to 1996-97	5.69	3.66	3.68
5. Ninth Plan 1997-98 to 2001-02	5.52	2.50	2.49
6. Tenth Plan period 2002-03 to 2006-07 of which	7.77	2.47	2.51
(a) 2002-03 to 2004-05	6.60	0.89	0.89
(b) 2005-06 to 2006-07	9.51	4.84	4.96

Source: National Accounts Statistics 2008 (New Series), Central Statistical Organization, Ministry of Statistics and Programme Implementation, New Delhi

Courtesy: Planning Commission, Government of India, Eleventh Five Year Plan (2007-12), Vol. III, p. 4.

Table 1 suggests that Growth of agricultural GDP decelerated from over 3.5% per year during 1981–82 and 1996–97 to only around 2% during 1997–98 and 2004–05. Growth of agricultural GDP has been well below the target of 4% set in both Ninth and Tenth Plans.

TABLE 2

Gross Capital Formation in Agriculture

(Figures in Rs. crore at 1999-2000 prices)

Year	*GDP*	*Agriculture and Allied Activities*		*GCF/GDP in agriculture and allied (%)*	*GCF in agriculture as % of total GDP*
		GCF	*GDP*		
2004-05	2388768	57849	482446	12	2.4
2005-06	2616101	66065	511013	12.9	2.5
2006-07	2871120	73285	531315	13.8	2.6
2007-08	3129717	79328	557122	14.2	2.5

Source: Econmic Survey, 2008-09, Ministry of Finance, Government of India, p. 172.

TABLE 3

Share of Agriculture and Allied Sector in Total GCF (%) (at 1999-2000 prices)

Year	*Public Sector*	*Private Sector*	*Total*
1999-2000	6	11.9	10.2
2000-01	5.8	11.3	9.7
2001-02	6.7	13.7	11.7
2002-03	6.5	11.5	10.3
2003-04	7.4	9.2	8.8
2004-05	7.8	7.7	7.7
2005-06	7.9	7.1	7.2
2006-07	8.2	6.6	7

Source: Agricultural Statistics at a Glance, 2008, Directorate of Economics and Statistics.

Courtesy: Econmic Survey, 2008-09, Ministry of Finance, Government of India. p. 172.

The Gross Capital Formation (GCF) in agriculture as a proportion to the total GDP has shown a decline from 2.9 per cent in 2001-02 to 2.5 per cent in 2007-08. However, the GCF in agriculture relative to GDP in this sector has shown an improvement from 11.23 per cent in 1999-2000 to 14.24 per cent in 2007-08 (Table 2). The share of agriculture and allied sector in total GCF after showing a marginal increase during 1999-2000 to 2001-02 has been continuously declining. It stood at 10.2 per cent in 1999-2000, increased to 11.7 per cent in 2001-02 and thereafter declined to 7 per cent in 2006-07. The decline was mainly attributed to decline in the private sector despite increase in the share of public sector (Table 3). (Economic Survey, 2008-09)

1.2. Climate Change and Agriculture

The continuously increasing concentration of GHG in atmosphere is forcing the shift in climate across the globe. This change in climate is changing the pattern of cultivation and growing conditions. Agriculture worldwide is under tremendous pressure to fulfil the need of the rapidly growing population. The pressure becomes more noticeable with degrading soil and water conditions.

TABLE 4

Variations in Monsoon

Year	*% deficiency in rainfall from LPA*				*% change in kharif*			
	Jun.-Sep. (Monsoon)	*Oct-Dec (Post-Monsoon)*	*Jan.-Feb. (Winter)*	*Mar.-May (Pre-Monsoon)*	*Overall*	*Area*	*Output*	*Yield*
1999-2000	-4	18.8	1.4	-0.5	-1.1	-1	2.5	3.6
2000-01	-7.6	-47.3	-61.6	0.3	-12.7	2.7	-3.2	-5.8
2001-02	-8.3	13.1	-15	-8	-6.3	-1.3	9.8	11.3
2002-03	-19.2	-32.6	38.9	-18.2	-18.6	-7.6	-22.2	-15.8
2003-04	4.9	7.7	-12	24.7	6.8	10	34.1	21.9
2004-05	-12.7	-11.1	59	-7	-12.5	-4.2	-11.7	-7.8
2008-09	-2	-31	-46	-32		27#		
2009-10*	-24					-25		

#Fourth Advance Estimate, MOA, GoI.
*As of 16 July 2009. LPA: Long Period Average.
Source: Indian Meteorological Division (IMD) and Ministry of Agriculture.
Courtesy: *The Economic Times*, 30 July, 2009.

The current rainfall is a cause for concern to the country's agriculture and overall economy (Table 4). The area sown under foodgrains has fallen by 28% as compared to last year. Area under cereals has decreased by 29% and pulses by 19%. Even the area under non-foodgrains like oilseeds also has declined by 35% (Sekhar, 2009). The number of districts affected has risen to 246 as poor monsoon has brought 29% less rainfall, damaging standing crop. Ten states have declared 246 districts as drought affected. It comes to about 46-47% of the country districts. Shortfall in area coverage of paddy by about 5.7 million hectare compared to last year. Production of rice in kharif may be reduced by 10 million tonnes (*Times of India*, 20 Aug., 2009).

1.3. Changes in Yield and Productivity

If we see the table 5, we can see that there has been practically no tangible increase in the yield of wheat, rice corn, soyabean or sugarcane in any part of the world over the last 10 years. Agriculture productivity has stagnated internationally, while the consumption of agricultural products has steadily increased with increase in income levels and population growth. The per capita availability of foodgrains in India has declined from about 500 grams per day to less than 400 grams per day over the last two decades.

Table 6 depicts the declining or stagnant growth rate for most of the crops. Countries like Brazil have large swathes of land available for agriculture. However, in countries like India, China, Russia and America, the potential to get new cultivable land is very limited. The land area available for agriculture in India is shrinking fast because of urbanisation, industrialization, and construction of Special Economic Zone (SEZ), the development of the real estate business, and the successive fragmentation of landholdings with the emergence of new generation. (Bajaj, 2009)

1.4. Research and Development

IFPRI research shows that investments in R&D have the highest impact on agricultural growth per million rupees invested. The rates of return to public investment in research have been as high as over 60 percent, and in extension, over 50 percent. India currently invests only about 0.5 percent of its agricultural GDP in agricultural research, compared with 0.7 percent in the developing countries as a whole and as much as 2-3 percent in the developed countries. These figures suggest

TABLE 5

Yield of Various Crops

	2002	*2003*	*2004*	*2005*	*2006*	*2007*
Wheat (MT/Hectare)						
India	2.71	2.77	2.62	2.71	2.59	2.63
China	3.81	3.78	3.93	4.25	4.28	4.55
USA	2.70	2.36	2.97	2.90	2.82	2.60
Turkey	1.82	1.96	1.95	2.15	2.15	2.03
Canada	1.94	1.83	2.26	2.64	2.74	2.61
Corn (MT/Hectare)						
China	4.7	4.92	4.81	5.12	5.29	5.39
USA	8.67	8.12	8.93	10.06	9.29	9.36
Argentina	6.00	6.33	6.52	7.37	6.48	8.04
South Africa	2.84	2.65	2.94	3.64	3.41	2.52
Rice (MT/Hectare)						
Brazil	3.30	3.25	3.43	3.37	3.86	3.81
India	3.14	2.67	3.13	2.95	3.17	3.18
China	6.16	6.19	6.06	6.31	6.26	6.23
Indonesia	4.41	4.5	4.56	4.64	4.59	4.6
Thailand	2.62	2.57	2.65	2.63	2.70	2.69
Soy (MT/Hectare)						
Brazil	2.66	2.82	2.37	2.31	2.56	2.85
India	0.90	0.71	1.05	0.73	0.90	0.95
Argentina	2.63	2.82	2.36	2.71	2.66	2.99
China	1.63	1.73	1.65	1.81	1.70	1.72
USA	2.66	2.56	2.28	2.84	2.89	2.87
Sugarcane (MT/Hectare)						
Brazil	70.00	71.00	73.00	75.00	66.90	71.10
India	67.00	66.00	58.00	63.00	66.90	71.10
China	50.25	49.50	43.50	47.25	50.18	53.33
Thailand	71.00	71.00	70.00	61.00	66.90	71.10
Australia	73.80	82.60	82.60	87.10	94.10	88.80

Source: Bajaj, K. (2009), *The Economic Times*, 21 July, 2009, p. 13.

TABLE 6

Growth Rate in Output of Various Sub-sectors of Agriculture

(Gross Value of Output at 1999-2000 Price)

Period	*Cereals*	*Pulses and Oilseeds*	*Fruits and Vegetables*	*Other Crops*	*All Crops*	*Live-stock*	*Fisheries*
1951-52 to 1967-68	4.19	2.98	2.67	2.42	3	1.02	4.68
1968-69 to 1980-81	3.43	0.97	4.82	2.98	3	3.26	3.08
1981-82 to 1990-91	3.52	5.41	2.84	1.71	2.97	4.78	5.74
1991-92 to 1996-97	2.36	2.92	6.07	2.18	3.09	4	7.05
1997-98 to 2001-02	1.49	-1.43	4.11	3.82	2.25	3.53	2.63
2002-03 to 2006-07	1.28	4.29	2.97	3.58	2.46	3.69	3.23

Source: New Series of National Accounts Statistics, Central Statistical Organization, Ministry of Statistics and Programme Implementation, New Delhi.

Courtesy: Planning Commission, Government of India, Eleventh Five Year Plan (2007-12), Vol. III, p. 5.

that government has been systematically under investing in a sector that offers a high social return and that there is considerable scope for diverting incremental outlays to priority areas in research (Braun *et. al.*, 2005)

1.5. Rural Health

India is facing a nutritional crisis according to the National Family Health Survey (NFHS-III), with 45.9% of children below the age of three-that is, about 45 million little girls and boys-are underweight or malnourished and among married women in the age group of 15-49 years, the prevalence of anaemia has risen to 56.1% in 2005-06. According to the Global Hunger Index 2008, India is ranked 66 among 88 developing countries—worse than nearly 25 Sub-Saharan African countries and all of South Asia, except Bangladesh (Mittal, 2009).

2. CROP BIOTECHNOLOGY

Thus there is urgent necessity of implementing effective measures to counter such structural changes in agriculture.

Improving agricultural productivity is must. We need to boost agricultural productivity on the size and scale that we have achieved in industry and services. Such a substantial enhancement of agricultural productivity is possible only through the introduction of large scale irrigation, increased and judicious use of genetically modified crops, multiple cropping, the deployment of combined harvesters and significant and widespread improvements in agricultural practices (Bajaj, 2009). Biotechnology can help meet the ever-increasing need by increasing yields, decreasing crop inputs such as water and fertilizer, and providing pest control methods that are more compatible with the environment.

In India where roughly 60% of cultivated land is not irrigated and which faces frequent droughts and pest attacks, the benefits of GM crops that could be drought and/or pest-resistance, could be enormous in improving the livelihood of farmers.

Bio-safety must precede the large scale application of biotechnology, including genetically modified (GM) crops. And the institutional system of bio-safety must be transparent, credible and effective. Without such an institution in place, the whole policy of bio-technology becomes hostage to fears, rumours, and ideological belief (Gulati, 2007). Transgenics, or genetically modified organisms (GMOs), are the result of transferring one or more genes, usually from a wild species or a bacterium, to a crop plant. In 2006, farmers in 22 countries planted transgenic seeds on about 100 million hectares, about 8 percent of the global crop area. Though transgenics have been taken up more rapidly in commercial farming, they have considerable potential for improving the productivity of small-holder farming systems and providing more nutritious foods to poor consumers in developing countries (World Development Report, 2008). But their use has been limited to certain crops (soybean and maize used for animal feed, and cotton), traits (insect resistance and herbicide tolerance), and countries with commercial farming (Argentina and Brazil). The only transgenic widely adopted by small-holders has been Bt cotton for insect resistance. An estimated 9.2 million farmers, mostly in China and India, planted Bt cotton on 7.3 million hectares in 2006 (World Development Report, 2008).

TABLE 7

Economic and Environmental Benefits from Bt Cotton

	Argentina[a]	*China*[a]	*India*[b]	*Mexico*[a]	*South Africa*[c]
Added Yield (%)	33	19	26	11	65
Added Profit (%)	31	340	47	12	198
Reduced Chemical Spray (Number)	2.4	—	2.7	2.2	—
Reduced Pest Management Cost (%)	47	67	73	77	58

a. Adapted from FAO 2004e.
b. Qaim and others, 2006. .Other recent studies include Gandhi and Namboodiri 2006, who reported similar trends except for a much higher increase in profits (88 percent).
c. Bennett, Morse, and Ismael, 2006. Other studies point to high variability in yields (Gouse, Kirsten, and Jenkins, 2003; Gouse and others, 2005; Hofs, Fok, and Vaissayre, 2006).
— = not available.
Note: The figures are based on farm-level surveys in important cotton producing regions within each country.
Source: World Development Report, 2008. Agricultuure for Development, p. 178.

Impressed by Gujarat's outstanding performance in agriculture (growing at 9.6% per annum since 2000-01), International Food Policy Research Institute points to three main reasons of growth in Gujarat's agriculture (Gulati *et. al.*, 2009):

(a) Cotton output soared from 3.05 million bales (of 170 kg each) in 202/03 to 11.2 million bales in 2007/08 primarily driven by Bt Cotton since 2002.
(b) The rapid growth of the high value segment, i.e. livestock, fruits and vegetables.
(c) Jump in the production of wheat.

Thus, crop biotechnology helps improve the crop production. It has many advantages (Guide to Biotechnology, 2007:

(a) Natural Protection for Plants

Biotechnology will open up new avenues for working with nature by providing new *biopesticides,* such as microorganisms and fatty acid compounds, that are toxic to targeted crop pests but do not harm humans, animals, fish, birds or beneficial insects. Because biopesticides act in unique ways, they can control pest populations that have developed resistance to conventional pesticides. Using the flexibility provided by biotechnology, we can transplant the genetic information that makes the Bt bacterium lethal to certain insects (but not to humans, animals or other insects) into plants on which that insect feeds. The plant that once was a food source for the insect now kills it, lessening the need to spray crops with chemical pesticides to control infestations

(b) Herbicide Tolerance

Using biotechnology, it is possible to make crop plants tolerant of specific herbicides. When the herbicide is sprayed, it will kill the weeds but have no effect on the crop plants. This lets farmers reduce the number of times herbicides have to be applied and reduces the cost of producing crops and damage to the environment.

(c) Resistance to Environmental Stresses

Scientists are making great strides in developing crops that can tolerate difficult growing conditions. For example, researchers have genetically modified tomato and canola plants that tolerate salt levels 300 percent greater than non-genetically modified varieties. Other researchers have identified many genes involved in cold, heat and drought tolerance found naturally in some plants and bacteria. Scientists in Mexico have produced maize and papaya that are tolerant to the high levels of aluminum that significantly impede crop plant productivity in many developing countries.

(d) Increasing Yields

Researchers at Japan's National Institute of Agrobiological Resources added maize photosynthesis genes to rice to increase its efficiency at converting sunlight to plant starch and increased yields by 30 percent.

According to the National Center for Food and Agricultural Policy's (NCFAP) 2004 report, in 2003 the 11 biotech crop varieties adopted by U.S. growers increased crop yields by

5.3 billion pounds, saved growers $1.5 billion by lowering production costs, and reduced pesticide use by 46.4 million pounds. Based on increased yields and reduced production costs, growers realized a net economic impact or savings of $1.9 billion. Three new traits for corn and cotton were introduced in 2003, and the NCFAP study takes into account six biotech crops—canola, corn, cotton, papaya, soybean and squash.

(e) Environmental and Economic Benefits

Beyond agricultural benefits, products of crop biotechnology offer many environmental and economic benefits. As described above, biotech crops allow us to increase crop yields by providing natural mechanisms of pest control in place of chemical pesticides. These increased yields can occur without clearing additional land, which is especially important in developing countries. In addition, because biotechnology provides pest-specific control, beneficial insects that assist in pest control will not be affected, facilitating the use of integrated pest management. Herbicide tolerant crops decrease soil erosion by permitting farmers to use conservation tillage.

In its report "Conservation Tillage and Plant Biotechnology," the Conservation Tillage Information Centre (CTIC) at Purdue University attributes the recent improvements in tillage reduction to the increased use of the herbicide tolerant varieties produced through biotechnology. CTIC concludes that the increase in conservation tillage associated with herbicide-tolerant crops decreases soil erosion by 1 billion tonnes of soil material per year, saves $3.5 billion per year in sedimentations costs and decreases fuel use by 3.9 gallons per acre. According to the International Service for the Acquisition of Agri-Biotech Applications, a single biotech crop, Bt cotton, has led to the following environmental and economic benefits for farmers in developing countries:

From 1999 to 2000 in China, insecticide usage decreased by 67 percent and yields increased by 10 percent, leading to income gains of $500 per hectare.

Extensive field trials in India from 1998 to 2001 demonstrated a 50 percent reduction in insecticide spraying and a 40 percent increase in yields, which equals an increase in income from $75 to $200 per hectare.

Small farmers in South Africa gained through a 25 percent yield increase and decreased number of insecticide sprays from 11 to four, reducing pesticide costs by $45 per acre. The higher cost of Bt seed (up to $15 per hectare for small farmers) resulted in an average economic advantage of $35 per hectare

2.1. Why the Slow Progress in Transgenics?

Growth of biotechnology in agriculture has been mar by apprehensions in general public. There are many reasons for the slow progress in transgenics (World Development Report, 2008).

Neglect of pro-poor traits and orphan crops

Investments in R&D on transgenics are concentrated largely in the private sector, driven by commercial interests in industrial countries. Because the private sector cannot appropriate benefits of R&D on small-holder food crops, this research must be led by the public sector. Yet the public sector has underinvested in R&D generally and in biotechnology specifically.

Risks

Continuing concerns about possible food safety and environmental risks have slowed release in many countries. These concerns have persisted even though available scientific evidence to date on food safety indicates that the transgenics now in the market are as safe as conventional varieties

Weak regulatory capacity

The capacity of regulatory bodies to assess environmental and food safety risks and approve the release of transgenics is limited in most developing countries. Weak regulatory systems, fuel public distrust and ignite opposition to transgenics. Low regulatory capacity is a major factor slowing approvals even of products that have already undergone extensive testing, such as Bt rice in China and Bt eggplant in India. Weak capacity also results in widespread use of unauthorized transgenic seeds in many settings (cotton in India and China, and soybean in Brazil in past years), which further reduces public confidence in the regulatory system.

Limited access to proprietary technologies

With an increasing share of genetic tools and technologies covered by intellectual property protection and largely controlled by a small group of multinational companies, the transaction cost of obtaining material transfer agreements and licenses can slow public research on and release of transgenics.

Complexity of trade in transgenics

Some countries worry about health effects of imports of transgenic foods, including food aid. Exporters fear the loss of overseas markets and of a "GMO-free" brand. They have to consider the costs of segregating the storage and shipments of transgenics from conventional varieties, and obtaining clearance for transgenics for consumption in the importing country. Countries and farmers slow to adopt transgenics may lose their competitiveness in global markets, however, if cost-reducing transgenics, such as Bt cotton, are widely adopted in large exporting countries

2.2. A Way Forward

The new agricultural technologies on the horizon are largely biotechnologies. Indian policy-makers, scientists, and regulators have long supported the development of biotechnology (including genetic modification) that provides new crops favourable to India's climatic areas and is suitable for use by farmers in rural communities. One of the most important technologies in the Indian context is one that produces drought resistance. Developing biotechnology appropriately, however, will require effective research and reforms of the regulatory structure and process, duly recognizing the local and international debate on biotechnology, particularly regarding genetically modified (GM) crops. In this context, setting up a body like the National Biotechnology Regulatory Authority (NBRA) would enhance regulation of biotechnology in India (Braun *et. al.*, 2005). According to peer reviewed comprehensive study by Graham Brookes, PG Economics of UK, GM crops introduced a little over a decade ago helped farmers around the world to be economically successful through an increased net income of $27 billions, produce healthier foods by reduced pesticide application by almost 500 million pounds, better animal feeds and more fibre, while reducing agriculture's impact on our environment through reduced green house emissions of 20 billion pounds equivalent to removing 4 millions cars from the road for one year.

GM crops are being grown on 252 million acres in 22 (11 industrial and 11 developing) countries by more than 10.3 million farmers, 90% being resource poor from developing countries. According to the 2006 ISAAA (International Service for the Acquisition of Agribiotechnology Applications) report, the 60-fold increase of GM between 1996 and 2006 makes it the fastest adopted crop technology in history. The statistics suggest farmers have given their verdict on biotech crops because of the significant agronomic, economic, environmental, and social benefits.

The biotech interventions can help break the shackles of a trend line agriculture growth of 1.5 to 2% in the last decade, improve the near-stagnant productivity levels and help farmers fight stresses relating to pests, weeds and climate changes. It can help India achieve 4% growth in agriculture imperative for sustained GDP growth of 8-9% (Ravi, 2007)

3. CONCLUSION

With inherent advantages in biotechnology, information technology, energy input-output ratio and labour costs, Indian agriculture has tremendous potential that can be unlocked through new opportunities thrown up by the current global food crisis which is again shifting the terms of trade in favour of agriculture. Although just a third of the geographical size of the United States, India has roughly the same cropped area. This is one area where India has a decisive comparative advantage over China, which is much bigger but has only about half the cropped area as India. Once investment, subsidy, price, labour and market distortions are addressed, and agricultural trade and markets, including the market for land, opened up, India can emerge as a new agricultural superpower through substantial productivity gains that could flow from technological advances such as genetically modified seeds, state of the art water aquifer) management and new ICT-based marketing infrastructure that integrates markets, makes price discovery more efficient and reduces parasitic intermediaries between the cultivator and the market (Sheel, 2008). Now it is in the hands of policy-makers how they treat biotechnology as significant tool for sustainable solution to reduce agriculture crisis.

References

Bajaj, K. 2009, "Improving Agricultural Productivity is Crucial", *The Economic Times*, 21 July, 2009, p. 13.

Braun, J.V. Gulati, A. Hazell, P. Rosegrant, M.W. Ruel, M. 2005, "Indian Agriculture and Rural Development: Strategic Issues and Reform Options". International Food Policy Research Institute. www.ifpri.org 2005, p. 2.

Economic Survey, 2008-09, Ministry of Finance, Department of Economic Affairs, Government of India, pp. 171-72.

Guide to Biotechnology, 2007, Compiled by Biotechnology Industry Organisation, pp. 65-68.

Gulati, A. 2007, *The Economic Times*, 22 May, 2007, p. 17.

Gulati, A. Shreedhar, G., 2009, "Emulate Gujarat's Agricultural Success", *The Economic Times*, 7 May, 2009, p. 11.

Ravi, K.C., 2007, *The Economic Times*, 22 May, 2007, p. 17.

Sekhar, C.S.C., 2009, "How Serious is Rainfall Deficiency for Kharif", *The Economic Times*, 30 July, 2009.

Sheel, A., 2008, "Industrial Revolution and Indian Agriculture", *The Economic Times*, 2 June, 2008, p. 13.

World Development Report, 2008, "Agriculture for Development", *The World Bank*, pp. 171-72.

Mittal, S. 2009, "Food Security Act: Is it well thought out?", *The Economic Times* 26 Aug., 2009, p. 16.

6

Trends in Investment in Indian Agriculture: Impact of Structural Reforms

POONAM SINGH

The economic reforms initiated in 1990-91 relied more on "set the prices right" to boost the agriculture sector. The liberalisation of the economy was anticipated to result in higher investment and growth in agriculture induced by favourable terms of trade. It was expected that the gains in terms of trade would increase investment in agriculture subsequent to the liberalisation of non-agriculture sector would be more important than efficiency gains flowing from the liberalisation of agricultural trade and reduction of input subsidies. The expectations, however, did not materialize. Agricultural growth slackened and investment in agriculture, particularly on public account, declined. By the late nineties the hopefulness with respect to reforms leading to a higher investment, growth and employment in agriculture had started to fade.

A great concern has been widely expressed by several economists that public investment in agriculture has declined in the recent years, particularly investment towards creation of irrigation potential and rural infrastructure (Dantwala, 1986; Rath, 1989; Misra and Chand,1995;. Shetty, 1990; Kumar, 1992; Misra, 1996; Alagh, 1994; Gulati and Bathla, 2001; Chand, 2000 and 2001; Roy and Pal, 2002; Chadha, 2003; Rao and Gulati, 2005). They stressed the importance of public investment in infrastructure consisting of transport, storage, energy, etc. for the development of the agriculture sector. As such investment "for" agriculture is more relevant than investment "in" agriculture for the growth of agriculture sector.

This paper deals with the analysis of trends in investment in Indian agriculture, with specific emphasis on the period of economic reforms and divided into four sections. First, the paper describes the trends in public and private investment in Indian agriculture at constant prices with its impact on agricultural GDP (Section 1). Secondly, it delineates the state level analysis of the trends in public investment and private investment in agriculture (Section 2). Thirdly, it extends the discussion by looking at investment "in" agriculture and investment "for" agriculture. Lastly, concluding remarks are described in Section 4.

I. TRENDS IN PUBLIC AND PRIVATE INVESTMENT IN INDIAN AGRICULTURE

Public investment in agriculture has played a vital role in promoting growth of agricultural output because it includes expenditures directed to agricultural infrastructure, research and development and education and training, etc. It has been observed that since the beginning of 1980s gross capital formation in agriculture in public sector started coming down gradually and continued falling till early 1990s while private investment followed this declining trend only up to 1986-87, but thereafter started rising and got accelerated from 1993-94 onwards. The declining trend in public investment in agriculture in the decade of 1980s as well as in 1990s was improved since 2000-01. On the contrary; private investment kept moving upward showing dissimilar movement in the two series since 1981-82. Ratio of gross capital formation in private sector to gross domestic product in agriculture persistently increased also with some fluctuations, while ratio of gross capital formation in public sector to gross domestic product in agriculture continuously declined in the whole period. There has been an apparent shift in the relationship of public investment and private investment in Indian agriculture in1990s and early-2000s (Table 1).

TABLE I

Gross Capital Formation in Public and Private Sector in Agriculture in Relation to Gross Domestic Product in Agriculture (At 1993-94 prices)

(Rs. Crore)

Years	*GDPag*	*GCFagPU*	*GCFagPvt.*	*GCFagPvt.as %of GDPag*	*GCFagPU as %of GDPag*
1980-81	159293	7301	6932	4.58	4.35
1981-82	167723	7130	6949	4.25	4.14
1982-83	166577	7092	7437	4.26	4.46
1983-84	182498	7196	7529	3.94	4.13
1984-85	185186	6921	8027	3.74	4.33
1985-86	186570	6213	7919	3.33	4.24
1986-87	185363	5864	7844	3.16	4.23
1987-88	182899	6045	8204	3.31	4.49
1988-89	211184	5699	9063	2.70	4.29
1989-90	214315	4972	8452	2.32	3.94
1990-91	223114	4992	11424	2.24	5.12
1991-92	219660	4376	10589	1.99	4.82
1992-93	232386	4539	11602	1.95	4.99
1993-94	241967	4918	10331	2.03	4.27
1994-95	254090	5397	11388	2.12	4.48
1995-96	251892	4849	10841	1.93	4.30
1996-97	276091	4668	11508	1.69	4.17
1997-98	269383	3979	11963	1.48	4.44
1998-99	286094	3870	11025	1.35	3.85
1999-00	286983	4756	13083	1.66	4.56
2000-01	286666	4435	12980	1.55	4.53
2001-02	305263	5488	12250	1.80	4.01
2002-03	283393	4760	13881	1.68	4.90
2003-04	310611	5923	15261	1.91	4.91
2004-05	310486	6051	19668	1.95	6.33
2005-06	329168	6385	22424	1.94	6.81

Source: National Account Statistics, 2000, 2001 (Back Series 1950-51 to 1992-93) 2004, 2005 and 2007, C.S.O., Government of India.

TABLE 2

Compound Annual Growth Rate (%) (At 1993-94 prices)

Periods	*GDPag*	*GCFagPU*	*GCFagPvt.*	*GFCFagPU*	*GFCFagPvt.*
1980-81 to 1989-90	3.35	-4.18	2.23	-4.39	2.31
1990-91 to 1999-00	2.84	-1.85	1.52	-0.25	2.22
2000-01 to 2005-06	2.80	7.56	11.55	7.14	6.56
1980-81 to 2005-06	2.95	-0.53	4.81	-0.61	4.56

In the recent years an intense debate has been waging among agricultural economists of the country about the trends in investment and the relationship between public and private investment in agriculture in the light of the declining trend in public investment in agriculture observed since the mid-eighties. The debate is mainly centered on the complementarity between public and private investment in agriculture. Both public and private investment in Indian agriculture had shown a rising trend till the end of 1970s in India. This led many researchers to conclude that there is a strong complementarity between public and private investment in Indian agriculture (Shetty, 1990; Mallick, 1993; Dhawan and Yadav, 1995; Gandhi, 1996). These researchers emphasized the 'crowding in' effect of public investment in agriculture in India. The opposite phenomena of a rising trend in private investment and a declining trend in public investment in agriculture observed since the 1980s has made the issue much debatable. Many scholars in recent years have challenged the operation of the 'crowding in' hypothesis of public investment in Indian agriculture (Mishra and Chand, 1995; Mishra and Hazell, 1996; Mishra, 1998).

The annual compound growth rates of gross capital formation and gross fixed capital formation in public sector were negative during 1980s and 1990s. On the contrary, the annual compound growth rates of gross capital formation and gross fixed capital formation in private sector show a high rate of growth during the period 1980-81 to 2005-06 (Table 2). Private capital formation grew at a substantially higher rate and compensated the fall in the public sector capital formation. But the deceleration in rate of increase in private capital formation in agriculture during 1990s as compared to 1980s was quite notable, which provide a strong support to complementarity between capital formation in public and private sector in agriculture. The declining growth rate of GDP in agriculture during the period due to declining public investment was also the cause of serious concern.

The falling public investment in agriculture during the 1980 was mainly because of a large proportion of the resource flows to the agriculture sector going in to current expenditure on subsidies for fertilizers, irrigation, electricity, credit and other agricultural inputs, rather than investment. The rising level of subsidies in agriculture and diversion of funds from irrigation to anti-poverty programmes were the real hindrances in the growth of public capital formation according to many scholars (Mallick, 1993, Rao, 1994, Gulati and Narayanan, 2003). Hardening resources and increasing pressure on revenue expenditure in payments of salaries and interest have crowded out capital expenditure in public account since 1980s. The deteriorating trend in central tax-GDP ratio started right from the mid-1980s was a major source of fiscal imbalances (Ahluwalia, 2000; Rao, 2002).

This fiscal crisis has negative impact on public investment of economy, particularly in agriculture sector. Public investment in agriculture began to decline in the 1980s, but initially the decline was offset by the fact that private investment in agriculture was increasing. Since the mid-1990s private investment in agriculture has stagnated while public investment has continued to decline. It is essential to reverse these trends, especially for public investment in irrigation and water resource management. It is also essential to increase public investment in rural roads and rural electrification. Success in these areas will stimulate private investment and contribute to a revival of growth momentum in agriculture.

II. STATE-WISE TRENDS IN PUBLIC AND PRIVATE INVESTMENT IN AGRICULTURE

Capital formation at state level assumes dominant importance in the context of policy-making and balanced regional development by economists. Public investment in agriculture is also the accountability of the States, but many

States have neglected investment in infrastructure for agriculture. There are many rural infrastructure projects, which have started but are lying incomplete for want of resources. The overall public expenditure on agriculture is dependent on the resources available to the States, which has declined in all the States over a period of years.

II.1 Public Investment

The trends in capital expenditure on agriculture and allied heads from public account in major states at constant prices (1993-94 Prices) are presented in Table 3. The investment series at 1993-94 prices have been prepared by deflating the current price series by implicit price deflator used by the CSO for capital formation in agriculture sector. For the sake of clarity, the study have classified the entire period into five sub-periods coinciding with the phases of agricultural development and declining public expenditure by states.

The data series are grouped in five years and divided in five sub-periods as:

I. (1980-81 to 1984-85),
II. (1985-86 to 1989-90),
III. (1990-91 to 1994-95),
IV. (1995-96 to 1999-2000), and
V. (2000-01 to 2004-05).

II.1.1 Per Hectare Public Investment

Capital expenditure was computed on per hectare basis also to evaluate the relative position of different states by dividing total capital expenditure at constant prices (1993-94 prices) by net sown area of the states. Among major states capital expenditure on agriculture remained highest in Jammu and Kashmir in all the five periods. As this state have the benefit of special status in the country, it has been receiving special aid for various agricultural development schemes (Chand, 2000). Variation in per hectare annual expenditure incurred on capital formation in agriculture by different states show not any consistent trend in per hectare capital expenditure for agriculture in most of the states. Punjab, Gujarat and Maharashtra allocated highest resources to development for agriculture during different periods. Per hectare public capital invested in agriculture was lowest in Rajasthan during the entire period. Other states with low per hectare investment are Tamil Nadu, Rajasthan, Uttar Pradesh and West Bengal. Punjab shows steep fall in capital expenditure since I period. Madhya Pradesh, Orissa and West Bengal has also been spending not only lesser resources but nearly stagnant amount since 1999-2000, for farm infrastructure.

TABLE 3

State Level Capital Expenditure on Agriculture and Allied Heads as Ratio of Net Sown Area At Constant Prices, Rs./Hectare Per Year

States	*1980-81 to 1984-85*	*1985-86 to 1989-90*	*1990-91 to 1994-95*	*1995-96 to 1999-2000*	*2000-01 to 2004-05*
Andhra Pradesh	351	365	482	513	1093
Assam	443	543	385	387	888
Bihar	492	646	365	402	839
Gujarat	400	287	492	931	910
Haryana	524	377	317	511	848
Himachal Pradesh	807	609	359	572	811
Jammu and Kashmir	2427	2980	1435	1330	2577
Karnataka	317	252	421	631	1022
Kerala	696	483	584	716	611
Madhya Pradesh	286	270	244	246	462
Maharashtra	678	726	740	743	1223
Orissa	538	363	342	574	486
Punjab	1760	881	1003	869	780
Rajasthan	174	150	189	304	292
Tamil Nadu	215	197	205	316	653
Uttar Pradesh	442	362	319	324	524
West Bengal	267	206	233	303	391
All India	498	407	340	339	317

II.2 Private Investment

There are no direct data available on annual basis for compilation of capital formation in agriculture in the private sector at state level. However, the RBI-NSSO has been conducting country-wide survey of debt and investment (AIDIS)

TABLE 4

State-wise Total and Per Hectare Private Capital Formation in Agriculture

States	*Total FCFA At Current Prices (Rs. Crore)*			*Per Hectare of Net Sown Area at 1993-94 prices*		
	1981-82	*1991-92*	*2002-03*	*1981-82*	*1991-92*	*2002-03*
Andhra Pradesh	110	283	684	362	307	347
Assam	12	19	44	163	83	88
Bihar	39	79	83	167	122	61
Gujarat	98	201	682	361	258	384
Haryana	82	169	761	802	577	1138
Himachal Pradesh	7	36	132	429	753	1299
Jammu and Kashmir	8	13	80	412	206	579
Karnataka	99	535	404	350	598	219
Kerala	54	157	328	868	839	809
Madhya Pradesh	112	716	911	210	443	332
Maharashtra	167	659	1292	326	445	399
Orissa	16	37	94	93	70	86
Punjab	129	198	597	1080	563	766
Rajasthan	99	499	1114	228	386	383
Tamil Nadu	89	382	692	586	799	821
Uttar Pradesh	267	685	1744	545	499	575
West Bengal	34	94	146	212	207	149
All India	1445	4801	11622	363	406	471

Sources: 1. RBI (1988), Household Capital Expenditure during 01.07.1981 to 30.06.1982: All India Debt and Investment Survey 1981-82, Reserve Bank of India, Bombay.

2. NSSO (1998), Household Capital Expenditure during 01.07.1991 to 30.06.1992: Debt and Investment Survey, 48th Round, Ministry of Planning and Programme Implementation, Govt. of India

3. NSSO (2005), Household Capital Expenditure during 01.07.2002 to 30.06.2003: Debt and Investment Survey, 58th Round, Ministry of Planning and Programme Implementation, Govt. of India.

at decennial intervals since 1951-52. To make inter-state comparison, fixed capital formation in agriculture has been computed on per hectare of net sown area basis at 1993-94 prices for all three points of time. During 1981-82, Punjab ranked number one and Haryana occupied the third place. All the BIMARU states like Orissa, Bihar, M.P., and Rajasthan were at the bottom. Investment in agriculture in private account was also low. During the years from 1981-82 to 1991-92, private investment in Orissa, Bihar, Gujarat, Andhra Pradesh and Assam further deteriorated. Madhya Pradesh marked highest growth in private fixed capital expenditure during this period. During 1991-92, Kerala has attained first position. In Punjab, Karnataka and Haryana compared to all India average Rs. 471 per hectare of net sown area in 2002-03, per hectare private investment was quite remarkable. Maharashtra also achieved impressive growth in fixed capital formation in agriculture but private investment in Haryana and Uttar Pradesh declined from 1981-82 to 1991-92. Himachal Pradesh continuously performed well and occupied the first place. Haryana and Tamil Nadu were at second and third place respectively during the 11 years, from 1991-92 to 2002-03, private investment in Bihar, Karnataka, Maharashtra, Madhya Pradesh and West Bengal went down and remained below the country average. In Kerala, per hectare private investment at constant prices remained almost constant in this period. Uttar Pradesh showed improvement rising from Rs. 499 in 1991-92 to Rs. 575 in 2002-03.

III. CAPITAL FORMATION "IN" AND "FOR" AGRICULTURE

In the strict definitional sense of the term, public investments in agriculture are associated with public sector gross fixed capital formation (GFCF) in agriculture, as defined in the National Accounts Statistics (NAS) of the Central Statistical Organisation. By this definition, which uses the asset-based approach as well as the industry-of-use approach; public sector GFCF in agriculture comprises mainly (about 90 percent) of the irrigation projects. The problem with this definition is that it does not capture the full range of public-sector investments that have significant influence on the growth of agriculture. Government expenditures in agricultural research and development (R&D), rural roads, rural electrification, education, and other infrastructure are as important as public expenditures on irrigation. This dual effect on agriculture is often expressed as the well-known dichotomy of investments "in" agriculture and investments "for" agriculture. A number of economists have stressed the importance of public investment in the production of a large number of modern inputs such as fertilizers, pump sets, tractors and in infrastructure consisting of transport, storage, energy, etc. for the development of the agriculture sector. According to them investment "for" agriculture is more relevant than investment "in" agriculture for the growth of agriculture sector (Dantwala, 1986). Later studies have also pointed out that the CSO estimates of public investment in agriculture have a narrow coverage as they include only investments "in" agriculture mainly on irrigation. CSO estimates thus leave out other investments "for" agriculture such as public expenditure on rural roads, rural electrification, rural markets, storage, rural education, etc. (Misra and Chand, 1995; Chand, 2000 and 2001).

The Report of the Committee on Capital Formation in Agriculture, GoI, March 2003 looks into the concept of capital formation and the limitation for adoption of the broader concept in national accounting and includes public sector, private corporate sector and household sector for data collection.

According to report, GFCF of Public sector in agriculture in real terms has declined during 80s and 90s, while GFCF for agriculture has been stagnated during the period. The share of GFCF in agriculture as well as for agriculture in GDP has also been declined over the years. Public sector GFCF in agriculture and GFCF for agriculture was continuously falling since 1980-81. It is notable that public sector GFCF "in" agriculture as well as "for" agriculture was less than 1.5% share of GDP after early 1990s and less than 1% share of GDP after mid-1990s, which reflect neglect of agriculture sector by Indian policy-makers.

The over-all annual compound growth rate of public sector gross fixed capital formation in agriculture was negative during 1980-81 to 2001-02. The compound growth rate of public sector gross fixed capital formation for agriculture was positive though very low as just 0.03% for the whole period. While there was some improvement in 1990s showing positive growth at the rate of 0.7 percent. Thus, the momentum of declining growth of public sector GFCF in agriculture as well as public sector GFCF for agriculture was slowed down in the decade of 1990s as compared to 1980s. Therefore, there has been a long-term

TABLE 5

Public Sector Gross Fixed Capital Formation "In" and "For" Agriculture At 1993-94 Prices

(Rs. Crore)

Year	*GDP*	*GFCF*	*GFCF*		*% Share in GDP of GFCF*	
			In Agriculture	*For Agriculture*	*In Agriculture*	*For Agriculture*
1980-81		401128	7358	9855	1.8	2.5
1981-82		425073	6998	9684	1.6	2.3
1982-83		438079	7020	9973	1.6	2.3
1983-84		471742	7089	10599	1.5	2.2
1984-85		492077	6699	9813	1.4	2.0
1985-86		513990	6005	9224	1.2	1.8
1986-87		536257	5738	9835	1.1	1.8
1987-88		556778	6004	9722	1.1	1.7
1988-89		615098	5733	9875	0.9	1.6
1989-90		656331	4911	8895	0.7	1.4
1990-91		692871	4871	8706	0.7	1.3
1991-92		701863	4400	8655	0.6	1.2
1992-93		737792	4549	8477	0.6	1.1
1993-94		781345	4996	9522	0.6	1.2
1994-95		838031	5406	10072	0.6	1.2
1995-96		899563	5318	9631	0.6	1.1
1996-97		970083	4942	6456	0.5	0.7
1997-98		1016594	4467	8995	0.4	0.9
1998-99		1082748	4459	9398	0.4	0.9
1999-00		1148442	4637	9902	0.4	0.9

Source: The Committee on Capital formation in agriculture, March 2003, Directorate of Economics and Statistics, Department of Agriculture and Cooperation, Ministry of Agriculture, Government of India.

deceleration in the share of capital formation in agriculture in GDP at both aggregate and public sector level. In fact the shares of GFCF in agriculture and for agriculture in GDP have declined much more sharply in the Public Sector, which was likely to have an adverse impact on growth of agricultural production and its contribution in National Income.

TABLE 6

Compound Annual Growth Rate (%) (At 1993-94 prices)

Period	*GFCF In Agriculture (Public Sector)*	*GFCF For Agriculture (Public Sector)*
1980-81 to 1990-91	-4.0	-1.2
1991-92 to 1999-00	0.7	1.7
1980-81 to 1999-00	-2.4	0.03

IV. CONCLUSION

Analysis with investment series has confirmed deceleration in public investment both at national and state level. During early phase, the share of public and private sectors in total investment was almost equal, and there has been a steady rise in the share of private investment since mid-eighties. There are undeniable evidences of decline in investment in real terms after the eighties. Public investment in agriculture began to decline in the 1980s, but initially the decline was offset by the fact that private investment in agriculture was increasing. Since the mid-1990s private investment in agriculture has stagnated while public investment has continued to decline. After 2000-01, public and private investment in agriculture moved in upward direction and revealed increasing trends. In state level analysis, declining trend of public investment in real terms across the board in most of the states since mid-1980s also has been reported. Share of GFCF in agricultural GDP was lower in 1990s than in 1980s. The falling public investment in agriculture during the 1980 was mainly because of a large proportion of the resource flows to the agriculture sector going into current expenditure on subsidies for fertilizers, irrigation, electricity, credit and other agricultural inputs, rather than investment. Diversion of funds from irrigation to anti-poverty programmes and increasing pressure on revenue expenditure in payments of salaries and interest were the real hindrances in the growth of public capital formation according to many scholars.

In Indian agriculture, which continues to provide livelihood for more than half of the population, pro-developed countries' policies after 1991 had acute adverse effects. The self-sufficiency in food production after green revolution was built with government support; like price supports, credit assistance and marketing facilities, which led to the creation of a network of institutional support structures in rural areas. The reform process in India significantly weakened the structural support through declining public investment "in" agriculture as well as "for" agriculture. As part of fiscal reforms, major input subsidies were brought down relative to the size of the agricultural economy. Public capital formation in agriculture continued to fall, and the growth of public expenditure on research and extension slowed down. The expansion of rural credit was arrested and informal sector again trapped the poor farmers. The new strategy of agriculture growth and diversification of agriculture from traditional crop cultivation to horticulture, etc. would require more investments on cold storage, rural roads, communication, marketing network and facilities, warehouses, etc. Simultaneously efforts should be made to revitalize agriculture through introduction of bio-technology and other innovations. This would require substantial increase in investment on research and development for agriculture.

Over the period of economic reforms, agricultural growth rates slowed down significantly. Most importantly, the rate of growth of foodgrain production slowed down, and fell behind the population growth rates for the first time after independence. The spate of farmers' suicides reported from some states reflects the distress condition of agriculture after 1991. A reversal of neo-liberal policies in agriculture has become absolutely essential to revive the livelihood systems of rural households in India.

References

Ahluwalia, Montek, S. (2000), "Economic Performances of States in Post-Reforms Period", *Economic and Political Weekly*, Vol. 35, May 6.

Alagh, Y.K. (1994), "Macro Policies for Indian Agriculture" in G.S. Bhalla (ed.), Economic Liberalisation and Indian Agriculture, Institute for Studies in Industrial Development, New Delhi.

Chadha (2003), "Indian Agriculture in the New Millennium: Human Response to Technology Challenges", *Indian Journal of Agricultural Economics*, Vol. 58, No. 1, January-March.

Chand, Ramesh (2000), "Emerging Trends and Regional Variations in Agricultural Investments and Their Implications for Growth and

Equity", Policy Paper-11, National Centre for Agricultural Economics and Policy Research, New Delhi.

Chand, Ramesh (2001), "Emerging Trends and Issues in Public and Private Investment in Indian Agriculture: A State-wise Analysis", *Indian Journal of Agricultural Economics*, Vol. 56, No. 2, April-June.

Dantwala, M.L. (1986), "Strategy of Agricultural Development Since Independence," in Dantwala, M.L. (ed.), Indian Agricultural Development Since Independence: A Collection of Essays, Oxford and IBH Publishing Co. Pvt. Ltd., New Delhi.

Dhawan, B.D. and S.S. Yadav (1995), "Private Fixed Capital Format in Agriculture: Some Aspects of Indian Farmers' Investment Behaviour", *Economic and Political Weekly*, Vol. 30, No. 30, September 30.

Gandhi, Vasant, P. (1996), "Investment Behaviour in Indian Agriculture", *Indian Journal of Agricultural Economics*, Vol. 51, No. 4, October-December.

Government of India (2000), (2004), (2005), (2007), National Account Statistics, Central Statistical Organisation, Department of Statistics, Ministry of Planning, New Delhi.

Government of India, (2001), National Account Statistics, (Back Series 1950-51 to 1992-93), Central Statistical Organisation, Department of Statistics, Ministry of Planning, New Delhi.

Government of India (2003), "Report of the Committee on Capital Formation in Agriculture", Directorate of Economics and Statistics, Department of Agriculture and Cooperation, Ministry of Agriculture, Government of India.

Gulati, A. and S. Narayanan (2003), Subsidy Syndrome in Indian Agriculture, Oxford University Press, New Delhi.

Gulati, Ashok and Seema Bathla (2001), "Capital Formation in Indian Agriculture: Re-visiting the Debate", *Economic and Political Weekly*, Vol. 36, No. 20, May 19.

Kumar, A. Ganesh (1992), "Falling Agricultural Investment and Its Consequences", *Economic and Political Weekly*, Vol. 27, No. 42, October 17.

Mallick, Sushanta, K. (1993), "Capital Formation in Indian Agriculture: Recent Trends", *Indian Journal of Agricultural Economics*, Vol. 48, No. 4, October-December.

Misra, V.N. (1998), "Economic Reforms, Terms of Trade, Aggregate Supply and Private Investment in Agriculture: Indian Experience", *Economic and Political Weekly*, Vol. 33, No. 31, August 1.

Misra, V.N. and M. Govinda Rao (2003). "Trade Policy, Agricultural Growth and Rural Poor: Indian Experience, 1978-79 to 1999-2000", *Economic and Political Weekly*, Vol. 38, No. 43, October 25.

Misra, V.N. and Peter, B.R. Hazell (1996), "Terms of Trade, Rural Poverty, Technology and Investment: The Indian Experience, 1952-53 to 1990-91", *Economic and Political Weekly*, Vol. 31, No. 13, March 30.

Misra, S.N. (1996), "Capital Formation and Accumulation in Indian Agriculture Since Independence", *Indian Journal of Agricultural Economics*, Vol. 51, Nos. 1 and 2, January-June.

Misra, S.N. and Ramesh Chand (1995), "Public and Private Capital Formation in

Indian Agriculture: Comments on the Complementarity Hypothesis and Others", *Economic and Political Weekly*, Vol. 30, No. 25, June 24.

NSSO (1998), Household Capital Expenditure during 1.7.1991 to 30.6.1992: Debt and Investment Survey, 48th Round, Ministry of Planning and Programme Implementation, Government of India.

NSSO (2005), Household Capital Expenditure during 1.7.2002 to 30.6.2003: Debt and Investment Survey, 58th Round, Ministry of Planning and Programme Implementation, Government of India.

Rao, C. Hanumantha (1994), Agricultural Growth, Rural Poverty and Environmental Degradation in India, Oxford University Press, Delhi.

Rao, C. Hanumantha (2001), "WTO and Viability of Indian Agriculture", *Economic and Political Weekly*, Vol. 36, No. 3, September 8.

Rao, M. Govind (2002), "State Finances in India: Issues and Challenges", *Economic and Political Weekly*, Vol. 37, August 3.

Rath, Neelkanth (1989), "Agricultural Growth and Investment in India", *Journal of Political Economy*, Vol. 11, No. 1, January-June.

Reserve Bank of India (1977), Household Capital Expenditure during 01.07.1971 to 30.06.1972: All India Debt and Investment Survey, 38th Round, Reserve Bank of India, Mumbai.

Reserve Bank of India (1988), Household Capital Expenditure during 01.07.1981 to 30.06.1982: All India Debt and Investment Survey, 1981-82, Reserve Bank of India, Mumbai.

Roy, B.C. and Suresh Pal (2002), "Investment, Agricultural Productivity and Rural Poverty in India: A State Level Analysis", *Indian Journal of Agricultural Economics*, Vol. 57, No. 4, October-December.

Shetty, S.L. (1990), "Investment in Agriculture: Brief Review of Recent Trends", *Economic and Political Weekly*, Vol. 25, Nos. 7 and 8, February 17-24.

7

Determinants of Capital Formation in Andhra Pradesh Agriculture

P. NARASIMHA RAO

INTRODUCTION

The root cause of the prevailing agrarian distress in the country has been attributed to declining capital formation in agriculture. The declining capital formation in agriculture sector which is a matter of serious concern and a major problem has become a major issue for debate. The question is whether the private sector can compensate for the declining public sector capital formation. This aspect assumes greater importance in the context of liberalization, where the role of the state is declining. So the problem is centered around the relationship between public and private capital formation in agriculture. Though number of scholars made studies on this aspect, these studies are concentrated the analysis of the relationship between public and private sector at all India level. But do not reflect the regional picture. It is known that there are substantial variations across the states in terms of agricultural development as well as capital formation.

The trends in capital formation differ among across the

states. Unless the factors influencing these trends in capital formation are identified, it may be difficult to conclude on the reasons for declining public investment and Gross Capital Formation. It is also difficult to estimate the relationship between public and private capital formation. The other related aspects are the role of public sector, and the role of private sector with regard to investment on agriculture.

The other aspect that is to be verified is whether the private investment can reduce inter- and intra-regional inequalities. In the light of these arguments make an attempt is made to address some of the above issues for the state level in detail in this study. The study has been conducted in Andhra Pradesh because of its dynamic agriculture production, where the traditional production system has been in the process of transformation into modern commercial agriculture. The main objectives of the study are: 1. To estimate the trends in capital formation, private and public and its composition in agriculture, and 2. To estimate the determinants of capital formation.

The details pertaining to the estimate of Gross fixed capital formation of public, private and state Gross Domestic Product in Agriculture in the period 1980-81 to 1991-92 at 1980-81 prices and for the period 1992-93 to 2003-04 at 1992-93 prices presented in Table 1. The break up of public, private and total Gross Fixed Capital Formation in agriculture sector is presented to analyze the relationship among them. The time series data reveals that the Gross fixed capital Formation in Andhra Pradesh Agriculture is found to be growing steadily during period 1980-81 to 2002-03. A similar trend is observed in case of public sector Capital Formation also. In case of private fixed capital formation in Agriculture, which was steadily rising during the period 1980-81 to 1991-92, reached a peak level in 1991-92 and thereafter fell sharply up to 1992-97 and later picked up marginally after 1997-98. To establish the functional relationship between public and private Gross Capital formation the following regression equation is used.

$$\text{Log } Y = \text{Log } A + B \times \text{Log } X$$

where

Y= Private fixed Capital formation in rupees

X = Public fixed capital formation

TABLE I

Capital Formation in Andhra Pradesh Agriculture

Rs. (Crores)

Year	*Public*	*Private*	*Total*	*All Sectors*	*Agriculture (GDP)*
Pre-Reform Period		**At 1980-81 prices**			
1980-81	67	100	167	9140	3391
1981-82	64	111	175	10953	4224
1982-83	149	121	270	11813	4240
1983-84	158	140	298	13692	4974
1984-85	215	181	396	14784	5024
1985-86	251	218	469	16619	5134
1986-87	314	257	571	17957	5106
1987-88	295	291	586	21249	6560
1988-89	324	347	671	26645	8652
1989-90	268	334	602	30480	9626
1990-91	280	382	662	35835	10615
1991-92	377	503	880	43636	13396
Post-Reform Period		**At 1992-93 prices**			
1992-93	506	407	913	47407	14505
1993-94	630	361	991	57867	14247
1994-95	644	433	1077	68923	16249
1995-96	609	471	1080	79853	18774
1996-97	599	501	1100	90147	21521
1997-98	826	568	1394	95782	18348
1998-99	883	747	1630	114937	26583
1999-00	1257	755	2012	125235	24707
2000-01	1242	615	1857	140119	27784
2001-02	1308	624	1932	151396	26223
2002-03	1682	629	2311	162310	21881
2003-04	N.A.	N.A.	N.A.	180812	26815

N.A. = Not available.

Source: Directorate of Economics and Statistics, Hyderabad.

$$Y = 143.19 + 0.426 \times X$$
$$(1.62)$$

The above results clearly indicate that there is a positive

and significant relationship between private fixed capital formation and public fixed capital formation. The results leads to the conclusion that the public capital formation stimulate the private investment in agriculture. A one per cent of growth of public investment creating 0.45 per cent growth in private investment. And also it is found that there is a positive relationship between agriculture Gross Domestic Product and gross fixed capital formation in agriculture. This clearly leads to conclusion that agriculture growth depends upon capital formation in agriculture, by enhancing the productive capacity of the agricultural sector.

The three yearly fluctuating averages of gross fixed capital formation since 1981-82 to 2001-02 is presented in the Table 2. The averages are centered at the end of the triennium. The averages of the three years are taken to eliminate year to year fluctuations in the values of the Gross Fixed Capital Formation. The composition of private and public sector capital formation reveals that the share of public capital formation was 45 per cent and the share of public sector capital formation was about 55 per cent during triennium ending from 1981-82 to 1991-92. After a decade the share of public sector capital formation increased to 47 per cent and the share of private capital formation declined to 53 per cent. A similar trend in capital formation continued during the period triennium ending in 2000-01. That is the share of public sector capital formation increase to nearly 65 per cent and the share of private fixed capital formation decreased to 35 per cent. Even in Post-Reform Period the share of public sector capital formation showed an increasing trend while the share of private sector capital formation started declining. This trend is contrary to the all India level, where the share of public sector capital formation has declined. Expenditure on public investment on irrigation in Andhra Pradesh may be the major component of public sector fixed capital formation in agriculture

The growth rates of capital formation for the last two decades for different sub-periods are presented Table 3. The trend reveals that there is a decrease in the growth rate of Gross Fixed Capital Formation in Agriculture. The simple annual growth rate of Gross Fixed Capital Formation, during the period 1982-83 to 1986-87 was about 26.36 per cent but was declined to 6.85 per cent during 1987-88 to 1991-92 and it further declined to

TABLE 2

Capital Formation in Andhra Pradesh Agriculture: Three Yearly Moving Average Series

(Rs. in Crores)

Year	*Public*	*Private*	*Total*	*All Sectors*	*Agriculture (GDP)*
Pre-Reform Period		**At 1980-81 prices**			
1. 1981-82	93.33	110.67	204.00	10635.34	3951.67
2. 1982-83	123.67	124.00	247.67	12152.67	4479.33
3. 1983-84	174.00	147.33	321.33	13429.67	4746.00
4. 1984-85	208.00	179.67	387.67	15031.67	5044.00
5. 1985-86	260.00	218.67	478.67	16453.34	5088.00
6. 1986-87	286.67	255.33	542.00	18608.34	5600.00
7. 1987-88	311.00	298.33	609.33	21950.34	6772.67
8. 1988-89	295.67	324.00	619.67	26124.67	8279.33
9. 1989-90	290.67	354.33	645.00	30986.67	9631.00
10. 1990-91	308.33	406.33	714.67	32650.34	11212.34
11. 1991-92	387.67	430.67	818.33	42292.67	12838.67
Post-Reform Period		**At 1992-93 prices**			
12.1992-93	504.33	423.66	928.00	49636.67	14047.33
13.1993-94	593.33	400.33	993.67	58065.67	15000.33
14.1994-95	627.07	421.67	1049.33	68881.00	16424.33
15.1995-96	617.33	428.33	1085.67	79641.00	18848.00
16.1996-97	678.00	513.33	1191.33	88594.00	19547.67
17.1997-98	769.33	605.33	1374.67	100288.67	22150.67
18.1998-99	988.67	690.00	1678.67	111984.67	23212.67
19.1999-00	1127.33	705.67	1833.00	126763.67	26358.00
20.2000-01	1269.00	664.67	1933.67	138916.67	26209.33
21.2001-02	1410.67	622.67	2033.33	151.275.00	25214.00
22.2002-03	N.A.	N.A.	N.A.	164839.34	24973.0

N.A. = Not Available.

Source: Same as in Table 1.

5.67 per cent during 1992-93 to 1996-97 and picked up to 9.58 per cent during the period 1997-98 to 2001-02. But the trend in public sector capital formation continued to increase from 26.36 per cent during 1982-83 to 1986-87, it declined to 4.93 per cent, during the period 1987-88 to 1991-92 and it picked up marginally

TABLE 3

Percent Change in Capital Formation in Andhra Pradesh Agriculture

(in percentage)

Sl. No.	*Year Triennium Ending (GFCF)*	*Public (GFCF)*	*Private (GFCF)*	*Total GFCF*	*All sectors (GFCF)*
1.	1982-83 to 1986-87	131.88	105.91	118.83	53.12
2.	1987-88 to 1991-92	24.65	44.36	34.29	92.65
3.	1992-93 to 1996-97	34.43	21.16	28.37	78.48
4.	1997-98 to 2001-02	83.36	02.86	47.91	50.83
Annual					
5.	1982-83 to 1986-87	26.36	21.18	23.76	10.62
6.	1987-88 to 1991-92	4.93	8.87	6.85	18.53
7.	1992-93 to 1996-97	6.88	4.23	5.67	15.69
8.	1997-98 to 2001-02	16.67	0.57	09.58	10.16
9.	1982-83 to 1991-92	21.37	24.67	23.04	24.80
10.	1992-93 to 2001-02	17.97	04.70	11.90	20.47

Source: Calculated from Table 2.

to 6.88 per cent per annum during 1992-93 to 1996-97. Again it increased to 16.67 per cent during the period 1997-98 to 2001-02. In the reforms period the decrease in the growth rate of public sector capital formation, found to be high when compared to pre-reform period.

While this decline in public sector capital formation is marginal the decline in private sector capital formation is very high. The decline in private sector capital formation depends upon a number of factors. The private sector capital formation depends upon pattern of public investment, terms of trade in agriculture in relation to manufacturing sector, rate of return in agriculture, technology subsidies and institutional credit. The contribution of above factors to the present decline in private sector capital formation has to be probed.

FACTORS INFLUENCING THE BEHAVIOUR OF CAPITAL FORMATION IN ANDHRA PRADESH AGRICULTURE

The behaviour of capital formation in agriculture has to be analyzed with respect to the major components of capital formation. The total expenditure on agriculture and irrigation under revenue account and capital account have to be examined to trace the behaviour of capital formation in agriculture. The expenditure on these components is presented in Table 4. The total expenditure incurred by agriculture and irrigation as a proportion of State Gross Domestic Product has fluctuated from 4.09 per cent to 14.53 per cent during the period of study. The share at first increased during the period from 1981-82 to 1986-87 and declined between 1987-88 and 1992-93. It continues to decrease thereafter and reached to a low level of 3.24 per cent in the year 2003-04. The total expenditure on agriculture and irrigation as a proportion of agricultural GDP during 2000-01 to 2004-05 ranged between 6.2 to 6.5 per cent. So it reflects that the total expenditure on agriculture as per cent of agriculture GDP drastically declined during Post-Reform Period and reached to a very low after 2000-01. The share of revenue expenditure total agricultural investment given in the table reveals that the share of revenue expenditure in total investment agriculture is 58 per cent in 1980-81 and increased to 68 per cent in 1991-92, and stagnated thereafter. It again decreased to 42.13 per cent in 2004-05.

This indicates that the share of revenue expenditure in agricultural investment was 35 per cent during 1980-81 and this increased to 36 per cent in 1991, later it again increased to 41 per cent in 2004-05. The higher share of revenue expenditure in total investment indicate that the large part of expenditure is to meet wages, share and maintenance expenditure. Further, the analysis of expenditure on sub-sector like irrigation reveals the government concern for capital investment in irrigation, after 2003-04, when the ratio between revenue and capital expenditure virtually become equal. The analysis of the ratio of expenditure on revenue account and capital account found to be alarming situation in agriculture for the last two decades. It is found that most of the period the revenue expenditure in total investment is alarmingly high. This indicates the increasing constraint on the share of funds available for capital investment.

TABLE 4

Expenditure on Agriculture and Irrigation in Andhra Pradesh

(Rs. in crores)

Year	Revenue Account			Capital Account			Total	Agricul-	Agricul-	C11=	C12=
	Agricultural	Irrigation	Total	Agricultural	Irrigation	Total	Agricultural	tural Investment	tural GDP	C4/C8 *100	C8/C10 *100
C1	C2	C3	C4	C5	C6	C7	C8	C9	C10	C11	C12
1980-81	54.56	100.61	151.17	15.51	91.67	107.18	258.35	1538.61	3314.86	58.51	7.79
1981-82	55.47	109.81	125.28	17.60	95.64	113.24	278.52	1628.44	4128.94	59.34	7.79
1982-83	65.18	134.68	199.86	23.61	177.21	200.82	400.68	2150.86	5135.59	49.88	7.79
1983-84	64.05	150.62	214.70	22.54	248.89	271.43	486.13	2619.84	4911.23	44.16	9.89
1984-85	84.00	161.00	245.00	29.93	268.42	298.35	543.35	2845.14	5018.22	45.09	10.82
1985-86	386.91	—	386.91	43.07	286.82	329.89	716.80	2851.1	4991.35	53.97	14.36
1986-87	163.16	212.29	375.45	19.24	297.19	298.43	673.88	9683.66	4991.35	55.71	13.50
1987-88	229.70	296.92	526.62	13.87	302.53	316.40	843.02	4952.96	6412.53	62.46	13.14
1988-89	241.94	352.46	594.40	14.41	314.40	328.81	923.21	5383.64	8457.77	64.38	10.91
1989-90	254.46	361.87	616.33	8.63	316.28	324.91	341.24	13930.98	9315.90	67.48	10.10
1990-91	242.77	416.17	658.95	11.52	288.58	300.1	859.05	7231.02	11138.21	68.70	8.60
1991-92	349.52	455.91	805.43	12.83	363.75	376.58	1182.01	8160.98	14833.28	68.14	7.96
1992-93	473.73	532.36	1006.09	14.19	509.22	523.41	1529.5	22793.94	13917.89	65.77	10.98
1993-94	484.13	591.72	1075.88	11082	492.73	504.55	1580.4	9857.16	10876.47	68.07	14.53

1994-95	433.85	654.02	1087.87	11.15	582.78	593.93	1681.8	10876.47	19752.52	64.68	8.51
1995-96	463.67	840.30	1303.97	10.63	634.93	645.56	1949.53	32217.61	22810.45	66.88	8.54
1996-97	490.13	991.54	1481.67	7.09	679.89	686.98	2168.65	17484.36	25336.41	68.32	8.55
1997-98	581.57	1105.50	1687.07	8.69	757.22	765.91	2452.98	19538.47	24035.70	68.77	10.20
1998-99	666.49	1176.94	1843.43	8.60	934.79	943.39	2787.22	24718.88	32351.91	66.13	8.61
1999-00	760.80	1664.14	2424.94	16.60	1006.36	1017.96	3442.9	27602.72	24706.65	70.43	13.93
2000-01	841.56	1492.24	2333.8	5.47	1097.57	1097.57	1130.0	59250.65	27569.91	206.97	4.09
2001-02	761.01	1584.37	5447.5	18.46	1143.42	1143.42	1661.8	75292.30	26569.91	468.88	4.37
2002-03	910.57	1816.09	2726.6	15.05	1398.75	1398.75	1413.8	37145.49	21721.59	192.85	6.50
2003-04	1105.22	1995.93	3101.50	31.61	2729.65	2761.28	5862.78	41362.23	180812.00	52.90	3.24
2004-05	1502.21	2139.46	3641.67	6.84	4872.4	4879.25	8520.92	87416.43	199075.00	42.73	4.28

Source: Directorate of Economics and Statistics, Government of Andhra Pradesh, Hyderabad.

The behaviour of private sector investment in agriculture in the absence of time series data can be explained in terms of institutional credit for long-term and medium-term purpose. The flow of institutional credit in Andhra Pradesh agriculture reveals that there is a tremendous growth of credit for the last two decades, and it accounts for nearly 2/3 of private capital formation in agriculture. However, it is reported by many scholars that the loans taken for capital expenditure do not get translated into investment for various reasons, such as repayment of old loans, diversion into consumption, etc., fragmentation of land, unavailable agricultural production, poor Ayucutt roads, poor communication, unfavourable terms of trade in agriculture and socio-political conditions reflect the situation of poor private investment.

The trends in private agriculture investment can also be explained in terms of investment on different sources of irrigation. Growth of groundwater irrigation largely depends upon investment on groundwater irrigation. The analysis of growth of groundwater and surface irrigation area reflect the trends in investment in agriculture.

From Table 5, It is found that an average of 0.75 lakh hectares are added every year to the gross irrigated area between 1980-81 and 2002-03 which was about 15 lakh hectares in the State. The growth in irrigation development in the state during the period 80's and 90's can be seen from the data on source-wise net irrigated area. The net irrigated area by canals is stagnant for the last two decades and in case of tanks it has declined. But the net irrigated area under groundwater source increased by 11 lakh hectares, in this period. Among the two sources, growth of area under surface water depends on public investment, on the other hand, the area irrigated by groundwater (tubewells and other wells), depends on private investment also. This is further confirmed by Linear Growth Rate of 2.03 and 0.77 per cent for groundwater and surface water irrigated area respectively. The growth in private investment on tubewells and other wells contributed in the absence of public investment in Andhra Pradesh.

EFFICIENCY OF CAPITAL USE

Capital formation creates new and better production facilities and enlarges and improves the existing ones. The relationship between the gross capital formation and the related increase in GDP is expressed as the incremental capital output ratio (ICOR). The term may be defined as the ratio of gross capital formation in a period to the related increase in GDP. The ICOR is an overall measure of the efficiency with which incremental or additional capital (that is, real investment) is being used to bring about a rise in output or GDP. The lower the ICOR the lower is the rate of gross capital formation and required to secure a particular growth rate of GDP.

The incremental capital output ratio (ICOR) measures the increase in output as a result of use of investment, whether it is made in public or private sector. The analysis of ICOR for the 4 sub-periods is given in Table 6. The ICOR was 1.93 per cent during the period 1982-83 to 1986-87. Thereafter it fell to 0.53 per cent during the 1987-88 to 1991-92. There has been a moderate increase between 1992-93 to 1996-97, i.e. increased to 0.86 per cent. There has been a tremendous growth during the period 1997-98 to 2001-02. The ICOR is 2.65 per cent during period 1997-98 to 2001-02. During this period increase of output in agriculture sector with respect to investment is higher. That is productivity of capital during 1997-98 to 2001-02 was higher. Private sector capital formation might have contributed to the growth of incremental capital output ratio.

The marginal efficiency of capital was being low of 0.51 per cent during the period 1982-83 to 1986-87. It has increased to about 1.85 per cent during the period 1987-88 to 1991-92. However, during the period 1992-93 to 1996-97, the marginal efficiency of capital decreased to 1.15 and reached to the lowest point of 0.37 during the 1997-98 to 2001-02. This indicates that even though the public capital formation in agriculture has not declined there is a tremendous decrease in the marginal efficiency of capital during the period 1997-98 to 2001-02. This indicates the distress conditions in agricultural production economy. Though the Marginal efficiency of capital is the highest for a decade from 1987-88 and 1996-97, it falls to very low-level during the period from 1987-88 and 2001-02. For the

TABLE 5

Gross and Net Irrigated Area in Andhra Pradesh

(Area in Hectares)

	Net Irrigated Area								
	Canals	*Tanks*	*Surface Water*	*Well and Tube Wells*	*Others*	*Total*	*Gross Irrig ated AreaGIA*	*Gross Cropped Area GCA*	*GIA/ GCA*
C1	*C2*	*C3*	*C4*	*C5*	*C6*	*C7*	*C8*	*C9*	*C10*
1980-81	1692792	899919	2592711	776763	93246	870009	4341561	12281695	.35
1981-82	1755898	1044838	2655817	786229	104816	3546862	4677825	13047106	.35
1982-83	1742649	852544	2595193	838481	93113	3526787	4717851	12768946	.35
1983-84	1839027	1086720	2925747	838117	113969	3877833	5058114	13393051	.37
1984-85	1793889	774426	2568315	836896	117276	3522487	4469542	12212264	.36
1985-86	1793889	774426	2568315	836896	117276	3522487	4337391	12100145	.35
1986-87	1779937	776504	2556441	883848	109979	3550268	4360070	11692817	.37
1987-88	1593511	662951	2256462	990881	121810	3369153	4298083	12154777	.35
1988-89	1870686	1104068	2974754	1133433	149976	4258163	5439979	13150607	.41
1989-90	1888583	1025807	2914390	1208229	162178	4284797	5453957	13257706	.41
1990-91	1868867	967844	2836711	1303221	165546	4305478	5369677	13192714	.40
1991-92	1825435	947994	2773429	1402997	174369	4350795	5377875	13192249	.40
1992-93	1726964	728499	2455463	1402997	162176	4020636	5085082	12754147	.39
1993-94	1659016	632595	2291611	1967974	156379	4415964	5019640	12689940	.39

1994-95	1606107	692021	2298128	2077083	182405	4557616	5184694	12783111	.40
1995-96	1538613	746631	2285284	1656814	181167	4123225	5304007	13042981	.40
1996-97	1628606	843890	843890	1728437	193986	4394919	5782246	13410147	.43
1997-98	1537708	562730	562730	1676460	167704	8145478	5158081	12134911	.42
1998-99	1634279	810487	810487	1896571	197148	4538485	6092074	13624671	.44
1999-00	1634252	651427	651427	1899929	198516	4384124	5745883	13023038	.44
2000-01	1649387	726809	726809	1954301	197232	4527729	5916147	13545263	.43
2001-02	1562413	567519	567519	1927438	180498	4237868	5548633	—	—
2002-03	1208538	425677	425677	1842285	137164	3613664	4536195	—	—

Source: Directorate of Economics and Statistics, Government of Andhra Pradesh, Hyderabad.

ratio of Gross Fixed Capital Formation in agriculture to Agriculture GDP in percentage terms clearly indicate a declining trend, considering a longer period the ratio decreased from 7.92 to 7.18 per cent during the period between 1982-83 to 2001-02.

Further, the share of agriculture in total GDP shows a continuous declining trend for the last two decades. It has decreased from 32.69 per cent during the period 1982-83 to 1986-87 to 19.7 per cent during the period 1997-98 to 2001-02. Due to the fall in the share of agriculture in total GDP the Gross Fixed Capital Formation has also declined over the period. This clearly reveals that though there is a growth in Gross Fixed Capital

TABLE 6

Estimates of Incremental Capital Output Ratio in Andhra Pradesh Agriculture Sector

(in percentage)

	Incremental GDP in Agriculture (crores)	*GDP Growth Rate Output (in Percentage)*	*Gross Fixed Capital Formation (crores)*	*Incremental Capital Output Ratio (ICOR)*	*Marginal Efficiency of Capital (MEC)*	*Gross Fixed Capital Formation as per cent of GDP in Agriculture*
1	*2*	*3*	*4*	*5*	*6*	*7*
1982-83 to 1986-87	280.41	6.25	542	1.93	0.51	7.92
1987-88 to 1991-92	1516.5	22.39	818	0.53	1.85	6.99
1992-93 to 1996-97	1375.08	9.78	1191	0.86	1.15	6.25
1997-98 to 2001-02	765.83	3.45	2033	2.65	0.37	7.18

MEC: Marginal Efficiency of Capital.
ICOR: Incremental Capital Output Ratio.
Source: Calculated from Table 2.

Formation, it is not in real terms. It has not contributed to the growth of agriculture output in the State.

The declining Gross Fixed Capital Formation in agriculture sector reflects on the policy for the development of this sector. The above analysis leads to the conclusion that there is lack of long-term perspectives for the development of the agricultural sector.

Thus the analysis reveals that the rate of return on private investment which in turn depends upon terms of trade is found to be the most important determinant of private capital formation. The public sector investments mainly depend upon fiscal resources. The increase in farm subsidies and decrease in revenue receipts from agriculture caused an adverse impact on public sector capital formation. GDP in agriculture is effected by both capital formation as well as terms of trade.

References

Brahm Prakash and Susila Srivastava (1990), "Capital Formation in Indian Agriculture". Trends, constraints and Prospects". *Indian Journal of Agricultural Economics*, Mumbai, Vol. 51, No. 4, p. 604.

Dhawan, B.D. (1992), "Trends and Determinants of Capital Investments in Agriculture". *Indian Journal of Agricultural Economics*, Mumbai, Vol. 51, No. 4, p. 529.

Dinger S.M. (1990), "Analysis of the Trends and Determinants of Capital Formation in Indian Agriculture". *Indian Journal of Agricultural Economics*, Mumbai, Vol. 51, No. 4, p. 612.

Indersain and Sharma, V.K. (1992), "Capital Formation in Punjab Agriculture: An Analysis of Private Investment". *Indian Journal of Agricultural Economics*, Mumbai, Vol. 51, No. 4, p. 605.

Jairath, M.S. and Brijesh, C. Porohit (1989), "Trends in Capital Formation in Agriculture—A case of Arid India". *Indian Journal of Agricultural Economics*, Mumbai, Vol. 51, No. 4, p. 587.

Kakde, S.J. and Alshi, M.R. (1984), "Capital Formation in Agriculture—A Study in Akola District (Maharashtra)". *Indian Journal of Agricultural Economics*, Vol. 51, No. 4, p. 632.

Majumdar and Menon (1991), "Capital Formation in Indian Agriculture: Recent Trends". *Indian Journal of Agricultural Economics*, Mumbai, Vol. 48, No. 4, p. 667.

Pal, P.K., Pal, G.P. and Pal, D.P. (1980), "Capital Formation in Indian Agriculture Private Versus Public Initiative", *Indian Journal of Agricultural Economics*, Vol. 51, No. 4, p. 627.

Pendse, N.G., Koshti, N.K. and Baghel, L.M.S. (1950), "Trends in Capital Formation in Indian Agriculture: A Comparison of pre and post-Green Revolution Period". *Indian Journal of Agricultural economics*, Vol. 51, No. 4, p, 633.

Rai, K.N. Karwa Sra, J.K. and Singh, S.P. (1993), "Capital Formation in Indian Agriculture: An Overview". *Indian Journal of Agricultural Economics*, Mumbai, Vol. 51, No. 4, p. 612.

Rekha, R. Gaonakar and Mundinamani P.S. (1996), "Private Sector Capital Formation in Agriculture: A Goan Experience". *Indian Journal of Agricultural Economics*, Mumbai, Vol. 51, No. 4, p. 621.

Sanjeeva Reddy P. (1996), "Determinants of Private Capital Formation Under Different Sources of Irrigation: A Case Study in Andhra Pradesh". *Indian Journal of Agricultural Economics*, Mumbai, Vol. 51, No. 4, p. 625.

Varadarajan S. and Sri Sankari (1993), "Private Capital Formation in Agriculture". *Indian Journal of Agricultural Economics*, Mumbai, Vol. 51, No. 4, p. 609.

8

Corporatisation of Contract Farming in Karnataka

S. Erappa

Given the Indian context, where changes in agrarian structure have constituted a major component of political and administrative history (pre and post-independence) leading to different forms of land revenue from the cultivators, which led to indebtedness, dispossession of land, levels of tenancy and increased impoverishment in rural society, it becomes essential to know how in the contemporary neo-liberal economy, the historical social relations are being changed. Indian agriculture moving towards the capitalist intensification of farming through contract farming, though marginally. This trend, should it be called as agricultural development or development of few MNCs or short-term gains of farming community.

The various state intervention strategies as well efforts by non-governmental organisations to arrest migration of the rural masses, which include promotion of income generation activities, have not succeeded in reversing this trend. One of the strong reasons could be the lack of well established forward and backward linkages such as extension advice, mechanisation services, supply of seeds, fertilisers and credit, as also guaranteed and profitable markets for their produce. Therefore, the need for contract farming, which would hopefully promote the linkages to the small-scale farming community to grow crops on commercial terms.

Contract farming can be defined as an agreement between farmers and processing and/or marketing firms for the production and supply of agricultural products under a forward agreement, generally at predetermined prices. The agreements also allow the purchaser to provide a degree of production support through inputs and technical guidance for the crop cultivation. From the farmer's side, there is a commitment to produce the specified agricultural products within the quality and quantity standards prescribed by the purchaser, and the firm supports, in turn, the farmer's production, and also purchases the produce.

The comparative picture of gherkin cultivation in India and abroad is given in Table 1. It indicates the cultivation of gherkin according to seasons, the availability of labour, wage rates, temperature and the type of irrigation in two different situations.

TABLE I

Comparative Study of Gherkin Cultivation in India and Abroad

Sl.. No	*India*	*Abroad*
1.	Can be Grown in Three Seasons	One Season: April-May
2.	Labour Abundance	Scarcity of Labour
3.	Low Wages Rs. 25-40	High Wages: $ 5 per hour
4.	Favourable Temperature	-20 Degree
5.	Manual Irrigation	Drip Irrigation with Fertigation

HISTORY OF CONTRACT FARMING IN KARNATAKA: A BRIEF NOTE

The practice of contract farming was prevalent in the sugar industry where farmers agreed to grow sugarcane at a pre-notified price for decades. Of late, MNCs have entered into the Indian agricultural sector and introduced a number of horticultural crops, and their products have a high demand in international markets. Contract farming, as it existed then, was different from the design and functioning of contract farming methods obtaining today. In other words, the state notifies the price and extends other facilities, i.e., supply of seeds, fertilisers, package of practices, and buy-back from the farmer's field, grade-wise price fixation, and, more importantly stands guarantee for the contract agreement between the farmer and the concerned MNCs. The liberalisation of seed policy has enabled the import of new varieties of crops, both hybrids and high-yielding, by corporate bodies through joint ventures.

Karnataka's agrarian structure is very conducive in promoting contract farming in the country. The distribution of number and area of operational holdings across gender and major size classes during 1995-96 and 2000-01 is given in Table 1. The aggregate pattern of percentage variation in the number of operational holdings and the area operated by size class, reveals 13.8 per cent and 1.6 per cent respectively in the 1995-96 and 2000-01 agricultural census. In other words, the number of operational holdings was increasing, while the area operated was declining during the successive agricultural census in the state. It is interesting to note that across all size classes the percentage variation in the medium and large holding categories indicates negative trends.

REVIEW OF LITERATURE

The social implications of contract farming promoted in small-holdings in a Chilean community. The article highlights the probable advantages of contract farming, such as to elevate the rich peasants into the status of peasants-capitalists rather than to cause the proletarianisation of the peasant community. The inherent advantages of contract agriculture (not importantly the higher returns from land) seen to have motivated Chilien farmers (Tanya Korovkin, 1992).

Behrooz Morvaridi's (1998) paper highlights the fact that only large farmers are in a position to invest in irrigation to maintain productivity though this trend was found to be short-lived and that "corporate profits are made at the expense of long-term productivity for farmers". Interestingly, irrigation costs were not included under the contract farming system and these were indeed a huge burden on the growers. Ben White (1997) study on "agri-industry and contract farmers in the hilly southern region of Upland West Java", covers two case studies, i.e., the nucleus in one case (a small holder dairy farming co-operative), and the other (a small holder growing hybrid coconuts) a large nationalised plantation corporation under contract farming schemes. In both the cases, "contract farming communities deviate markedly from the neo-populist vision of homogeneous, modernising family farms, and the differentiation is quite marked and wage labour common". while evaluating the agro-industrial enterprises and plantation labour in Cameroon, focuses on the role of contract farmers co-operatives associated with Palm oil, a subsidiary of the giant Unilever Company, in the southern west province of Anglophone Cameroon. A small number of large producers of palm oil dominates the co-operatives under the guidance of the Pamol company management and the State (Piet Konings,1998). The contract between farmers and the processor viz., Denisco Foods who had 50 years of experience behind them and have 4,100 ha. (Olesen, 2003)

Clapp (1994) examines the unequal representation of contract farming in Latin America. This could be because of this politics of representation, which is the prime reason for the social relations of contract farming. He suggests that an alternative representation of contract farming, which focuses on the contradictions of wage labour, has an indirect control over labour and an uncertain supply to farmers and that lead to disguised proletarianisation. The politics of representation can be absolved through regulating 'the moral economy of the contract' between the company and peasant community. Another remedy put forth by the committee was to adopt contract farming to reduce the burden on Punjab Agro Industries Corporation. The book on "Green Revolution Reconsidered", highlights the need for crop diversification. Several other researches, too, have endorsed the above opinion. Since then, contract farming has expanded considerably—from 12,000 acres in 2002-03 to 25,000 acres in 2003-04. (Ranju Sarkar: 2004). With this unique contract farming experiment, Punjab is trying to develop a diversified portfolio of crops that can compete with wheat and paddy. The high yielding varieties of oilseeds such as Hyola can give higher returns of Rs. 13,300 per acre as compared Rs. 10,000 from wheat. Crops grown under contract farming are generally short duration crops, while some are traditional crops.

OBJECTIVES OF THE STUDY

The main focus of the paper is to know the company's involved in promoting gheirkin crop under contract farming in Karnataka. Further to understand the respondents profiles like landholding pattern, age composition, educational levels, family members involved in agriculture, cost of cultivation, production and productivity, pre-fixed prices, income and employment, contract system and the available facilities provided by the companies.

METHODOLOGY

There are 25 firms currently involved in contract farming in Karnataka. All the 25 firms have selected Gherkin (small cucumber) as a crop to cultivate under contract farming, spread over districts of Tumkur, Bellary and Haveri. Tumkur has been selected because of its proximity to the study area. The reference year for the study is 2002-03. Revisits were conducted during 2005-06 to understand the changes witnessed at the households of contract farmers that have been covered in the initial years of the survey. There are 10 companies involved in promoting Gherkin in Tumkur district. The field visits confirm that firms like Global Green Company (GGCL), Unicorn, Reitzel, Vishal and Intergarden are leaders in contract farming business in the district. Table 2 gives the details of company, taluk/s, village/s and the number of contract farmers covered in the study. Contract farming is concentrated in taluks like Gubbi, Tiptur and Sira of Tumkur district. Gubbi and Sira taluks form the hub of contract farming activities in the district. Five leading companies are chosen and these covers 11 villages and 30 contract farmers, representing different sizes of holdings. Executives of the above companies extended their co-operation in furnishing relevant details for the study. Therefore, the above companies are chosen for the in-depth study.

TABLE 2

Selected Taluks, Companies, Villages and Sample Contract Farmers in Tumkur District

Sl. No.	*Name of the Taluk*	*Name of the Company*	*Name of the Village*	*No. of Sample HHs*
1.	Gubbi	UNICORN	Appanahalli	11
			Unaganahalli	10
			Hosakere	9
2.	Tiptur	REITZEL	Gowdanakatte	16
			Shivapura	14
3.	Gubbi	VISHAL	Ankasandra	15
			Dasappanahalli	15
4.	Sira	GGCL	Gopikunte	8
			Hosahalli	5
			Kammanahalli	6
5.	Gubbi		Hosakere	11
6.	Gubbi	INTERGARDEN	Bidare	30

All the above companies caters to an export market and in order to match the demand for gherkins abroad, seeds are supplied to farmers in advance. In other words, higher the demand abroad higher is the extent of land sought to be brought under gherkin. The company plans in such a way that the officials concerned has work throughout the year. One of the staff member said that in western countries, the government would provide subsidy to farmers (Rs. 9/per kg) who grew gherkin.

RESPONDENTS PROFILES

The distribution of contract farmers (Head of the Household) by selected company and size class is given in Table 3. Of the total 150 contract farmers selected, small and marginal farmers constitute 52 per cent, medium farmers 38 per cent, and large farmers 10 per cent. And from each of the five companies, 30 contract farmers representing all the sizes of holdings were selected and interviewed for the study.

Table 4 provide the age profile of CFs (HHs) by size class and company affiliation in the study area. Seventy per cent of

TABLE 3

Distribution of Contract Farmers (CFs) by Company and Size Class

Size Class	*Name of the Companies*					*Total*
	IG	*GGCL*	*REITZEL*	*UNICORN*	*VISHAAL*	
Marginal	10	9	5	7	6	37
Small	7	7	7	10	9	40
Medium	10	11	14	11	11	57
Large	3	3	4	2	4	16
Total	30	30	30	30	30	150

heads of households of CFs are in the age group of 26 to 50 years, 25 per cent are above 51 years, and less than five per cent below 25 years. Similar are the trends observed across the size of holdings in the case of small and medium farmers. In the case of large farmers, 50 per cent of CFs are in the age group of around 50 or 50 plus: and eight out of 150 CFs are below 25 years. All the five companies taken together, around 75 per cent of the CFs are in the age group of 26 to 50 years. REITZEL and UNICORN selected CFs around 40 per cent in the age group of 51 plus years. The distribution of CFs within the company across the size

TABLE 4

Age Classification by Name of the Company and Size Class

		Name of the company					*Total*
Age	*Age*	*IG*	*GGCL*	*REITZEL*	*UNICORN*	*VISHAL*	
Total <25		7	-	-	1	-	8
	%	23			3		5
26 to 50		22	23	18	18	24	105
	%	3	23	40	37	20	25
51 to 75		1	7	12	11	6	37
	%	3	23	40	37	20	25
Grand		30	30	30	30	30	150
Total	%	100	100	100	100	100	100

of holdings, small and marginal CFs constitute around 55 per cent, medium CFs category 35 per cent and large CFs 10 per cent in the study area.

Table 5 indicate the educational status of CFs by size class. By and large, CFs have a high literacy rate (99 per cent). CFs who have studied beyond primary and high school levels account for 69 per cent and 19 per cent respectively. It is interesting to note that almost all the CFs identified by the companies were literates. Table 6 furnish details of male and female members of CFs involved in agriculture by size class and affiliated companies. Of the total population of 1,001, 71 per cent (709) are into agriculture. All the companies put together, 52 per cent of the total members involved in agriculture were females and the rest male. A similar trend exists across the five companies operating in the study area.

TABLE 5

Educational Level of the CFs by Selected Companies

Name of the	*Educational Level*				
Company	*Illiterate*	*Primary*	*High School*	*Graduation*	*Total*
IG		9	18	3	30
GGCL	2	4	20	4	30
REITZEL		5	17	8	30
UNICORN		5	21	4	30
VISHAAL		6	14	10	30
Total	2	29	90	29	150

TABLE 6

Population into Agriculture by Company

Name of the company	*Males Involved in Agriculture (%)*	*Females Involved in Agriculture (%)*	*Total*	*Actual*
IG	48	52	100	118
GGCL	47	53	100	132
REITZEL	49	50	100	157
UNICORN	46	54	100	143
VISHAAL	46	54	100	159
Total	48	53	100	709

Table 7 gives the break-up of the cost of cultivation per acre of gherkin. To cultivate one acre of gherkin, the gross cost comes to Rs. 26,500, of which 48 per cent is spent on harvesting of the produce. The other major cost components are fertilisers (16 per cent); seeds (11 per cent); farm yard manure (5 per cent); and pesticides (4 per cent) (see Appendix 2). Establishment costs like staking and GI wire, jute thread and plastic thread account for 10 per cent of the gross cost. Across the size of holdings, cost components do not show much variation. The gross and net returns approximately are Rs. 47,000 and Rs. 20,000 respectively. The average yield of gherkins per acre is 6,300 kgs.

TABLE 7

Cost of Cultivation (Per Acre) of Gherkin Crop in the Study Area

Sl. No		*Particular Total*	*Marginal Farmers*	*Small Farmers*	*Medium Farmers*	*Large Farmers*
1.	Land Development	750	800	900	1000	852
2.	Farm Yard Manure	1300	1250	1400	1450	1350
3.	Seeds	3000	3000	3000	3000	3000
4.	Sowing	200	200	200	200	200
5.	Fertiliser	4194	4236	4250	4585	4150
6.	Weeding	500	550	600	800	620
7.	Staking/GI Wire	718	666	684	630	678
8.	Jute thread	1126	1117	1200	1200	1150
9.	Plastic thread	595	583	591	533	582
10.	Pesticides	1000	940	938	909	947
11.	Irrigation	400	400	400	400	400
12.	Harvesting	12400	12650	12800	13000	12680
13.	Gross Cost	26183	26392	26963	27707	26309
14.	Gross Returns	46228	46526	47558	47723	46992
15.	Net Returns	20045	20134	20595	20016	20683
16.	Output (Kgs)	5963	6423	6339	6505	6295

Tables 8 and 9 give details of the output of gherkin by crops, grades and size classes. The average output of gherkins for crop 1 and 2 are 3,434 kgs and 2,594 kgs, respectively. The gross returns for crop 1 and 2 are Rs. 25,668 and Rs. 18,423 respectively. The output for grade 1 accounts for 53 per cent of the total output for crop 1; and for grade 2 and 3, 33 per cent and 14 per cent respectively.

TABLE 8

Output of Gherkins per Acre by Crop and Size Class

Size Class	CROP 1		CROP 2	
	Qty Kgs	*Value (Rs.)*	*Qty Kgs*	*Value (Rs.)*
Marginal	3060	23782	2195	15550
Small	3609	26300	2258	16344
Medium	3316	24879	2677	19268
Large	4282	31256	4063	27257
Total	3434	25668	2594	18423

TABLE 9

Output of Gherkins Per Acre by Grades and Size Class

Grades	Number of Gherkins	
	CROP 1	*CROP 2*
Grade 1	1802	1385
Grade 2	1130	922
Grade 3	501	287
Total	3433	2594

Gherkins were made grades depending on the size of the produce (Table 10). Further, depending on the grades the pre-fixed prices are also been mentioned in the contractual agreement which has been accepted both by the company and the farmer. It is observed that the pre-fixed prices by grades are almost similar by the above companies. As per determined grades, filters are manufactured and weighed by the buying assistants and entered into the Passbook. Later, the buyers take the gherkins to the Collection Centre and after securing a gate pass, take the produce to the main factory for processing and export to the contracted country/s.

Details of harvest days of gherkin as reported by CFs by size class are given in Table 11. A large number of CFs, i.e., 103 CFs out of 146 sample households, reported that the harvesting period ranges from 41 to 60 days, whereas, 28 per cent of the CFs reported to have harvested gherkins for 20 to 40 days.

TABLE 10

Gherkin Grade/s and the Prices

GRADES	*PRICE (Rs. Per Kg)*
160+ = 160-180	10.50+0.50=11
60+ = 100-160	7.00
30+ = 60-100	4.00
-30-60	2.00

TABLE 11

Employment Generation during Harvest of Gherkin Crop

Size Class	*Number of days of Harvest*			
	20 to 40	*41 to 60*	*61 and above*	*Total*
Marginal	9 (24)	27 (73)	1 (3)	37 (100)
Small	8 (20)	32 (80)	--	40 (100)
Medium	19 (36)	33 (62)	1 (2)	53 (100)
Large	5 (31)	11 (69)	--	16 (100)
Total	41 (28)	103 (71)	2 (1)	146 (100)

Tables 12 and 13 give the average annual income of contract farmers both BCF and ACF by size class. Of the 150 CFs, 131 (87%) reported an average annual income of less than Rs. 20,000 per year before contract farming. The average annual income of eight per cent of the total CFs was in the range of Rs 20,000-Rs. 30,000. There were only seven CFs whose average annual income was Rs. 30,000 and above BCF. It was observed that 10 per cent of the CFs, whose average annual income was less than Rs. 20,000, had moved to the next income bracket ACF. Further, the number of CFs whose average annual income was Rs. 30,000 and above registered an income of 15 per cent ACF.

The contract document between the company and the CF is in three formats, i.e., Kannada, English and both. About 80 per cent of the CFs reported having signed the CD in Kannada, five per cent in English only and 15 per cent in both English and Kannada (Table 14).

TABLE 12

Average Annual Income (Per HH) Agriculture Before Contract Farming by Size Class

Size Class	*Average Annual Income BCF (agri)*						
	<20000	*20001 to 30000*	*30001 to 40000*	*40001 to 50000*	*50001 to 60000*	*60001 and above*	*Total*
Marginal	36	-	1	-	-	-	37
Small	37	3	-	-	-	-	40
Medium	51	4	-	2	-	-	57
Large	7	5	-	2	1	1	16
Total	131	12	1	4	1	1	150

TABLE 13

Average Annual Income (per HH) During Contract Farming by Size Class

Size Class	*Average Annual Income BCF (agri)*						
	<20000	*20001 to 30000*	*30001 to 40000*	*40001 to 50000*	*50001 to 60000*	*60001 and above*	*Total*
Marginal	34	1	-	1	-	1	37
Small	34	4	1	1	-	-	40
Medium	43	9	2	1	1	1	57
Large	5	3	4		1	3	16
Total	116	17	7	3	2	5	150

TABLE 14

Contract Document in Kannada/English or Both

Size Class	*Kannada*	*English*	*Both*	*Total*
Marginal	28	5	4	37
Small	33	2	5	40
Medium	46	-	11	57
Large	13	-	3	16
Total	120	7	23	150

TABLE 15

Availability and Utilisation of Services for the Produce

Services	Quality Criteria	Marginal		Small		Medium		Large		Total	
		Yes	No	Yes	No	Yes	No	Yes	No	Yes	No
Transport	Available	*	-	*	-	*	-	*	-	*	-
	Utilised	*	-	*	-	*	-	*	-	*	-
Accounts/	Available	*	-	*	-	*	-	*	-	*	-
Audits	Utilised	*	-	*	-	*	-	*	-	*	-
Technical	Available	*	-	97	3	95	5	94	6	97	3
Support	Utilised	97	3	97	3	90	10	*	-	95	5
Market	Available	-	-	-	-	-	-	-	-	-	-
Access	Utilised	-	-	-	-	-	-	-	-	-	-
Traihing	Available	*	-	*	-	*	-	*	-	*	-
	Utilised	*	-	*	-	*	-	*	-	*	-

*Denote 100 per cent.

TABLE 16

Services are Available for Primary Producers

Services	Quality Criteria	Marginal		Small		Medium		Large		Total	
		VG	G	VG	G	VG	G	VG	G	VG	G
Transport	Availability	100	-	100	-	100	-	100	-	100	-
	Accessibility	92	8	95	5	84	16	81	19	89	11
	Cost of Service (%)	-	3	-	3	-	3	-	3	-	3
	Quality of Service	100	-	100	-	100	-	100	-	100	-
Accounts/	Availability	100	-	100	-	100	-	100	-	100	-
Audits	Accessibility	100	-	100	-	100	-	100	-	100	-
	Cost of Service	-	-	-	-	-	-	-	-	-	-
	Quality of Service	-	100	-	100	-	100	-	100	-	100
Technical	Availability	100	-	97	3	88	12	100	-	95	5
Support	Accessibility	100	-	100	-	91	9	100	-	97	3
(Maintenance	Cost of Service	-	-	-	-	-	-	-	-	-	-
etc.)	Quality of Service	100	-	100	-	100	-	100	-	100	-
Market	Availability	-	-	-	-	-	-	-	-	-	-
Access	Accessibility	-	-	-	-	-	-	-	-	-	-
(Linkages)	Cost of Service	-	-	-	-	-	-	-	-	-	-
	Quality of Service	-	-	-	-	-	-	-	-	-	-
Training	Availability	100	-	100	-	100	-	100	-	100	-
	Accessibility	-	100	-	100	-	100	-	100	-	100
	Cost of Service	-	-	-	-	-	-	-	-	-	-
	Quality of Service	-	100	-	100	-	100	-	100	-	100

The availability and utilisation pattern of services provided by companies is given in Table 15. The services provided by companies such as transport (lifting gherkins from the field), training facilities (dissemination of knowledge on the package of practices), technical support, and their utilisation by CFs, were found to be totally satisfactory (Table 16).

CONCLUSION AND POLICY OPTIONS

Liberalisation, globalisation, privatisation and the fast expansion of agri-business , small farmeRs. may find it difficult to cope up with the resultant volatility in the economy. Therefore, the need of the hour is to mitigate the difficulties in the contract farming system, which would hopefully popularise it further among small farmers. The agreements between the farmer and the firm provides for the purchaser to extend a degree of production support through inputs and technical guidance for crop cultivation. There is a commitment from the farmer's side to produce the specified agricultural products by conforming to the quality and quantity prescribed by the purchaser, and the firm supports, in turn, the farmer's production, and also purchases the produce.

Contract farming, as it existed then was different from the design and functioning of contract farming method today. Karnataka will shortly emerge as one of the food park centres in the food basket of India. Karnataka has already given an indication of that. Gherkin revolution has brought much needed income to impoverished farmers. Gherkin is a much sought after delicacy in US and in Europe. Currently Karnataka has a 90 per cent share in India's gherkin exports.

The objectives of the study are: to make an inventory of firms involved in contract farming in Karnataka, the structure of agreement between the primary producer and the firm, the type of crop promotion under contract farming, to assess the impact on income and employment generation for contract farmers, finally, to suggest policies for its sustainability. There are around 25 firms involved in contract farming and promoting gherkin spread over districts of Tumkur, Bellary and Haveri in Karnataka. Tumkur district is purposely selected for the in-depth study.

MAJOR FINDINGS

By and large, the selected five companies fix price per kilo of gherkins by grade, i.e., first Rs. 11 to Rs. 10.50; second Rs. 7 to Rs. 6; third Rs. 4 to Rs. 2; and lost grade Rs. 2 to Re 1. And above companies supply inputs like seeds, fertilisers, pesticides and technical guidance to contract farmers (CFs). Of the total 150 CFs selected, small and marginal farmers constitute 52 per cent, medium farmers 38 per cent, and large farmers 10 per cent. Seventy per cent of the heads of households (HHs) of CFs are in the age group 26 to 50 years. Almost all CFs (99 per cent) are literate. Around 70 per cent of the total population in the study area is involved in agriculture. The average annual income mobility observed before contract farming and after contract farming is between 10 and 15 per cent.

The average landholding of CF is 4.78 acres, of which dry and irrigated land account for 2.32 acres and 2.46 acres respectively. The area under gherkin ranges between 0.50 acre and 1 acre, and the majority of CFs cultivate gherkin in an area of 0.50 acre to 0.75 acre. To cultivate one acre of gherkin, the gross cost comes to Rs. 26,500, of which 48 per cent is spent on harvesting of the produce. Gross returns and net returns account for approximately Rs. 47,000 and Rs. 20,000 respectively. The average yield of gherkins per acre is 6,300 kgs. The average number of harvested days of gherkins ranges from 41 to 60 days, and the labour cost ranges from Rs. 7,000 to Rs. 8,694.

About 80 per cent of CFs reported to have signed contract documents in Kannada, five per cent in English and 15 per cent in both English and Kannada. Around 73 per cent of CFs have been cultivating gherkin for a year, while 25 per cent have been into it for two years. The availability and utilisation pattern of services, i.e., the package of practices, input supplies and a buy-back system were found to be totally satisfactory. Gherkin crop provides employment opportunities to landless rural labourers. Pre-fixed prices for gherkins largely eliminate the risk to growers, middlemen are totally absent.

Financial institutions should step in to extend credit/loan facilities to CFs. Provision should be made to purchase the entire produce. And in the case of any lapse from the companies, the Government should come to the rescue of CFs. Private insurance companies should insure the crop in the event of crop failure or natural calamities. The role of NGOs/VOs in closely monitoring CFs and companies in maintaining a cordial relationship, which benefit them mutually.

References

Allen, G.R., 1972. An Appraisal of Contract Farming, *International Journal of Agricultural Economics* (IJAE), 23, 89-98.

Clapp, Roger A., 1994. The Moral Economy of the Contract in Living under Contract eds. Peter D. Little and Micheal J. Watts, The University of Wisconsin Press, Wisconsin.

Eaton, C.S., 1998. Directed Small-holder Farming in Fiji: A Case Study of Virginia Tobacco Production (Unpublished M.A. thesis), School of Social and Economic Development, University of the South Pacific, Suva.

Eaton, Charles and Andrew W. Shepherd, 2001. Contract farming: Partners for Growth, *Agricultural Services Bulletin*, 145, FAO, Rome.

Glover, D., 1984. Contract Farming and Smaller-holder Out-grower Schemes in the Less Developed Countries, World Development, pp. 1143-57.

Little. P.D. and Watts, M.J., 1994. Living under Contract: Contract Farming and Agrarian Transformation in Sub-Saharan Africa, Madison, University of Wisconsin Press.

National Bank for Agriculture and Rural Development (NABARD), 1999, *News Review*, Jan-March, Volume 15, No. 1, p. 56.

Singh, Gurdev, S.R. Asokan and Asopa, V.N., 1990. Seed Industry in India: A Management Perspective, Oxford and IBH, New Delhi.

Singh, Sukpal, 2000. Contract Farming and Agricultural Diversification in the Indian Punjab: A Study of Performance and Problems, *Indian Journal of Agricultural Economics*, 55(3), July-September, pp. 283-94.

Watts, M.J., 1994. Life under Contract Farming, Agrarian Restructuring, and Flexible Accumulation in P.D. Little and M.J. Watts, eds. Living under Contract: Contract Farming and Agrarian Transformation in Sub-Saharan Africa, Madison, University of Wisconsin Press, pp. 21-77.

9

Impact of Institutional Credit on Aggregate Agricultural Production in India during Post-Reform Period

MD. IZHAR AHMAD AND TARIQ MASOOD

INTRODUCTION

The Indian economy has been experiencing high growth rate especially after the various reforms measures adopted by the successive Governments. The sustainability of the growth momentum however critically depends on the growth of the agriculture sector. Though the share of agriculture sector in the Gross Domestic Product (GDP) declines considerably over the period it still provide livelihood to almost two-third of the country's population. Finance in agriculture is as important as development of technologies. Technical inputs can be purchased and used by farmer only if he has money (funds). But his own money is always inadequate and he needs outside finance or credit. Credit is not only a critical input in agriculture but also an effective means of economic transformation.

Professional money lenders were one of the main sources of credit to agriculture till 1935. They usually charge unduly high rates of interest and follow serious practices while giving loans and recovering them. As a result, farmers were heavily burdened with debts and many of them perpetuated debts. There were widespread discontents among farmers against these practices and there were instances of riots also. With the passing of Reserve Bank of India Act, 1934, District Central Co-op. Banks Act and Land Development Banks Act, agricultural credit received impetus and there were improvements in agricultural credit. A powerful alternative agency came into being. Large-scale credit became available with reasonable rates of interest at easy terms, both in terms of granting loans and recovery of them. Both the co-operative banks advance credit mostly to agriculture. First bank advances short-term and medium-term loans while the second bank advances long-term loans. The Reserve Bank of India as the Central bank of the country took lead in making credit available to agriculture through these banks by laying down suitable policies.

Although the co-operative banks started financing agriculture with their establishments in 1930's real impetus was received only after Independence when suitable legislations were passed and policies were formulated. Thereafter, bank credit to agriculture made phenomenal progress by opening branches in rural areas and attracting deposits. Till 14 major commercial banks were nationalized in 1969, co-operative banks were the main institutional agencies providing finance to agriculture. After nationalization, it was made mandatory for these banks to provide finance to agriculture as a priority sector. These banks undertook special programs of branch expansion and created a network of banking services throughout the country and started financing agriculture on large scale. Thus agriculture credit acquired multi-agency dimension. Development and adoption of new technologies and availability of finance go hand in hand. In bringing "Green Revolution", "White Revolution" and now "Yellow Revolution" finance has played a crucial role. Now the agriculture credit, through multi-agency approach has come to stay. The procedures and amount of loans for various purposes have been standardized. Among the various purposes "Crop loans" (Short-term loan) has the major share. In addition, farmers get loans for purchase of electric motor with pump, tractor and other machinery, digging wells or boring wells, installation of pipe lines, drip irrigation, planting fruit orchards, purchase of dairy animals and feeds/ fodder for them, poultry, sheep/goat keeping and for many other allied enterprises.

A large Number of agencies including Co-operatives, Regional Rural Banks (RRBs), Scheduled Commercial Banks (SCBs), Non-Banking Financial Corporations (NBFCs), Self-Help Group and well spread informal credit market together constitute Indian Agricultural credit delivery system. According to all India debt and investment survey the share of non institutional credit for agriculture sector was around 92.7% during year 1950-51 which decreases to 38.9% during 2001-02 and the share of institutional credit increases from 7.3% during 1950-51 to 61.1% during 2001-02.

FIGURE I

Structure of Agricultural Credit In India

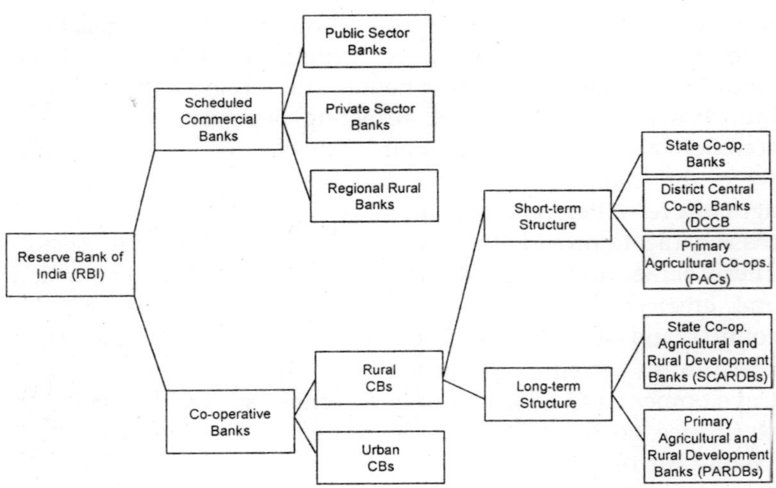

The findings of the National Sample Survey Organistion (NSSO) 59th Round (2003) revealed that only 27% of the total number of cultivated households received credit from formal sources while 22% received credit from informal sources. The remaining households comprising mainly small and marginal farmers had no credit outstanding.

In light of the above discussion the objective of the study is to·

- Analyse the trends and pattern of institutional credit for agricultural sector during pre- and post-reform period.
- Estimate the production function in order to determine the impact of institutional credit on agricultural production separately during pre and post-reform period.

The paper has been divided in four sections. First section discusses the trends and pattern of institutional credit for agricultural sector during pre and post-reform period in India. Second section describes data source, variables included and the methodology used for the estimation of the aggregate agricultural production function. The results are explained in the third section. The last section briefly concludes the findings of the study.

ANALYSIS OF TRENDS AND PATTERN OF AGRICULTURAL CREDIT

We have constructed some indicators to understand the pattern of agricultural credit during pre and post-reform period in India. Table 1 shows the growth rate of nominal institutional credit to agricultural sector for different time periods. Growth rate of direct Institutional during 1971-80 was 16.7% which decreases to 13.9% during 1981-90 and again to 12.8%. During the period 2001-05 there was some improvement in the growth rate of nominal direct institutional credit (18.4%). Growth rate of nominal indirect institutional credit was highest during 70's (11.4%) and lowest during 80's. During reform period growth rate of indirect institutional credit was more or less 9% which was better than the 80's. Total nominal institutional credit (Direct + indirect) grows fastest during 70's and slowest during the 90's. Hence various reform measures adopted by the successive Governments to liberalize the economy have retarded the growth rate of agricultural credit.

TABLE I

Annual Average Growth Rate of Agricultural Credit

Period	*Direct Institutional Credit (%)*	*Indirect Institutional Credit (%)*	*Total (Direct +Indirect) Institutional (%)*
1971-80	16.7	11.4	16.5
1981-90	13.9	4.7	13.5
1991-00	12.8	9.5	12.7
2001-05	18.4	8.6	13.6
1971-05	15.1	8.3	14.1

Source: Handbook of Statistics on Indian Economy, 2007-08.

Figure 2. depicts the behaviour of institutional credit as percentage of agricultural gross domestic Product (AGDP) over the period 1971-2005. Direct institutional credit as percent of agricultural GDP was 5.04% which increases to 8% in 1980-81 and again to 10.69% in 1987-88. It decreases to 6.89% in 1992-93 and during 1998-99 it was 8.45%. After the year 1999 direct institutional credit as percentage of agricultural GDP increases rapidly and it was 21% during 2004-05. The indirect institutional credit as percentage of agricultural GDP was around 2 to 3 percent during seventies which increases during 80's and it was 5.66% in 1985-86. After 1985-86 it decreases continuously and it was 1.49% in 1992-93. After 1993-94 indirect institutional credit as percentage of agricultural GDP increases continuously and it was 6.47% in 1998-99 and 28.58% in 2004-05. Total (Direct + Indirect) Institutional credit as percentage of agricultural GDP was 7.1% in 1971-72 it increases to 11.6% in 1979-80.

Direct Institutional credit per cultivated area was Rupees 5.8 crore during 1971-72 which increases to Rupees 18.88 crore during 1979-80, Rupees 65.34 crore during 1989-90 and reaches up to 668.63 during 2004-05. Indirect institutional credit per cultivated area was Rupees 2.37 crore during 1971-72 and it was Rupees 16.1 crore during 1989-90. Indirect credit increases tremendously during post-reform period from Rupees 16.01 crore during 1990-91 it increase to Rupees 149.78 crore and again to Rupees 909.91 crore during 2004-05. Total institutional credit

FIGURE 2

Agricultural Credit as Percent of Agricultural GDP

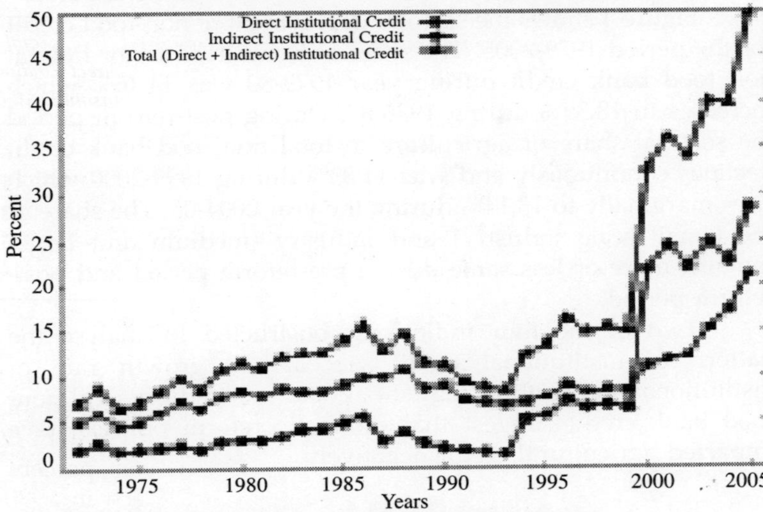

Source: Handbook of Statistics on Indian Economy, 2007-08.

FIGURE 3

Agricultural Credit per Cultivated Area (Million Hectares)

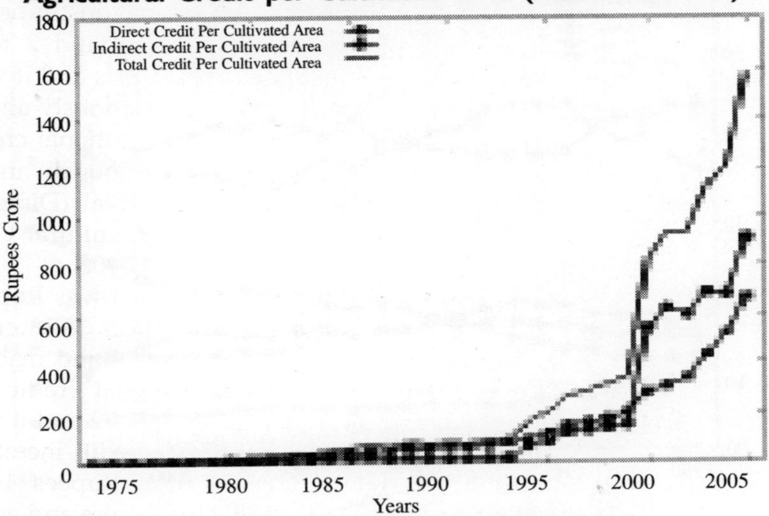

Source: Handbook of Statistics on Indian Economy, 2007-08.

per cultivated area increases significantly during post-reform period due to the rapid increase in both direct and indirect credit per cultivated area and constant level of total cultivated area.

Figure 4 shows the sectoral deployment of non-food credit for the period 1979-2005. The share of agriculture sector in total non food bank credit during year 1979-80 was 14.46% which increases to 18.39% during 1986-87. During post-reform period the sectoral share of agriculture in total non food bank credit declines continuously and was 11.83% during 1999-2000 which rises marginally to 13.14% during the year 2004-05. The share of SSI (small scale industry) and industry (medium and large) remains more or less same during pre-reform period and post-reform period.

Two of the four indicators constructed to analyse the pattern of institutional credit viz. annual growth rate of institutional and sectoral share of agriculture credit in total non-food bank credit suggest that economic reform policies have impacted agricultural credit negatively.

FIGURE 4

Trends in Sectoral Deployment of Non-Food Credit

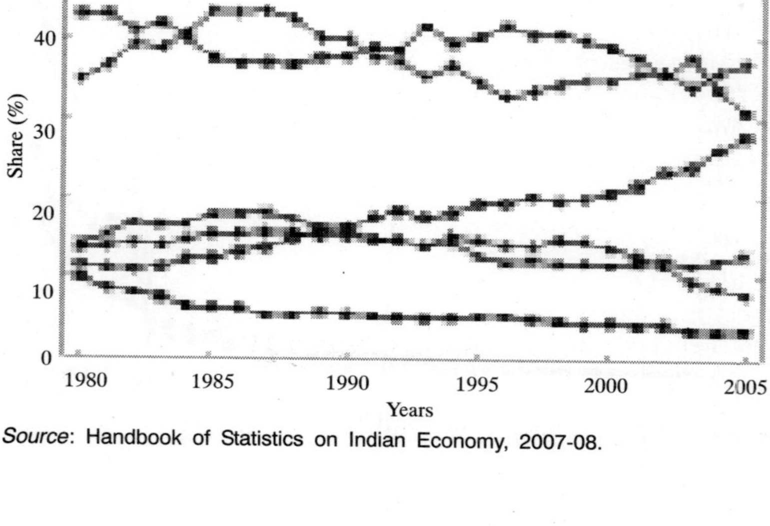

Source: Handbook of Statistics on Indian Economy, 2007-08.

DATA SOURCE AND METHODOLOGY

The study attempts to access the impact of institutional credit on agricultural production in India using time series data during pre and post-reform period. To investigate the impact of institutional credit on aggregate agricultural production we have estimated Cob Douglas Production function with agricultural gross domestic product (ADGP) as dependent variable and Institutional credit (IC) for agriculture sector as one of the independent variable. Institutional credit includes direct credit and indirect credit to agriculture sector. Other explanatory variables included in the study to estimate the Cobb Douglas production function besides institutional credit are total cultivated area (CULT), agricultural labour force (ALF), net irrigated area (IA), and consumption of fertilizers (FR). Selection of the explanatory variables has been made on the basis of literature surveyed and some previous studies. There are some other important determinant of agricultural production like use of pesticides, use of electricity, use of machinery, etc. but these variables are not included in the model since they can be purchased with the availability of credit. Institutional credit has been directly introduced in the model.

Data regarding variables ADGP, IC, CULT, IA, and FR have been taken from Handbook of Statistics on Indian Economy 2007-08, RBI. Data of the variable ALF has been taken from Food and Agriculture Organization of the United Nations (FAO), 2006. Agricultural gross domestic product and Institutional credit are measured in Rupees crore, total cultivated area and net irrigated area is measured in million hectares, consumption of fertilizers is measured in lakh tonnes and agricultural labour force is measured in thousand persons. Institutional Credit to Agriculture comprises of direct (short-term and long-term) credit issued by Cooperative, State governments, Scheduled Commercial Banks and Regional Rural Banks to agriculture and allied sector. Consumption of Fertilizers (FR) includes $N+P+K$. Agricultural labour force is the number of economically active persons engaged in agriculture, hunting, forestry or fishing.

Agricultural production function shows the technical relationship between agricultural output and various determinant of agricultural output. We have included agricultural gross domestic product (AGDP) as dependent variable and explanatory variables are institutional credit to agriculture sector, total cultivated area, agricultural labour force, net irrigated area and consumption of fertilizers. To avoid the problem of multicolinearity and to overcome the problem of degree of freedom all the variables are transformed to per cultivated million hectares. To estimate the Cobb Douglas production function all the variables are transformed to logarithmic form. The model used in the study is:

$$LAGDPCULT = \beta_0 + \beta_1 LICPCULT + \beta_2 LALFPCULT + \beta_3 LIRPCULT + \beta_4 LFRPCULT$$

Where

LAGDPCULT = Natural Logarithm of agricultural gross domestic product per cultivated Million Hectares

LICPCULT = Natural logarithm of institutional credit per cultivated million hectares

LALFPCULT = Natural logarithm of agricultural labour force per cultivated million hectares

LIRPCULT = Natural logarithm of net irrigated area per cultivated million hectares

LFRPCULT = Natural logarithm of consumption of fertilizers per cultivated million hectares

We have estimated Cobb Douglas production function for pre-reform period (1971-91) and post-reform period (1992-2005) separately to assess the impact of institutional credit on agriculture production during pre-reform period and post-reform period and to assess whether the relationship between the two variables undergone a significant change due to the various banking reform measures adopted by the Government.

RESULTS AND DISCUSSION

To overcome the problem of Multicollinearity all the variables are transformed to per cultivated million hectares. In original form some of the variables are highly multicollinear, in transformed model variables are not highly correlated although some degree of multicollinearity is still present in the model. As there are only few options before us to reduce the problem of multicollinearity we will accept moderate degree of multicollinearity among variables. The Cobb Douglas agricultural production function estimated using the ordinary least square method exhibits the problem of autocorrelation. To

TABLE 2

Regression Results Using Cochrane Orcutt Regression Method

Dependent Variable—LAGDPCULT—(Log of Agricultural Gross Domestic Product Per Cultivated Area)

Time Period	*Model I for period 1972-2005*			*Model II for period 1972-91*			*Model III for period 1993-2005*		
Variables	*Cofficients*	*t-Values*	*p-Values*	*Coefficients*	*t-values*	*p-values*	*Coefficients*	*t-values*	*p-values*
Constant	36.8417	4.0873	0.00030	10.3625	0.7931	0.4401	16.0128	6.0246	0.0003
LICPCULT	0.66174	4.4690	0.00010	0.60665	2.4780	0.0255	0.08978	0.9147	0.3870
LALFPCULT	-3.7057	2.9198	0.00659	-0.90501	-0.5651	0.5803	-1.0006	-2.6640	0.0286
LIRPCULT	5.0726	5.8081	<0.00001	-0.23611	-0.1273	0.9003	0.6479	2.1296	0.0658
LFRPCULT	-0.48006	2.6896	0.01157	0.35358	2.8781	0.0114	-0.0855	-0.4820	0.6427
N	34	20	13						
Adjusted R-squared	0.987242	0.968147	0.992821						
Durbin-Watson	1.847321	1.599801	2.347473						

reduce the problem of autocorrelation we have applied Cochrane Orcutt regression method for estimating all the three models. The Cochrane Orcutt iterative procedure requires the transformation of the regression model to a form in which the ordinary least square procedure is applicable.

First model for the period 1972-2005 is estimated using Cochrane Orcutt iterative procedure. The period of study as mentioned above is 1971-2005 but due to the transformation of the model in Cochrane Orcutt iterative procedure one observation is lost. All the coefficients of the model are highly significant. LICPCULT and LIRPCULT affect agriculture production positively. Sign of the coefficients of the variables LALFPCULT and LFRPCULT are significant but negative. Adjusted R-squared for the model is 0.987, which means log of the variables included in the model are able to explain 98% variation of the log of agricultural production over the period 1972-2005. The coefficient of the variable LICPCULT is 0.6617 which implies that for a percent change in institutional credit per cultivated million hectare agricultural GDP per cultivated million hectare increases by 0.66%. Another variable which has positive impact on the agricultural production is net irrigated area.

Second model is estimated for the period 1972-91. The model is representative of the pre-reform period and attempts to analyse the association between agricultural production and various determinant of it during pre-reform period. Coefficients of the variables LICPCULT and LFRPCULT have significant impact on agriculture production but two other variables included in the model viz. LALFPCULT and LIRPCULT are not impacting agricultural production significantly. Coefficient of the variable LICPCULT suggest that for one percent increase in institutional credit agricultural GDP increases by around 0.60 percent. For one percent increase in the consumption of fertilizers per cultivated area agricultural GDP increases by around 0.35 percent. Two other variables included LALFPCULT and LIRPCULT does not have any significant impact on agricultural product. Adjusted R-squared for the model is 0.968, i.e. around 96 percent variation of the log of agricultural gross domestic product has been explained by the log of the variables included in the model.

The third model for the period 1993-2005 has been estimated to assess the impact of institutional credit on agricultural production during post-reform period. Coefficient of the variable LICPCULT is not significant. The p-value for the coefficient of LICPCULT is 0.387 which is quite high. The value of the coefficient is 0.08 which means for one percent increase in the institutional credit per cultivated area agricultural production per cultivated area increases by 0.08 percent. The value of the coefficient of LICPCULT differs significantly from the coefficient of the same variable for the pre-reform period 1972-91 (0.60) and also from the overall period (0.66). During post-reform period LIRPCULT is the only variable which affects agricultural production significantly. LALFPCULT impacted agricultural production negatively. The value of the adjusted R-squared is quite high (0.995) for this model.

CONCLUSION

First part of the study analyses the trend and pattern of institutional credit in India during pre-reform and post-reform period. We have constructed four indicators annual growth rate of institutional credit, institutional credit as percentage of agricultural GDP, Institutional credit per cultivated area and sectoral share of agricultural credit to understand the trends and pattern of agricultural credit. Two indicators viz. annual growth rate of institutional credit and sectoral share of agricultural credit in total non-food bank credit suggest that economic reform policies are unfavourable for agricultural credit. Institutional credit as percentage of agricultural GDP increases rapidly during the post-reform period which may be due to the slow growth rate of the agricultural GDP during the period. Institutional credit per cultivated area increases tremendously during post-reform period which is due to the constant level of the total cultivated area which remains almost same during the whole reform period.

In the second section we have estimated Cobb Douglas production Function separately for the pre-reform period and post-reform period. Estimated coefficient of the institutional credit in model II suggests that it was one of the most important determinants of the aggregate agricultural production during pre-reform period. The estimated coefficient of the institutional credit is not significant in model III. During post-reform period institutional credit does not affects agricultural production.

Hence various reform measures including banking reform measures are not fruitful for agriculture finance. Not only annual growth rate of the agricultural credit retarded during post-reform period but sectoral share of agricultural credit also declines. During pre-reform period agricultural credit is one of the determinants of agricultural production but during post-reform period such association does not exists.

References

Acharya, S.S. (2006), "Agricultural Marketing and Rural Credit for Strengthening India Agriculture", INMR Policy Brief No. 3, Asian Development Bank.

Economic Survey, Government of India, various issues.

Golait, Ramesh (2007), "Current Issues in Agriculture Credit in India: An Assessment", Reserve Bank of India, Occasional Papers, Vol. 28, No. 1, Summer 2007.

Government of India, Economic Survey, Ministry of Finance, New Delhi, various issues.

Gulati, Ashok and Bathla, Seema (2002), "Institutional Credit to Indian Agriculture: Defaults and Policy Options", Occasional Paper 23, Nabard, Mumbai, 2002.

Iqbal, Muhammad, Ahmad, Munir and Abbas, Kalbe, "The Impact of Institutional Credit on agricultural production in Pakistan", The Pakistan Development Review, 42: 4, Part II (Winter 2003), pp. 469-85.

Kalamkar, S.S., and Narayanmurthy, A. (2003), 'Impact of Liberlisation on Domestic Agricultural Prices and Farm Income', *Indian Journal Agricultural Economics*, Vol. 3.

Mohan, Rakesh (2004), "Agricultural Credit in India: Status, Issues and Future Agenda", *RBI Bulletin*, November.

Reddy, Y.V. (2001), "Indian Agriculture and Reform: Concern, Issues and Agenda", *RBI Bulletin*, March.

"Handbook of Statistics on the Indian Economy", 2007-08.

"Report of the Advisory Committee on Flow of Credit to Agriculture and Related Activities from the Banking System" (2004), Chairman: Prof. Vyas.

Reserve Bank of India (2005), Draft Technical Paper on Priority Sector Lending. RPCD, Mumbai.

Roy, M. (2006), A Review of Bank Lending to Priority and Retail Sectors, *Economic and Political Weekly*, 41, 1035-40.

Sahu, Gagan Bihari and Rajasekhar, D. (2005), "Banking Sector Reform and Credit Flow to Indian Agriculture", *EPW*, December 31, 2005.

APPENDIX TABLE I

Institutional Credit as Percent of Agricultural GDP and Institutional Credit per Cropped Area/Cultivated Area

(Million hectares)

Years	*Institutional Credit as Percentage of Agricultural GDP*			*Institutional Credit per Cultivated Area (million hectares)*		
	Direct Credit	*Indirect Credit*	*Total Credit*	*Direct Credit*	*Indirect Credit*	*Total Credit*
1971-72	5.04	2.06	7.1	5.8	2.37	8.18
1972-73	6.02	2.79	8.8	7.86	3.64	11.5
1973-74	4.67	1.89	6.56	7.61	3.09	10.7
1974-75	5.02	2.13	7.15	9.23	3.91	13.14
1975-76	6.14	2.32	8.46	10.67	4.03	14.7
1976-77	7.34	2.54	9.88	13.35	4.62	17.97
1977-78	6.53	2.07	8.6	13.65	4.33	17.98
1978-79	7.86	2.96	10.83	16.49	6.22	22.71
1979-80	8.52	3.09	11.6	18.88	6.84	25.72
1980-81	7.9	3.08	10.98	21.87	8.51	30.39
1981-82	8.8	3.48	12.28	26.61	10.52	37.12
1982-83	8.32	4.24	12.55	27.86	14.19	42.05
1983-84	8.33	4.31	12.64	32.22	16.66	48.88
1984-85	9.11	4.92	14.03	39.01	21.05	60.06
1985-86	9.88	5.66	15.54	44.76	25.63	70.39
1986-87	9.97	2.98	12.95	48.88	14.59	63.46
1987-88	10.69	3.93	14.62	60.72	22.34	83.07
1988-89	8.76	2.75	11.51	57.85	18.2	76.04
1989-90	9.02	2.22	11.24	65.34	16.1	81.44
1990-91	7.39	1.92	9.3	61.67	16.01	77.69
1991-92	7.1	1.72	8.83	71.47	17.31	88.78
1992-93	6.89	1.49	8.38	77.59	16.78	94.36
1993-94	7.13	5.27	12.4	92.49	68.39	160.88
1994-95	7.76	5.74	13.5	115.37	85.34	200.71
1995-96	8.99	7.3	16.3	146.11	118.64	264.75
1996-97	8.27	6.59	14.86	159.26	126.86	286.13
1997-98	8.56	6.86	15.43	173.61	139.2	312.81
1998-99	8.45	6.47	14.92	195.68	149.78	345.46
1999-00	11.12	21.65	32.76	280.05	545.39	825.44
2000-01	11.78	24.31	36.09	303.52	626.18	929.71
2001-02	12.25	21.88	34.13	335.61	599.47	935.09
2002-03	15.32	24.68	40	427.99	689.64	1117.64
2003-04	17.27	22.47	39.74	523.55	681.01	1204.56
2004-05	21	28.58	49.58	668.63	909.91	1578.54

APPENDIX TABLE.2

Sectoral Share of Non-food Bank Credit

(% of total non-food bank credit)

Year	*Priority Sector*	*Agriculture*	*SSI*	*Industry*	*Trade*	*Other Sectors*
1979-80	35.17	14.46	13.77	43.21	10.01	11.61
1980-81	36.9	15.55	14.01	43.22	8.65	11.23
1981-82	39.49	17.07	14.43	41.26	8.13	11.12
1982-83	39.08	16.73	14.23	42.11	7.46	11.34
1983-84	40.93	16.88	14.96	40.17	6.44	12.46
1984-85	43.53	18.11	15.63	37.69	6.26	12.52
1985-86	43.41	18.23	15.73	37.08	6.17	13.33
1986-87	43.59	18.39	15.85	37.16	5.36	13.88
1987-88	42.71	17.64	15.9	36.95	5.29	15.06
1988-89	40.28	16.42	15.46	37.88	5.61	16.23
1989-90	40.12	16.42	15.44	38.01	5.44	16.44
1990-91	37.81	14.76	15.14	39.21	5.21	17.7
1991-92	37.44	14.96	14.96	38.81	5.07	18.68
1992-93	35.49	14.22	14.26	41.76	4.96	17.78
1993-94	36.92	14.53	15.5	39.65	5.02	18.41
1994-95	34.74	12.98	14.96	40.43	5.28	19.56
1995-96	33.02	12.18	14.36	41.9	5.39	19.68
1996-97	33.76	12.51	14.3	40.81	4.91	20.51
1997-98	34.58	12.12	15.12	40.84	4.59	19.99
1998-99	35.24	12.19	14.91	40.13	4.29	20.33
1999-00	35.14	11.83	14.08	39.27	4.48	21.1
2000-01	35.98	12.1	13.05	37.94	4.16	21.92
2001-02	36.3	12.59	11.85	35.7	4.24	23.76
2002-03	34.13	11.86	9.74	37.93	3.64	24.3
2003-04	36.22	12.43	9.04	33.94	3.41	26.43
2004-05	37.11	13.14	8.17	31.15	3.63	28.11

10

Analysis of the Impact of Terms of Trade on Rural Poverty in India

Roli Mishra, P.S. Tripathi and Rajesh Nigam

INTRODUCTION

The concept of poverty is closely associated with the price indices particularly those related to agricultural sector. This is because poverty in India is defined in terms of caloric intake and these calories a person can derive mainly through consumption of commodities produced in agricultural and allied sectors. If the prices of these commodities are rising fast then though terms of trade may move in favour of the farm sector but its impact on poverty will be highly adverse. The purpose of this paper therefore, is to establish the effects of terms of trade on rural poverty.

According to J.S. Uppal (1983), "Poverty like beauty is easier to recognise than to define". Poverty has been defined in absolute and relative terms. The extent to which a poor person falls short of the average level of well-being may be considered a more important determinant of poverty. In this context, rural poverty may be defined in terms of the subsistence level of lack of income to acquire the minimum necessities of life. The poverty line has been defined in rupees for various years both for the rural population and for the urban population (per capita per month).

Poverty Line with Base 1973-74

(Monthly expenditure of Rs. Per Capita)

at 1973–74 prices	Rural	Rs. 49.63 per capita per month
	Urban	Rs. 56.76 per capita per month
at 1977–78 prices	Rural	Rs. 56.84 per capita per month
	Urban	Rs. 70.33 per capita per month
at 1983–84 prices	Rural	Rs. 89.50 per capita per month
	Urban	Rs. 115.65 per capita per month
at 1987–88 prices	Rural	Rs. 115.20 per capita per month
	Urban	Rs. 162.16 per capita per month
at 1993–94 prices	Rural	Rs. 205.84 per capita per month
	Urban	Rs. 281.35 per capita per month
at 1999–00 prices	Rural	Rs. 326.56 per capita per month
	Urban	Rs. 454.11 per capita per month
at 2004-05 prices	Rural	Rs. 368.0 per capita per month
	Urban	Rs. 559.0 per capita per month

Source: Planning Commission.

Tendulkar and Sundaram (2003) show that the average annual reduction in poverty was higher in the last six years of the 1990s than that recorded during the ten and a half years preceding 1993-94. Sen (2004) using NSS data has come to the conclusions that the reforms have only benefited the elite and affluent classes. Considering such an extent of poverty and taking a humane approach, various economists have expressed their concern for the poor and their upliftment and to fulfil this criterion. The terms of trade has been introduced in 1970s in the agriculture price policy formulated as an important parameter. This itself suggests that "the variable of terms of trade is a concern of the government to decide its appropriate level which may be in the interests of both the producer and consumer and particularly the rural poor".

The interest of this paper centres on the effect of terms of trade on rural poverty. Some more studies (Dharam Narain, 1972, M.S. Ahluwalia, 1978) have also focused on this kind of relationship between the changes in price level and rural poverty but on account of certain specification problems, the conclusions are different. For instance, the study conducted by Narain highlights that the rural poverty is a function of price index, index of average real income of rural population and change over time. He concluded *inter alia* that the influence of price index on rural poverty was substantially reduced during the 70s while the variations in income per head became more important and this was mainly on account of the expansion of public distribution system into rural areas. Ahluwalia on the other hand gives an alternative specification of using relative price level, i.e. the ratio of prices paid by the poor to analyse the effect of the price variable on rural poverty. He further opines that the effect of inflation on rural poverty as focused by Narain may be right but there are however, technical difficulties in analysing this effect and further adds, "Our measure of poverty aggregates across two socio-economic groups that constitute the bulk of the rural poor—landless labourers and marginal farmers and inflation affects these two groups somewhat differently. Landless labourers may be hard hit by inflation because money wages lag behind price rises, but small farmers may not be similarly affected, since they consume what they produce, so that with given production levels, they are not adversely affected if the rate of inflation is higher. Indeed, where there is a small surplus, they may even benefit from inflation if it turns the terms of trade in their favour". The review of the aforementioned studies provides an insight about the importance of the parameter of the net barter terms of trade to influence rural poverty. Although, the net barter terms of trade reflects the importance of price movements of each sector of the economy. But a farmer who seeks to increase the level of output on his farm, wishes to maximise his revenue. As a consequence, the concept of income terms of trade become important as it reflects the changes in the absorbing capacity of the farmer over a period of time. Thamarajakshi (1969) suggested that income terms of trade is much more relevant and important than the net barter terms of trade. This is because the net barter terms of trade during the period of crisis no doubt remained favourable to the agriculture sector but the farmer suffered during this period because of crop failure on many occasions during the IInd Phase (1964–65 to 1974–75) of our analysis. However, during the Ist phase (1950–51 to 1964–95) and IIIrd phase (1974–74 to 1995–96) the farmers condition was better than the IInd phase despite the fact that net barter terms of trade remained unfavourable. This contradiction can only be resolved through the analysis of the income terms of trade which not only takes into account the price indices but also the quantity of output produced during each year. The income terms of trade over a period of time have remained favourable to the agricultural sector *vis-à-vis* industrial or non-agricultural sectors and this point has been reflected through increase in agricultural production index over the years due to technical change which boosted up the foodgrains production in particular, bringing better returns and prosperity for the farmers, enhancing their revenues and thus, witnessing favourable income terms of trade all through the period of analysis We have, therefore, analysed the impact of net barter as well as income terms of trade on rural poverty. The inferences that will be obtained from the analysis will be relevant for the government to use them while formulating agricultural price policy.

HYPOTHESES FORMULATION

We have formulated two separate hypotheses to analyse the relationship of net barter as well as income terms of trade with rural poverty.

If the net barter terms of trade are favourable to the agricultural sector, then the rural poverty will aggravate since the prices of the agricultural commodities will affect the rural poor adversely. Therefore, we expect a positive sign between net barter terms of trade and rural poverty.

If the income terms of trade turn in favour to agricultural sector, the rural poverty will tend to decline. With the increasing purchasing power of the farmers, their absorbing capacity will also improve and hence rural poverty will decrease. Therefore, in this case, we expect a negative sign between the coefficient associated with income terms of trade and rural poverty.

METHODOLOGY

We have analysed the impact of terms of trade on rural poverty with the help of linear regression model. The series of net barter and income terms of trade has been derived from National Accounts Statistics of India 1950–51 to 1995–96 (refer Appendix 1) and poverty estimates are derived from the household consumer expenditure data collected by NSSO every fifth year (refer Appendix 2). Planning Commission does not take cognizance of the annual surveys conducted by NSSO. The quinquennial survey of 1993-94 and annual survey throughout the 1990s indicated that the declining trend in poverty ratio was halted in the reform era. However, 55th round results (1999-2000) took every one by surprise as the poverty ratio came down from 36 percent in 1993-94 to 26 percent in 1999-2000. However, the results of 55th round created a serious controversy with respect to reference period. The existing National Account Series with base 1980-81 was replaced by new series in 1999 with base 1993-94 which implied higher 1990s growth of both consumer expenditure and rural income. The data of consumer expenditure was being collected on the basis of uniform 30 day recall period since 1950. In the 55th round, the data was recorded for two reference periods—one week recall and one month recall. This changed reference period, increased the expenditure estimates and reduced poverty figure in one stroke. Planning Commission while releasing the results of 55th round qualified that "estimates may not be strictly comparable to earlier estimates of poverty". In this paper, we are not going into details of the reasons of non-comparability of 50th and 55th rounds but this point has been taken up to corroborates the limitations of extending our time series data further from 1995-96 onwards and thus analysis using the statistical model could be taken up for the period 1950-51 to 1995-96. However, impact of terms of trade on rural poverty on the basis of available literature in the post-reform era is taken up in a separate paragraph.

EFFECT OF TERMS OF TRADE ON RURAL POVERTY IN TERMS OF BIVARIATE ANALYSIS

In this section, we have tried to assess the combined effect of the net barter and income terms of trade on rural poverty with the help of bivariate regression model of the following type:

$$y = a + b_1x_1 + b_2x_2$$

Our phase-wise analysis of this regression model is as follows:

(a) Analysis for the Period 1951-52 to 1964-65 (Phase I)

The first phase that extended from 1951–52 to 1964–65 witnessed unfavourable net barter terms of trade but favourable income terms of trade. As per our hypothesis, rise in prices of agricultural commodities aggravates rural poverty and therefore we once again expect a positive sign associated with the value of b_1 (net barter terms of trade). On the other hand the rise in income of the farmers helps in reducing poverty and hence we expect a negative sign associated with value of b_2 (income terms of trade). In order to test these hypotheses, the regression equation fitted for the first phase is given below:

$$y = 7.38 + 137.35\ x_1 - 57.04\ x_2$$
$$(0.96)\ (0.49)$$
$$R^2 = 0.99\ F_{cal} = 1100 \qquad F_{0.95(1,11)} = 4.84$$

where

x_1 = Index of Net barter terms of trade
x_2 = Index of Income terms of trade
y = Index of Rural poverty

From the equation it is obvious that the sign of coefficient with net barter terms of trade (x_1) corroborates our hypothesis. The value of coefficient is significant also due to very low value of standard error indicating that unfavourable net barter terms of trade have been able to exercise a significant downward effect on poverty. With regard to income terms of trade the sign of b_2 is negative as expected and the value of b_2 is also significant implying that income terms of trade have also exercised significant effect on curtailing rural poverty, and therefore has also helped in uplifting the farming community living below poverty line in a significant way particularly the small and marginal farmers. The value of R^2 is very high explaining 99 percent variation in rural poverty due to the combined effect of net barter and income terms of trade. However, the effect of b_1 is more than b_2, i.e. whatever little reduction in rural poverty has taken place during this phase is on account of unfavourable net barter terms of trade than on account of favourable income terms of trade.

(b) Analysis for the Period 1964-65 to 1974-75 (Phase II)

The second phase covered a period from 1964–65 to 1974–75. During this phase, the net barter terms of trade were favourable to the agricultural sector implying an increase in the prices of agricultural commodities thus, hurting the agricultural poor. This view point is substantiated by the estimated bivariate linear regression equation which is stated as follows:

$$y = 38.44 + 90.23\, x_1 - 18.92\, x_2$$
$$(0.24) \quad (0.10)$$
$$R^2 = 0.86 \quad F_{cal} = 57.33 \qquad F_{0.95(1,9)} = 5.12$$

where

x_1 = Index of Net barter terms of trade
x_2 = Index of Income terms of trade
y = Index of Rural poverty

The values of the coefficients associated with net barter and income terms of trade have the positive and negative signs respectively and these signs are as expected. Further, these values are significant also and R^2 is fairly high explaining 86 percent change in poverty due to the combined effect of these two terms of trade. Hence, due to favourable net barter terms of trade, rural poverty has tended to increase although the favourable income terms of trade have tried to reduce it. But this improvement in income terms of trade is mainly because of favourable net barter terms of trade, which affected the poverty adversely and therefore, the overall impact of income terms of trade did not help much in reducing rural poverty.

(c) Analysis for the Period 1974-75 to 1995-96 (Phase III)

In the third phase from 1974-75 to 1995-96, the net barter terms of trade turned against the agricultural sector but the income terms of trade were more favourable to the same during this time period. Hence, the values of b_1 and b_2 obtained during this phase corroborates the positive and negative sign as expected from our priori hypothesis. The estimated regression equation is given below:

$$y = 49.96 + 65.49\,x_1 - 39.48\,x_2$$
$$(0.21) \quad (0.07)$$
$$R^2 = 0.85 \quad F_{cal} = 250 \qquad F_{0.95(1,43)} = 4.38$$

where

x_1 = Index of Net barter terms of trade
x_2 = Index of Income terms of trade
y = Index of Rural poverty

It is inferred from the above equation that the value of coefficient associated with our independent variable x_1 (net barter terms of trade) is significant, thus, highlighting the fact that with a slower rise in food prices *vis-à-vis* industrial prices poverty has not witnessed an increasing trend. Similarly, the value of our other independent variable x_2 (income terms of trade) is also significant indicating that the improvement in income terms of trade have tended to curtail the poverty level and have also benefited small and marginal farmers substantially. The value of R^2 is high at 0.86 explaining 86 percent variation in rural poverty due to the combined effect of net barter and income terms of trade.

This sharp increase in procurement prices may be a reason for rise in agricultural prices. An observation had also been made by Commission for Agricultural Costs and Prices (CACP) in 1975 implicating that "the appropriateness of an administered price for the grain in the Indian context can not be detached from the paying capacity of the vast mass of the low income consumers in the country". Therefore, there is a need for an appropriate agriculture price policy to secure the vested interests of the producers and not hurting the common rural masses

Tendulkar and Jain (1995) were first to evaluate the impact of economic reforms on poverty as early as 1995. It may be emphasized that a major objective of economic reform was to initiate policies that would end discrimination against agriculture and improve its terms of trade *vis-a-vis* other sectors of economy. The net barter terms of trade were biased against agriculture since 1996-97 because the policies of input subsidies and output support prices had suppressed domestic prices. According to Parikh (1997) subsidies in agriculture were fiscally unsustainable .... inefficient and costly to farmers. In the background of greater integration between domestic and international markets, absence of quota controls as in the pre-WTO period and the ineffectiveness of low tariffs, the surge in the imports of various crops contributed in different degrees to the decline in their domestic prices (Bhalla, 2004, Ghosh, 2005). The volatility of domestic prices resulted in varied kinds of problems in their internal adjustments while on one hand it increase the uncertainties in cultivation and on other hand it also provided mis-leading price signals to domestic producers of specific crops. Thus our initial hypothesis that if terms of trade are unfavourable to agriculture sector, rural poverty will decline holds good looking at this general overview and data on poverty estimates.

CONCLUSIONS AND POLICY IMPLICATION

We have tested our hypothesis for the phasal and total analysis with the help of bivariate regression model to see the combined effect of net barter and income terms of trade on rural poverty. The results obtained from the fitted regression equations for net barter terms of trade, income terms of trade and rural poverty suggests that in all the three sub-phases as well as in the total phase the value of coefficients associated with net barter terms of trade and income terms of trade have the expected positive and negative signs respectively and these values have been significant too indicating that both the net barter terms of trade and income terms of trade have facilitated to reduce rural poverty with net barter terms of trade causing more dominant impact than the income terms of trade on rural poverty.

An important policy implication that has surfaced from our analysis of terms of trade and rural poverty is that government should not allow agricultural production to fall, particularly the foodgrains production otherwise substantial increase in agricultural prices will trigger the poverty level. It may also be mentioned that government had decided to phase out subsidies on all types of chemical fertilizers by 2006. This is not a welcome step because not only the cost of production and price of agricultural production will increase but at the same time, it may have an adverse effect on agricultural output which may further escalate prices of agricultural commodities, thus, aggravating rural poverty in the years to come.

References

Agriculture and Rural Development—Stock Subsidies and food security. Ranade Ajit and Dev Mahendra S., 1997, Oxford University Press.

Ahluwalia, S. Montek (1986) 'Rural Poverty, Agricultural Production and Prices: A Reexamination' in Agricultural Change and Rural Poverty: Variations on a Theme by Dharam Narain eds. Mellor W. John and Desai M. Gunvant, Oxford University Press, New Delhi.

Alagh K. Yoginder, 1995, 'A Note on Measurement and Use of Poverty Estimates', *The Indian Journal of Labour Economics*, Vol. 38, No. 1, January-March.

Balkrishnan, P. *et. al.* (2008), "Agricultural Growth in India Since 1991", Study no. 2, Department of Economic Analysis and Policy, Reserve Bank of India, Mumbai.

Ghosh, Jayatyi (2005), "Trade Liberalization in Agriculture: An Examination of Impact and Policy Strategies with Special Reference to India", Background Paper for Human Development Report, 2005, New Delhi.

Government of India, Ministry of Agriculture, New Delhi, Report of the task force on Terms of Trade between Agricultural and Non-Agricultural Sectors (Chairman Prof. A.S. Kahlon, 1995).

Gupta, S.P., 1995, 'Economic Reforms and its Impact on Poor', *Economic and Political Weekly*, June 3.

Handbook of Statistics on Indian Economy, 1998.

Jhonson, Richard, A.. and Wichen Dean, W. (1996), 'Applied Multivariate Statistical Analysis', Printice Hall of India Private Ltd., New Delhi.

Kahlon, A.S. and Tyagi, D.S., 1980, 'Intersectoral Terms of Trade', *Economic and Political Weekly*, Vol. 15, No. 22, December.

Mahendra Dev, S. and Ranade, Ajit, 1998, 'Rising Food Prices and Rural Poverty: Going Beyond Correlations', *Economic and Political Weekly*, September 26.

Misra, V.N. and Hazell, B.R. Peter, 1996, 'Terms of Trade, Rural Poverty, Technology and Investment—The Indian Experience, 1952–53 to 1990–91', *Economic and Political Weekly*, Vol. XXXI, No. 13.

Mitra, Ashok (1997), 'Terms of Trade and Class Relations: An Essay in Political Economy, Frank Class London.

Mugrenkar, B.L. (1997) 'Terms of Trade, Technology and Agricultural Development in B.M. Desai (ed.) Agricultural Paradigm for the Ninth Plan under New Economic Environment, CMA Monograph No. 179, Oxford IBH Publishing, New Delhi

Mungrekar, B.L., 1993, 'Inter-Sectoral Terms of Trade – Issues of Concept and Method', *Economic and Political Weekly*, Vol. XXXVIII, No. 39, (Review of Agriculture), September 25.

Nambiar, A.C.K. (1992), 'Rural Poverty Problems and Prospects', Ashish Publishing House, Delhi.

National Account Statistics of India 1950–51 to 1995–96, *Economic and Political Weekly* Research Foundation, Mumbai.

Parikh, Kirit (1997), "Overview: Prospects and Retrospects", in Parikh Kirit ed., India Development Report, 1997, Oxford University Press, Mumbai.

Popli, Gurleen *et. al.* (2005), "Are the 2000 Poverty Estimates for India A Myth, Artefact or Real", *Economic and Political Weekly*, October 22–28, 2005, Vol. XL, No. 43.

Prasad, K.N. (1991), 'India's Rural Problems', Concept Publishing Company, New Delhi.

Rao, Hanumantha C.H., 1998, 'Agricultural Growth, Sustainability and Poverty Alleviation—Recent Trends and Major Issues of Reform' *Economic and Political Weekly*, July 18.

Rao, C.H. Hanumantha (1975), 'Technological Change and Distribution of Gains in Indian Agriculture, Mac Millan, Delhi.

Ravallion, M., 1998, 'Reforms, Food Prices and Poverty in India', *Economic and Political Weekly*, Vol. 33, Nos. 1 and 2.

Singh, M.L. (1976), 'Sectoral Terms of Trade and Economic Growth in India', Sterling Publishers Pvt. Ltd., New Delhi.

Subramaniam, 1993, 'Impact of Economic Reforms on Inter-sectoral Terms of Trade in India', Occasional papers, *RBI Bulletin*, Reserve Bank of India, Mumbai.

Tendulkar, Suresh D. and L.R. Jain (1995), "Economic Reforms and Poverty", *Economic and Political Weekly*, June 10.

Thamarajakshi, R. (1994) 'Intersectoral Relationships in a Developing Economy: The Indian Experience', Academic Foundation, New Delhi.

Thamarajakshi, R., 1990, "Intersectoral Terms of Trade Revisited', *Economic and Political Weekly*, Volume 25, No. 13, March 31.

Thamarajakshi, R., 1999, 'Agriculture and Economic Reforms', *Economic and Political Weekly*, August 14.

Thamarajakshi, R., 2000, 'National Agricultural Policy – Confusion on Ends and Means', *Economic and Political Weekly*, Vol. XXXV, Nos. 35 and 36, August 26.

The implications of the Uruguay Round Agreement on Agriculture for Developing Countries, 1998.

Tyagi, D.S., 1982, 'How Valid Are the Estimates of Trends in Rural Poverty ?' *Economic and Political Weekly*, (Review of Agriculture), June.

Tyagi, D.S., 1987, 'Domestic Terms of Trade and Their Effect on Supply and Demand of Agricultural Sector', *Economic and Political Weekly*, Vol. XXII, No. 13, (Review of Agriculture), March 28.

Uppal, J.S. (1983), 'Indian Economic Problems', Tata McGraw Hill Publishing Company Limited, New Delhi.

Wizarat, S., 'Technical Change in Pakistan's Agriculture, 1953–54 to 1977–78, February 1981, Report No. 120, Pakistan Institute of Development.

World Bank, India: Achievements and Challenges in Reducing Poverty, Country Study, 1997, Washington.

11

Food Security of India under WTO Regime: Availability Access and Affordability of Food, PDS and Food Subsidy

Ravi Ranjan

In these days of scientific and technological development, when an information revolution has ushered globally and world has becoming more and more accessible economically and politically both, to develop in isolation by any country has become an utter impossibility. Numerous economic factors like industrial production, agricultural marketing, finance capital, trade and commerce, etc. are more and more globalized, making one country dependent on another in several matters. In this newly emerged scenario no country, whatever position it has acquired, can shut its eyes to the developing trends of globalization and its all embracing impacts on it. But together with all such phenomenal development equally erroneous would be to shut one's eyes to the national goal formulated as growth with equality and social justice, the very cardinalities which have been accepted by the Indian people as their prime motive in all the decades since India's Independence.

The GATT, now terminologised as the World Trade Organization (WTO) has certain specific objectives which read as: 1. To help all countries to expand their production and trades in goods and services, 2. To promote the use of world's resources in a manner conducive to sustainable development and with a strong bias in favour of protection and preservation of environment. To ensure that the relation among the contracting parties in the fields of trade and economic development are so negotiated and settled with due considerations for and with a view (a) To achieve a raise in the standard of living of the people; (b) To ensure the people full employment; and (c) To secure for the people growth in their real income and effective demand.

The positive steps spelt out in GATT of fulfilling those objectives are:

1. Reduction in tarift and other barriers to trade throughly mutually advantageous arrangements, and
2. Elimination of discriminatory treatment in International treade.

To pursue the above treaty and in pursuit of achieving the objective set forth the contracting parties of GATT have entered into 15 agreements, namely

1. Agreement establishing the Mutual Trade Organization (MTO), now World Trade Organization (WTO),
2. Agreement on tariff and trade in goods,
3. Agreement on agriculture, in Agreement on textile,
4. Agreement on sanitary and phytosanitary measures,
5. Agreement on technical barriers to trade,
6. Agreement on trade-related investment measures,
7. Agreement on auto-dumping,
8. Agreement on custom valuation,
9. Agreement on pre-shipment inspection,
10. Agreement on rules of origin,
11. Agreement on import licensing procedure,
12. Agreement on subsidies and countervailing measures,

13. Agreement on safeguard,
14. General agreement on trade and services, and
15. Agreement on trade-related aspect of intellectual property rights including trade in counterfeit goods.

It is often stated on behalf the GATT, that ever since its formation in 1947 till 1991 the tariffs were lowered down by about 40 to 50 percent it helped international trade long period of high growth. It created conducive environment for trading communities to invest with more confidence and trade in goods and services in an increasingly open market.

Another claim made on behalf of GATT is that it helped to multiply the volume of merchandise involved in the international trade by 12 times and in volume international trade rote from 57 billion dollar in 1947 to 3,500 billion dollar in 1991. The GATT regime introduced in 1995 is likely to raise the world's annual income by an addition to 510 billion dollar to 2 billion annually up to 2005.

There is no data available to substantiate whether the claims, thus made by the proponents of GATT, have been materialised and to what extent.

However, this type of claims have not been ceased and there are elements who are tirelessly propagating the inevitability of WTO as its economic inseparability in economic growth of every nation in present day world economic scenario. It has since become clear that India need not have to reduce any tariff now because it has reduced since the beginning of the New Economic Policy in 1991. India need not also have to reduce an account of any export subsidy in agricultural export as India has not been granting any such subsidies. India also claim that all the subsidies it provides to agriculture fall within the exception of Green Box Policies. On this basis India claims that they are all aids to promote agriculture and not aids to export affecting agricultural trade.

Sustainable agricultural growth requires capital investment and capital formation in agricultural sector has been approaching its lowest odd due to withdrawal from the sector of public investment. Private investment, although has been increasing, is unable to meet certain investment which require huge amount for their accomplishment. Export-oriented agricultural growth, which is being emphasized by the government, has created new difficulties to the sector, and first of them being endangering the food security of the country. Notwithstanding that the existing food store of more than 30 million tonnes is enough to give food security to Indian people even in this year of mansoon failure in many states like Bihar, yet there is a huge population in India which can not get required food due to lack of their purchasing power. The allowance by government of wayada business in agricultural produces has accelerated the prices of foodgrains to such a high extent as was never expected by the Indian people. The policy of government to encourage export-oriented crops with new dispensation of cultivation WTO has posed serious problem of food security. In an estimation it has been indicated that in the next few years that is, till 2010 the total population of India will be approaching to 1180 million and the total foodgrains production would be 220 million tonnes. The table gives the projection of foodgrain in India till 2025 (Table 1).

TABLE I

Population and Foodgrains Projection for India

Year	*Population in million*	*Production*	*Market demand*	*Import*	*Hidden needs*
		Million Tones			
1988	853	147	142	5	+118
2010	1178	220	229	9	+129
2025	1467	289	313	26	+133

POPULATION AND FOODGRAINS PROJECTION FOR INDIA

In India, a country in which more than 50 percent or nearly 70 crores out of its total population like less than Rs. 20 per day, the problem is not that of less calories intake but also of poor intake of protein. Among the poor section of people living in rural segment the main sources for poor people of protein intake are pulses, hence the production of pulses require special attention. According to an estimate the total annual requirements of pulses in India is in between 16 to 19 million tonnes. But the consumption of pulses in India is not only low but its availability is also scarce, and to that sequel its consumption has gradually been decelerating in the years of globalization. In the years 1992-95 of Rs. 53.44 crore in 1993-94 of Rs. 73.5 crore and in 1994-95 of Rs. 90.56 crores of pulses have been exported. The prices of pulses have increased at faster rate than other foodgrains. In 2009 the unprecedented price hike in pulses approaching Rs. 90 per kg in retail market has made pulses consumption an impossibilities for majority of the Indian population. Under such an odd condition government has allowed wayada business and through it, an artificial scarcity of pulses and other foodgrains has been created by hoarders, and black marketers and government pays no any heed to ameliorate the condition.

Food, being the prime necessity for the people, can not be removed from government intervention. In India, barring a few states like Kerala, West Bengal, etc. the system of public distribution, as it was previously organized, has been dismantled by the government and as its substitute a more new system with much severe hotchpotch has been introduced. The subsidised food supply through public distribution system, as it exists today has not been properly targeted. It is estimated that not more than 40 percent of the foodgrains allocated under PDS are distributed through fair price shops and its major shares go to metropolitan cities like Delhi, Mumbai, etc. as shows in the Table 2.

TABLE 2

Percentage Relative Share of Some States in Total Population, Poor and PDS Share in Distribution of Foodgrains

(percentage)

Stare	*Share in total Population*	*Share in Poor*	*Share in PDS food grains distribution*
UP, Bihar MP	34.5	42.2	13.7
AP, Kerala, Delhi	11.4	10.5	28.7
Bihar	10		4.7

In an another estimation it has been accepted that except Kerala PDS provides only 10 to 20 percent of the total required foodgrains to most of the poor in the lowest three income deciles. It clearly evidences that nearly 70 to 75 percent underdogs are dependent on open market to meet their food requirements, as these two labels given in Tables 3 and 4.

TABLE 3

Share of Different Sources in Total Consumption of Foodgrains

(Percentage)

Income Docile (%)	*Open Market*		*PDS*		*Home grown*	
Poorest	*Past*	*Present*	*Past*	*Present*	*Past*	*Present*
0-10	71	73	21	20	8	7
10-20	71	70	18	20	11	9
20-30	58	75	17	16	11	10
Richest						
70-80	45	63	16	6	28	30
80-90	45	48	11	10	44	41
90-100	50	54	9	8	41	37

TABLE 4

Percentage Share of PDS in Different States

Income Docile (%)	*AP*		*Karnataka*		*Kerala*		*Tamil Nadu*	
Poorest	*Past*	*Present*	*Past*	*Present*	*Past*	*Present*	*Past*	*Present*
0-10	20	21	10	12	36	52	19	20
10-20	20	15	11	13	39	55	13	17
20-30	16	16	9	10	47	63	8	19
Richest								
70-80	7	16	11	11	33	33	14	13
80-90	20	11	6	5	25	25	9	11
90-100	8	9	4		35	55	8	9

The data on Tables 3 and 4 is the situation of PDS which does not provide any relief to 80 to 90 percent people who are illegible and needy for foodgrains on subsidised prices. To accommodate them all in the PDS system there is required a more efficient system free from various irregularities about which complaints are often made. Besides it there is also need to make arrangement for the supply of other necessary commodities through PDS on subsidised prices.

Under the price policy of the government both reduction in the real wages and purchasing power of the people have been experienced by the people on one hand and on the other government has gradually been reducing subsidies received by the peasant and consumers. Consequently, the agricultural sector in India has become un-remunerative. To have the sector advanced peasants should be guaranteed remunerative prices not by enhancing the prices of agricultural commodities and thus endangering the food security of poor people but by reducing the cost of production by making them available agricultural inputs on lower prices, and credit for lower interest rate.

In official circle and among the apologist of globalization there is rampant propoganda about a myth that Indian peasants are averse to the adoption of new technology as they believe it not profitable. Hence it is advised that setting agrarian policy minimal government intervention is right step to help larger section of the society. However, to ensure remunerative prices to farmers is necessary but it is not all to encourage production of foodgrains. There should be a clearly spelt out agrarian policy to ensure remunerative prices to the cultivators and also to make available all sorts of agricultural inputs in time and for cheap prices, so that the unit cost of the products may be reduced. In the rural segment peasants are both the producers and consumers of foodgrains, but besides them there is a huge population which does not produce any agrarian commodity and live on wages earned. They are also consumers of foodgrains, and in fixing the prices of consumer goods this vulnerable section must be kept in the mind of policy-makers. This vulnerable section of people require cheaper, subsidised foodgrains along with the urban poor.

In WTO regime government of India is reducing subsidies on agriculture pleading that the subsidies, thus given to the sector is huge and colossal, to such an extent as state exchequer is unable to bear the financial burden thus incurred upon it. To give huge subsidies to agriculture is not an isolated case for India rather many developed nations like USA and European countries provide to their agriculture larger amount as subsidies than what the government of India usually gives to its farm sector but the steps under the New Economic Policy initiated in the direction of subsidy reduction has created new problems for marginal and poor peasants.

In the citation of data on food subsidy the Government of India claimed that the amount of subsidy on food, which was Rs. 3995 crore in 1981-86 increased to Rs. 2348 crore in the year 1991-95. The figure presented by the government cannot be denied by what confused the government propaganda was the fact that most of the amount of subsidies went to the Food Corporation of India (FCI) instead of being availed by the vulnerable section of rural population.

It has been observed that PDS, on average, distributed 16,000 tonnes of foodgrains which in sufficient for 10 crore people at the rate of 160 kgs. per capita per year and Rs. 5250 crore is spent as subsidy, this can help to serve 26 crore people if it is targeted properly and efficiency is improved. Often it is said that fiscal deficit has been caused due to subsidies to poor people, but such version on the part of government seldom bears any truth. Most of the subsidies are hidden which go to protect the interest of rich people. A single example is enough to disclose the truth. It has been estimated that 75 out of 100 Indian companies located in backward area (75 percent of our country is backward) do not pay any tax at all. The average income or profit of these companies is over Rs. 5000 crores. If they are taxed the government could have collected Rs. 3000 crores a year as tax. But in the pro-corporate sector, Prime Minister of India Dr. Manmohan Singh and his government seldom have any political will to touch these people. This is a type of hidden subsidy extended to big capital and the total amount lying with various companies from the length and breadth of India would be commendably higher than the amount given as subsidy to poor people.

Under the WTO regime the agricultural policy has been shaped by the Central Government for execution of a new development strategy which is detrimental to the peasant and that strategy is of contract agriculture by allowing multinationals to agricultural sector and providing the sector and export-oriented sector. It would endauger the food security of India and dependence on imperialist nations for foodgrains means compromising on our sovereignty. This policy must be defeated.

REFERENCES

GATT, Part (1V) of the GATT containing articles 36, 37, 38, added in 1965. (The estimation has been based on the assumption of minimum requirement of 3000 calorie/person/day including storage loses) IFPRI, world cereals.

The Ministry of Food, govt. of India, has estimated 16 million tonnes while the Planning Commission's estimate is of 19 million tonnes.

R.P. Singh, "Agricultural Development, Food Security, Price Policy and Technological options: Some issues", (Ed.) Y.V. Krishna Rao, The impact of GATT and New Economic Policy on Indian Agricultural (Delhi, PPH, 1997), pp. 48-49.

The Indian Observer, 10 January, 1995.

12

Agriculture Diversification in India: Emerging Trends and Policy Implications

SANJEEV KUMAR

INTRODUCTION

Agricultural sector is the backbone of Indian economy. The structure of the Indian economy has achieved a remarkable change after independence. It has been transformed from traditional agriculture-based economy to high value agriculture. With the advent of the green revolution, India has transformed itself from a country of shortages to a land of surpluses. With the rapid growth of the economy, a shift is also being seen in the consumption pattern, from cereals to more varied and nutritious diet of fruit and vegetables, milk, fish, meat and poultry products. This has resulted in the development of diversification of Indian agriculture.

Many developing countries like India are moving from traditional subsistence agriculture to commercial agriculture. India has tremendous potential to unleash large scale process based farm activities to exploit the emerging global business opportunities. If agriculture could be diversified and the agri-business industry developed, it would boost rural incomes and have a major impact on employment and equitable income growth throughout the economy. Agriculture diversification can, therefore, play a vital role in diversifying and commercializing agriculture, adding value to agricultural produce, generate employment, enhance income of farmers, and create surplus for export of processed products.

Crop diversification is intended to give a wider choice in the production of a variety of crops in a given area so as to expand production-related activities on various crops and also to lessen risk. Crop diversification in India is generally viewed as a shift from traditionally grown less remunerative crops to more remunerative crops. The crop diversification also takes place due to governmental policies and thrust on some crops over a given time.

Agriculture diversification in favour of more competitive and high value commodities is considered an important strategy to overcome many of these emerging challenges. If carried out appropriately, diversification can be used as a tool to augment farm income generate employment, alleviate poverty and conservation resources (Von Braun, 1995; Pingali and Rosegrant, 1995 and Ryan and Spencer, 2001).

The emerging trends of agriculture diversification and the constraints it faces would help in making appropriate policies regarding institutional arrangements and creation of suitable infrastructure, which could benefit a large mass small and marginal farmer. The main objectives of the present paper are;

- To examine the emerging trends, nature and speed of agricultural diversification in India.
- To assess the implications of agricultural diversification on food security, employment and export.

Rest of this paper is organized as follows: The next section discusses the methodological framework and data sources. This is followed by emerging trends of agriculture diversification in India and Implications of agriculture diversification. Conclusions and policy implications are made in the final section.

METHODOLOGY AND DATA SOURCES

The level of crop diversification effects the extent of economic development in the rural sector of India. It varies among regions because of varied agro-climatic conditions and resource endowment of the farms. The introduction of new-seed-fertliser technology has not only led to intensification of farming but also results in large scale diversification of crop farming and the benefits gradually accrued to the whole farming community (De, 2000). There are few methods, which explain the diversification of the commodities or activities in a given time and space by a single quantitative indicator. These ones include: (i) Index of maximum proportion, (ii) Herfindal Index, (iii) Simpson Index, (iv) Ogive Index, (v) Entropy Index, (vi) Modified Entropy Index, and (vii) Composite Entropy Index (Shiyani and Pandva, 1998; Kelley Ryan and Patel, 1995; Ramesh Chand, 1996).

Each method has some superiority and/or limitation over the other. The Simpson Index approach used in this study for considering our objectives of assessing the extent of diversity in crop sector, livestock, forestry and fisheries activity. This index provides a clear dispersion of commodities in a geographical region. It ranges between 0 and 1. If there exists complete specialization, the value of index moves towards zero. The index is easy to compute and interpret.

The Simpson index is given by;

$$\text{SID} = 1 - \sum_{i=1}^{n} \text{P}_{\text{i}}^{2}$$

where, SID ®Simpson index of diversification.

Pi ®Proportionate area (or value) of tth crop/livestock/ fisheries activity in the gross cropped area (or total value of output).

The nature and patterns of diversification in India were examined by looking into temporal changes in area of different crops. It was also examined for different activities of agriculture sector, i.e. value of crops, livestock, forestry and fisheries activities. To estimate the speed of diversification in favour of high value commodities, compound annual growth rate (CAGR) of area, production and yield of different crops were computed.

In this study, diversification is measured at three Triennium Ending, i.e. TE 1990-91, TE 1999-2000 and 2006-07. For analytical convenience this period has been divided into two sub-periods, namely, 1990/91 to 1999/2000 (first sub-period) and 2000/01 to 2006/07 (second sub-period).

A widely accepted exponential model, $y = a\, b^t e^u$, has been fitted to the time series data for estimating growth rates. The logarithmic form of this function is given by;

$$\ln(y) = \ln(a) + t\ln(b) + u$$

where,

$y \rightarrow$ Dependent variable whose growth rate is to be estimated.

$t \rightarrow$ Independent variable (Time).

$u \rightarrow$ Disturbance or error term.

a and b are the parameters to be estimated from sample observations. The regression coefficient b is estimated by ordinary least squares (OLS) technique.

The Compound Average Growth Rate (CAGR) in % term is estimated as:

$$CAGR = \{\text{antilog}(b) - 1\}*100$$

Data Sources

This study was based on the secondary data sources. The values for various agricultural/allied agriculture commodities come from the National Accounts Statistics prepared by the Central Statistical Organization (CSO), Ministry of Statistics and Program Implementation, Government of India. The data on crop areas, production and yield are from the publications of the Directorate of Economics and Statistics, Ministry of Agriculture, Government of India. For analysis of per capita consumption patterns of food items come from the various round of National Sample Survey Organization (NSSO). The data on some other variables are collected from Directorate General of Commercial Intelligence and Statistics, Government of India (GoI) and Department of Animal Husbandry, Dairying and Fisheries, Ministry of Agriculture, Government of India (GoI).

EMERGING TRENDS, NATURE AND SPEED OF AGRICULTURAL DIVERSIFICATION

Diversification of agriculture in India is gradually transferred in favour of non-food crops to augment incomes rather than a coping strategy to manage risk and uncertainty. The Simpson index of diversification and share of food crops and non-food crops in India at three triennium ending, i.e. TE 1990-91, TE 1999-2000 and 2006-07 are presented in Table 1. The results show that crop sector is gradually diversifying in India. The value of Simpson index of diversification (SID) increased from 0.43 in TE 1990-91 to 0.47 in TE 2006-07. The trends also showed that the non-food crops have gradually replaced food crops. The share of food crops in India at three triennium ending, i.e. TE 1990-91, TE 1999-2000 and 2006-07 are decreased, i.e.

TABLE 1

SID and Share of Food Crops and Non-Food Crops in India

Period	*Simpson Index of Crop Diversity*	*Share of Food Crops and Non-Food Crops*	
		Food Crops (Area)	*Non-Food Crops (Area)*
TE 1990-91	0.43	67.90	32.10
TE 1999-2000	0.45	66.31	33.69
TE 2006-07	0.47	63.79	36.21

Sources: Directorate of Economics and Statistics (DES), Ministry of Agriculture.

67.90, 66.31 and 63.79 per cent respectively, while the share of non-food crops in India at TE 1990-91, TE 1999-2000 and 2006-07 are gradually increased, i.e. 32.10, 33.69 and 36.21 per cent respectively. It means that non-food crops like oilseeds, fruits, vegetables, spices and sugarcane have mainly substituted coarse cereals while in search for higher incomes. Figure 1 presents the index number of area under foodgrains, non-foodgrains and all crops for the study period, i.e. 1990-91 to 2006-07. The figure showed that the gap between foodgrains and non-foodgrains are gradually increased. This shows that India is gradually diversifying in favour of high value commodities. i.e non-food crops.

FIGURE (A)

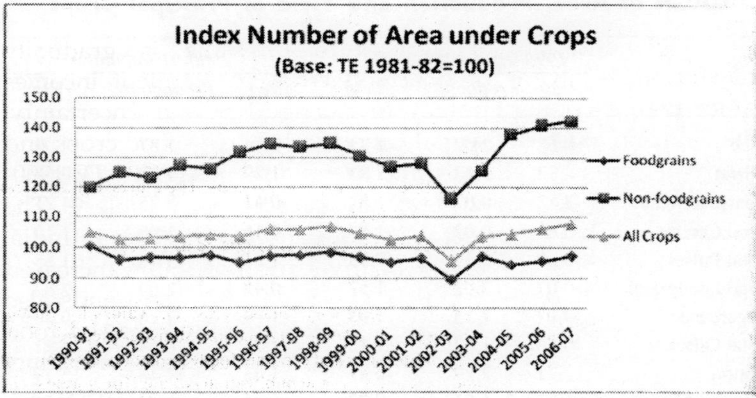

To examine the nature and speed of agricultural diversification, production performance and area expension of different commodities was assessed. The compound average growth rates (CAGR) of area, production and yield in India with respect of major commodity for the two sub-periods: 1990/91-1999/2000 and 2000/01-2006/07 as also for the complete period are presented in Table 2. The results showed that production performance of non-food commodities was superior to the food commodities. Among foodgrain group, cereals performed better than coarse cereals. Cereals sector was specializing in favour of rice and wheat. It was because of overriding concerned for food self-sufficiency in India. Rice and wheat replaced sorghum, millets and barley. The performance of pulses was better in second period as comparison to first period.

Indian farm output has been diversifying away from cereals and towards high value crop after 1990s. The performance of high-value products, including fruits and vegetables, sugar and fiber crops, sugarcane, cotton, and tobacco, has significantly better than foodgrains crop in specially in second period of the study. The results indicates that the speed of diversification is higher in second sub-period as comparison to first sub-period of the study.

Diversification of agriculture in India is gradually transferred in favour of commercial agriculture, i.e. high value

TABLE 2

CAGR of Area, Production and Yield of Principal Crops

Crop	*1990-91 to 1999-2000*			*2000-01 to 2006-07*		
	Area	*Production*	*Yield*	*Area*	*Production*	*Yield*
Rice	0.68	2.02	1.34	0.14	1.87	2.00
Wheat	72	3.57	1.83	1.29	1.36	0.08
Coarse Cereals	-2.12	-0.02	1.82	-0.41	3.25	4.25
Total Cereals	0.04	-0.02	1.59	0.16	1.95	3.10
Total Pulses	-0.60	0.59	0.93	1.91	3.42	1.65
Total Foodgrains	-0.07	2.02	1.52	0.48	2.09	2.82
Sugarcane	-0.07	2.73	1.05	1.89	2.20	0.30
Total Oilseeds	-0.86	1.63	1.15	2.71	6.69	4.91
Cotton	2.71	2.29	-0.41	1.45	17.48	15.79
Jute and Mesta	1.81	1.81	0.87	-1.75	0.04	2.51
Total Fibres	2.45	2.21	-0.27	1.09	15.23	14.14
Potato	3.84	5.44	1.54	3.05	-0.50	-3.44
Tobacco	1.56	1.00	-0.55	3.71	3.54	-0.17
Non-Foodgrains	1.18	2.69	1.09	2.46	5.09	3.87
All Principal Crops	0.27	2.29	1.33	1.06	3.17	3.88

Sources: DES, Ministry of Agriculture, Government of India (GoI).

crop/livestock/fishery activities to enhance the incomes of farmers and reduce the poverty. The share of individual sector in gross value of agricultural output in India and Simpion diversification index (SID) India at three triennium ending, i.e. TE 1990-91, TE 1999-2000 and 2006-07 are presented in Table 3. The table shows that there are four core sub-sector of agriculture i. e. crop, livestock, fisheries and forestry. Crop sub-sector is the principal sources of generating income in agriculture followed by livestock, forestry and fisheries sub-sector. The results indicate that the share of crop sector in agricultural gross domestic product marginally declined during the study period, i.e. form 73.65 in TE 1990-91 to 70.56 in TE 2006-07. On the other side the share of livestock, forestry and fisheries sub-sector has marginal increase in the same period. The results also indicate that the crop sector is gradually diversifying towards livestock, forestry and fisheries sub-sector. The value of Simpson index of diversification (SID) increased from 0.46 in TE 1990-91 to 0.50 in

TE 2006-07.. This showed that the crop sub-sector have gradually shifts towards livestock, forestry and fisheries sub-sector.

TABLE 3

Share of Individual Sector in Gross Value of Agricultural Output in India at Constant Prices

(per cent)

Period	*Crops Sector*	*Livestock*	*Forestry*	*Fishing*	*Simpson Index*
TE 1990-91	73.65	23.09	1.91	1.35	0.46
TE 1999-2000	71.11	24.28	2.36	2.25	0.49
TE 2006-07	70.56	25.24	2.02	2.18	0.50

Sources: CSO.

FIGURE 2

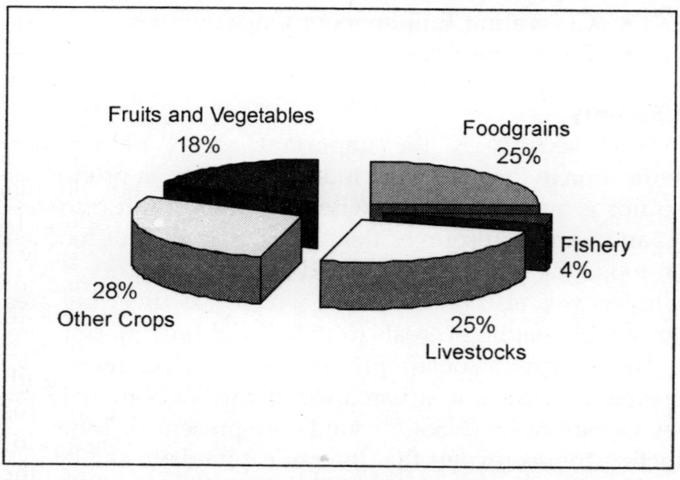

Figure 2 shows the recent conditions of distribution of total agriculture value in India. The potential for gains from foodgrain production are now limited, although more than 60 percent of gross cropped area is under cereals and pulses; their share of the value of total agricultural output is now less than 25 percent (TE 2006-07). High value commodities, particularly horticulture, livestock, and marine products, are highly expenditure elastic compared with grains. Given rising incomes and higher expenditure elasticity for these commodities, future growth is likely to come from the high value sector (Gulati and Ganguly, 2008). The share of high value commodities, including horticulture, livestock, and fisheries, in the total value of agricultural output has already increased from 40.2 percent in TE 1990-91 to 47.5 percent in TE 2006-07.

IMPLICATIONS OF AGRICULTURAL DIVERSIFICATION

There are several benefits of agricultural diversification in India. These are shifting concomption pattern, improve food security, increase income, generating employment opportunity, reduce poverty, improving productivity, promoting exports, etc. In this section the present study have assessed implication of diversification on foolwing aspect;

- Improving Food Security
- Generating Employment Oppertunities
- Promoting Export

Food Security

Food security is the important aspect of agricultural diversification in the context of India. Increasing in production of foodgrains is major challenge, when population and incomes are rising, and natural resources degrading. The shift of food crops to non-food crop portfollio may lead to food insecurity. The crop substitution was also taking place, which was diverting area in favour of high yielding cereals from low yielding inferior cereals.

The per capita consumption pattern of food items in India with respect to rural and urban areas of various National Sample Survey Organisation (NSSO) rounds are present in Table 4. The production trends reveals that the per capita daily availability of foodgrains has increased during the study period.

Given sustained increases in per capita incomes of about 4 percent per year during the past two decades, consumption patterns in India are changing away from cereals to high-value agricultural products. The results showed that per capita

TABLE 4

Per Capita Consumption Pattern of Food Items in India (Rs./per month)

Item Group	*1987/ 88*	*1993/ 94*	*1999/ 2000*	*2004/ 05*	*2005/ 06*	*2006 /07*
Rural						
Total cereals	41.92	68.9	108.75	101.77	107.68	116.44
Pulses	6.27	10.7	18.51	7.18	20.02	22.67
Milk and milk products	13.63	26.7	42.56	47.31	50.94	56.23
Edible oils	7.88	12.5	18.16	25.72	25.46	27.22
Egg, fish and meat	5.11	9.4	16.14	18.62	4.31	24.32
Vegetables	8.23	17.0	29.98	34.07	37.88	43.06
Fruits and nuts	2.57	4.9	8.36	10.42	11.75	12.47
Sugar	4.51	8.6	11.57	13.25	14.83	14.04
Urban						
Total cereals	37.55	65.4	106.87	107.44	111.54	120.98
Pulses	8.44	13.9	24.25	22.51	25.57	30.06
Milk and milk products	23.84	44.9	74.178	3.384	.949	7.49
Edible oils	3.23	20.1	26.81	36.37	35.02	37.52
Egg, fish and meat	8.85	15.5	26.78	28.47	32.28	34.2
Vegetables	3.12	25.0	43.9	46.84	49.73	56.87
Fruits and nuts	6.27	12.2	20.68	23.65	25.52	28.0
Sugar	5.86	10.9	14.0	15.88	17.45	17.25

Source: Various rounds of NSSO.

consumption of cereals from 1993-94 to 2006-07 have marginal increase from Rs. 70 to Rs. 116 per month in rural areas and from Rs. 65 to Rs. 120 in urban areas. The consumption of fruits, vegetables, milk and milk product, meat and meat product, eggs, and fish have rapidly increased in urban areas as well as rural areas over the study period. Similar changes occurred in urban diets. These dramatic changes indicate a structural shift in Indian diets.

Employment

Employment generation in rural areas is the tough task. Now is a question that, can agricultural diversification help in generate additional employment opportunities in rural areas? Some information was collated on average labour use in cereal, non-cereal and vegetables and presented in Table 5. This table showed that labour used for cultivation of vegetables is sustaintially higher than cereals. Area shift from cereals to vegetables would generate additional employment in rural areas. So we can say that high-value agricultural products have higher employment elasticity.

TABLE 1.5

Average Labour Use in Cereal, Non-Cereal and Vegetables (Man-days per hectare)

Cereals and Non-Cereals		*Vegetables*	
Crop	*Labour Use*	*Crop*	*Labour Use*
Rice	105	Potato	200
Wheat	55	Onion	125
Sorghum	55	Cabbage	110
Pearl Millet	50	Cauliflower	120
Cotton	100	Egg Plant	70
Sugarcane	190	Tomato	195

Source: Subramanian *et al* (2000) and GoI (2000).

Exports

International trade of India in high-value food products has expanded enormously over the last decades, fueled by changing consumer tastes and advances in production. The performance of agriculture and allied product exports in India are given in Table 6.

The results showed that share agricultural exports in India decline at 12.66 per cent in second sub-period, as against 18.56 per cent during first sub-period. The share of foodgrains crops is very lower in agriculture exports, i.e. around 12 per cent. A large share of agriculture export was contributed by diversification of crop and livestock sector. It was noted that diversification of agriculture commodities has promoted export of many non-traditional items. The progress of high value agriculture items during the study period was quite impressive. This implies that agriculture diversification can substantially contribute to export provided a congenial environment trough infrastrure development and institutional innovation is created.

TABLE 6

Share and Growth of Exports of Agriculture and Allied Product of India

(in percentage)

Agriculture and allied products	*1990-91*	*1995-96*	*2000-01*	*2006-07*	*CAGR*	
					First Period	*Second Period*
Cereals (Rice and Wheat)	8.19	24.26	12.27	12.32	28.36	11.87
Plantation Crops	21.97	13.14	10.90	6.86	13.63	4.63
Fruits and vegetables	14.50	13.04	15.44	12.94	16.42	10.24
Oil meals	10.11	11.54	7.49	9.59	12.62	20.69
Spices	3.89	3.90	5.93	5.50	25.47	10.63
Marine products	15.95	16.62	23.33	13.94	19.12	3.52
Meat and meat preparations	2.32	3.08	5.39	5.77	22.03	17.16
Fibres (Cotton)	14.05	1.00	0.81	10.64	-7.98	108.13
Tobacco	4.38	2.20	3.18	2.94	15.05	12.09
Sugar and mollases	0.62	2.49	1.85	5.68	-3.9	03.46
Others	4.02	8.73	13.41	13.81	33.59	17.69
Total	100.00	100.00	100.00	100.00	18.58	12.66

* First Period: 1990/91-1999/2000 and Second Period: 2000/01-2006/07.
Sources Reserve Bank of India (RBI).

CONCLUSION AND POLICY IMPLICATIONS

The present study shows that India is moving from traditional subsistence agriculture to high value agriculture. Agriculture diversification in India play a vital role in diversifying and commercializing agriculture, adding value to agricultural produce, generate employment, enhance income of farmers, and create surplus for export of processed products. The result shows that consumption patterns are changing towards high value agricultural commodities from traditional agriculture and this is driving the process of agricultural diversification in India.

Consumption patterns are changing towards high value agricultural commodities and this is driving the process of agricultural diversification in India. The share of high value agriculture is increasing in the total value of agricultural output and these commodities being highly expenditure elastic are the potential sources of future income. This demand-led phenomenon can help achieve many strides for the agricultural sector in India, provided policy can look beyond farming and better integrate production agriculture with other components of the agri-structure.

The present study also highlighted the implications of agriculture diversification on food security; generate employment and earnings form exports. The results showed that food security was not so adversely affected as a consequence of agricultural diversification. Similarly the high value crops have substantial potential for generating employment opportunities. Most of the high value crops are high labour requirement crops. The high value commodities have also witness good performance in the international trades. The structure of India's agricultural exports has been gradually changing in favour of high-value food products (horticultural and animal foods), international food safety and quality standards are becoming stringent. Their compliance will be a key to the growth of exports of high-value food products. Thus, appropriate quality testing and certification procedures will have to be put in place.

References

Birthal, P.S., P.K. Joshi and Ashok Gulati (2005), Vertical Coordination in High Value Commodities: Implications for Smallholders. Markets, Trade and Institutions Division, Discussion Paper No. 85, International Food Policy Research Institute, Washington D.C.

Chand, Ramesh (1996), Diversification through high value crops in western Himalayan region: evidence from Himachal Pradesh. *Indian Journal of Agricultural Economics*, Vol. 41(4): 652-63.

Directorate of Economics and Statistics (DES), Ministry of Agriculture, Government of India (GoI), New Delhi.

Government of India (2008), National Accounts Statistics, Central Statistical Organization, Ministry of Statistics and Program Implementation, Government of India (GoI).

Gulati, Ashok and Kavery Ganguly (2008), Beyond Grain Security: Agriculture Tomorrow, *The Business Standard*, New Delhi.

Joshi, P.K., Gulati, A., Birthal, P.S. and Tiwari, L. (2005), Agriculture Diversification in South Asia: Patterns, Determinants, and Policy

Implications. In S.C. Babu and A. Gulati (Eds.), Economic Reforms and Food Security. USA: The Haworth Press, Inc.

National Sample Survey Organization (various rounds), Household Consumer Expenditure in India, Ministry of Statistics and Programme Implementation, Government of India.

Pingali, P.L. and Rosegrant, M.W. (1995), Agricultural commercialization and diversification: processes and policies. *Food Policy*, 20(3): 644-651.

Rao, C.H.H. (2000), "Declining Demand for Foodgrains in Rural India: Census and Implications", *Economic and Political Weekly*, January 22.

Ryan, J.G. and D.C. Spencer. (2001), Future Challenges and Opportunities for Agricultural R&D in the Semi-Arid Tropics, Patancheru-502 324, Andhra Pradesh, India: International Crops Research Institute for the Semi-Arid Tropics.

Von Braun, J. (1995), Agricultural commercialization: impacts on income and nutrition and implications for policy, *Food Policy*, Vol. 20(3): 187-202.

13

Globalisation, Food Security and Sustainable Agriculture in India

S.S. Kalamkar

INTRODUCTION

The global food security is in question today with ever increasing food prices resulting from adverse climatic effects on agricultural production, rise in oil prices, increasing use of grains for biofuels, and almost half reduction in public spending on agricultural sector over the last three decades. The environmental sustainability has also become more elusive due to rapid industrial and population growth, urbanization, and with the lack of public realization about the sheer effects of environmental pollution. The world food situation is currently being rapidly redefined by new driving forces. Income growth, climate change, high energy prices, globalization, and urbanization are transforming food consumption, production, and markets. The influence of the private sector in the world food system, especially the leverage of food retailers, is also rapidly increasing (Braun, 2007). The world has experienced an unprecedented increase in population during the past century, with a billion people added every decade during the last three decades alone. Dramatic shifts in production and consumption of food have accompanied this population explosion, including a surge in grain production, a spectacular rise in meat production and consumption, and the emergence of an increasingly vital role for international trade (Rosegrant, *et al*, 2001). Changes in food availability, rising commodity prices, and new producer–consumer linkages have crucial implications for the livelihoods of poor and food-insecure people (Braun, 2007). Global food prices witnessed a very sharp increase in 2007 and they are continuing to rise. Initially it was thought that the increase in food prices was a part of their cyclical nature, aggravated by the adverse impact of weather on production in some parts of the world. However, the continuing surge and the high level of global food prices seen so far in 2008 make it abundantly clear that the recent trend cannot be attributed to any volatility of international prices and there are fears that food prices may stay at these levels or may rise even more. This is causing worldwide concern. The severity of the problem can be seen from the fact that food prices-based on the International Monetary Fund (IMF), food price index increased by 9.5 per cent between April 2006 and April 2007 and by 45.6 per cent over the next 12 months. The increase has been particularly very sharp for staple foods. Rice prices doubled in the five months between November 2007 and March 2008, wheat prices increased more than two-fold in the 12 months after March 2007 and maize prices doubled in one and half year after August 2006. These increases in prices of staple foods have led to emergencies and rationing in a large number of countries and there are frequent reports of food riots from various parts of the globe. The picture is turning gloomier day by day. The factors being held responsible for high food inflation are diversion of foodgrains for biofuel; adverse weather and climate change; increase in crude oil prices; dietary shifts in China and India following an improvement in income and living standards, and neglect of agriculture for a long time, etc. (Chand, 2008).

Importance of food management and maintaining food security the world over has been abundantly recognized since long. Food security theme has been a consistent raised in specific contexts in a number of world conference convened by the United Nations in the 1990s (George, 2006). The necessity of having the food security at global level was first recognized at the 1974 World Food Conference where Food and Agriculture Organisation (FAO) was called upon to establish Committee on review and to recommend any action necessary in case of problems in particular areas. The World Food Summit was called in response to the continued existence of widespread under-nutrition and growing concern about the capacity of agriculture to meet future food needs. In 1974, governments attending the World Food Conference had proclaimed that "every man, woman and child has the inalienable right to be free from hunger and malnutrition in order to develop their physical and mental faculties." Subsequently, an International Undertaking on World Food Security was set-up in which Member Nations committed themselves to food stocks at levels necessary to ensure continuity of supplies and to meet emergency needs in the event of crop failure or natural disaster. Monitoring of implementation of the Undertaking has since then become the responsibility of the Committee on World Food Security. World Food Summit (1996) had set a target of reducing the number of hungry and food insecure to half (842 million in the base period of 1990-92) by 2015. Also, the first goal of UN Millennium Development Goals (MDGs) was to reduce the proportion of hungry (from a base level of around 20 percent) to half by 2015 (Acharya, 2009). Though the world has been changing remarkable over the past 25 years, food security still remains an unfulfilled dream for more than 800 million people living in the developing countries. The global food security is in question today with ever-increasing food prices resulting from adverse climatic effects on agricultural production, rise in oil prices, increasing use of grains for biofules, and almost 50 percent reduction in public spending on agricultural sector over the last three decades. The environmental sustainability has also become more elusive due to rapid industrial and population growth, urbanization and with lack of public realization about the sheer effects of environmental pollution.

The food security has become increasingly important globally as well as at domestic front as the global foodgrains production is not keeping pace with increasing population (Singh and Mishra, 2008). From 1984 to 1994 annual growth in World foodgrain production was only one per cent. Infact, the global per capita availability of foodgrains has fallen substantially during the last decade of reforms, and the maximum decline has taken place during the first five years. The per capita annual production of cereals in the world increased from 271 kg during 1961-65 to 295 kg during 1966-70, which were the initial years of the green revolution (see Table 1). The uptrend in production continued for about next two decades and per capita cereal production peaked by the mid-1980s at a level of 334 kg per person per year, which was the highest one till date. After mid-1980s, the growth rate of cereal production decelerated to 1.09 per cent, compared to 2.51 per cent in 1961-85. The recent growth rate turned out to be lower than the growth rate in population even though the growth rate in population was coming down. The per capita production of cereals declined to less than 315 kg in the first eight years of the current decade. Though there is some improvement in per capita availability of cereals during the last four years (2003-07), this increase has not been available for use as food and feed, due to diversion of foodgrain for production of biofuel in United States and other countries. When total production is netted out for the corn used for biofuel, then per capita production falls to 307 kg, the lowest in any five-year period after 1966-70. This shows that the shortage of staple food has been building up over several years and it became quite large in the recent years (Chand, 2008).

TABLE 1

Global Trends in Per Capita Cereals Production—1961-2007

(kg)

Period	*Wheat*	*Rice/Milled*	*Maize*	*Total Cereals*
1961-65	67	50	77	271
1966-70	74	54	87	295
1971-75	90	56	81	308
1976-80	98	58	90	324
1981-85	104	63	93	334
1986-90	104	64	90	327
1991-95	100	64	94	317
1996-00	100	66	101	319
2001-05	95	63	104	310
2003-07	94	65	108	314

Source: FAOSTAT and FAO Food Outlook, various issues (as quoted in Chand, 2008).

The world has experience an unprecedented increase in population during the past century, with a billion people added every decade during the last three decades. Dramatic shifts in production and consumption of food have accompanied this population explosion, including a surge in grain production, spectacular rise in meat production and consumption, and the emergence of an increasingly vital role for international trade (Rosegrant, *et al.*, 2001). The world food situation is currently being rapidly redefined by new driving forces. Income growth, climate change, high-energy prices, globalization, and urbanization are transforming food consumption, production and markets. Of the world's 34 most food-insecure countries, 22 had average annual growth rates ranging from 5 to 16 percent between 2004 and 2006. Global economic growth, however, is projected to slow from 5.2 percent in 2007 to 4.8 percent in 2008. Beyond 2008, world growth is expected to remain in the 4 percent range while developing county growth is expected to average 6 percent. This growth is a central force of change on the demand side of the world food equation (Braun, 2007). The United Nations population projections indicate that World population will increase to 8.3 billion in 2025 and 10 billion in 2050 from the present level of 5.8 billion. Such unprecedented growth in population necessitates food production to be almost doubled by 2050. However, the strategies biased toward urban and industrial growth, together with the neglect of the agricultural sector, have led to significant damage to prime agricultural land (Bhadra and Brandao, 1993) and there is little evidence that the process of converting land to urban uses poses a serious threat to future global food production (Rosegrant, *et al.*, 2001). The UN estimates indicate that almost 800 million people in developing countries today face chronic under nutrition and some 200 million children under the age of five suffer from protein and energy deficiencies. At present as many as 88 nations fall into the category of low-income food deficit countries: 42 in sub-Saharan Africa, 19 in Asia and the pacific, 9 in Latin America and the Caribbean, 6 in North East/North Africa and 12 in Europe/commonwealth of independent states.

India plays a very important role by its contribution in world's food production, accounts for 10.8 percent of total world's total cereals production, rank third next to China and

USA in 2006. Infact, India ranks first in world's total pulses production (23.3 percent) and second in rice and wheat production, accounts 21.6 and 11.4 percent respectively. India accounts for 16.7 percent of the world's food consumers. India's size in terms of food consumers is many times larger than the average size of the rest of the countries, except China (Acharya, 2007). Due to deep rooted poverty, rapidly growing population, low agricultural productivity and resultant food and nutritional insecurity during early independence periods, country had to give high priority to make our population food secure which would in turn mean economic growth and reduce poverty. India has made impressive strides on the agricultural front during the last three decades. Foodgrain production more than doubled from 102 million tonnes in triennium ending 1973 to 227.3 million tonnes in 2007-08. Virtually all of the increase in the production resulted from yield gains rather than expansion of cultivated area under foodgrains which remain stagnant at around 124 million hectares. India has emerged as one of the leading producer of fruits, vegetables and milk. Despite the impressive growth and development, India is still home to the largest number of poor people of the world. With about 251 million below the poverty line, India accounts for about one-fifth of the world's poor (Kumar, 2005). Food availability and price stability, which are considered as a good measure of food security till 1970, were achieved through green revolution and Public Distribution System (PDS), however, the chronic food security which is primary associated with poverty, still persisted in the country. In addition to this, per capita per day availability of foodgrains in India is almost stagnant; it was 468.8 gm/capita/day in 1971 and decreased to 462.4 in 2004. Though physical access to food was achieved, economic access at micro-level lagged behind indicating food and nutritional insecurity. One quarter of the world's hungry people live in India. *The State of Food Insecurity in the World, 2008* just released by the FAO estimated that India is home to more than 230 million undernourished people, which is 21 percent of the national population. India is home to the greatest population of severely malnourished children in the world. Four hundred million children suffer daily, which is grater problem than in Sub-Saharan Africa. Accordingly to the *National Family Health Survey of India,* 55 percent children living in rural areas suffer from malnutrition compared to 45 percent of children in urban areas.

Though the structure of food basket is undergoing change as diets are diversifying from basic cereals to fruits, milk and milk products, meat, fish and eggs, etc.; the population growth, rise in per capita income, urbanization, change in taste and preference, economic growth, etc. are likely to change the supply and demand prospects of food in the years to come. Because of high population pressure, India's land and other resources to meet its food and development needs are under severe pressure. Providing food at the household level for ensuring food security is the major policy concern of the country (Goyal and Singh, 2002). Although many Indians still do not have an adequate diet, the national food situation is dramatically better today than five decades ago. In 1960, India's population was 2.34 times less than of its current size, but foodgrains population was almost three times less and country was critically dependent on food aid to prevent widespread famine, particularly in drought years. Today, India is self-sufficient in foodgrains production. The nation produces and consumes about 170 million metric tonnes of cereals each year including seed and waste (Bhall, et.al, 1999). But will India continue to be self-sufficient in foodgrains production in the years ahead? And will national production of foodgrains continue to keep pace with demand. In developing counties like India, where majority of population lives in rural areas, derive their livelihood from agricultural sector, sustainability of agriculture can not be achieved in isolation of the issue of food and livelihood security. Therefore, it becomes imperative to discuss the actual food security scenario in the country in global perspective and sustainability of agriculture along with the options to make it more rational.

DATA AND METHODOLOGY

The study is based on secondary data collected from the different sources such as government publications, reports, websites and published papers. The entire data-related to area, production and yield of crops, per capita foodgrains availability and related data have been compiled from *Agricultural Statistics at a Glance* published by Agricultural Statistics Division,

Directorate of Economics and Statistics, Department of Agriculture and Cooperation, Ministry of Agriculture, Government of India and related website. Besides tabular analysis, growth rates were calculated to indicate an increase or decrease in various parameters.

RESULTS AND DISCUSSION

Food Security and Sustainable Agriculture: the Concept

The concept of food security has evolved during last three decades to include not only food availability, but also economic access to food and biological absorption of food in the body. Infact adequate per capita availability of food is a function of the balance between food production on the one hand, and growth in population and purchasing power, on the other (Swaminathan, 2009). Food security and food insecurity are the terms used to describe whether or not all people at all time have physical and economic access to sufficient, safe and nutritious food for a healthy and active life (World Food Summit, 1996). Food security is multi dimensional and its major components are: (a) availability of food, (b) access to food, (c) quality and nutritional adequacy of food, and (d) utilization of food. Food in-security, can therefore, be a failure of one of these factors or some combination of these factors. Food security is an essential foundation for meeting various Millennium Development Goals (MDGs) related to hunger, child mortality, mental health, disease, gender equality and primary education (Gill *et al.*, 2003). Availability of sufficient food at the country or local level does not mean that all people within that geographical unit are food secure. Food security implies that food intake must be adequate in both qualitative and quantitative terms. However, the issue of quality of diet has received little attention in the food security debate at all levels (Bose and Dey, 2007). It is argued that continuing to improve access to carbohydrates when they are no longer limiting factor, will lead to increasing food utilization by the poor (Gill *et al.*, 2003; Ferro-Luzzi, 2002). An estimated 850 million people in the world today suffer from hunger. Of those, about 820 million live in developing countries, the very countries expected to be most affected by climate change. Governments, international organizations, civil society, the private sector and other actors, must work together to address these challenges and to devise appropriate strategies.

Sustainable development has become inevitable in all the spheres, including agriculture (Bhatia, 2006). Sustainability is not an option but imperative (GoI, 2001). *The World Commission on Environment and Development* (the Brundtland Commission, 1987) has defined the term 'Sustainable Development' as 'development that means the needs of the present without compromising the ability of future generations to meet their own needs'. Sustainability of agriculture has been interpreted in a number of ways in the recent literature. It is however, not a new concept. Organic methods of farming or 'permanent agriculture' which respected the integrity of the soil and related ecological systems have been referred to as 'sustainable' (Chopra, 1993). Jodha (1991) treats sustainability as a characteristics of the agricultural system and defined as 'it is the ability of the system, to maintain a certain well-defined level of performance over time, and if required to enhance the same through linkages with other systems without damaging the ecological integrity of the system'. At the farmers' level, sustainability concerns are expressed that the input levels have to be continuously increased in order to maintain the yield at the old level. This poses a threat to the economic viability and sustainability of crop production. A sustainable farming system is a system in which natural resources are managed so that potential yield and the stock of natural resources do not decline over time (Kumar and Mittal, 2006). The sustainable agriculture development is non-degrading, technologically appropriate, economically viable and socially acceptable and it ought to view in the context of need for enhancement of productivity, production and profitability of agriculture and above all, for improvement in the economic conditions of the farmers (Bhatia, 2006).

NEED FOR FOOD SECURITY

The need for food security arises primarily due to the fluctuations in food production and non-availability of sufficient food from domestic sources. The growth in foodgrain production has stagnated during recent past while the consumption need of the growing population is increasing. Large proportion of the world's underfed population starves not because of general food shortage but because of the insufficient access to food supplies or insufficient income to purchase good. Dr. Amartya Sen, the eminent economist, in his scholarly work on the Great Bengal Famine, has attributed the death of millions to the inadequacy, or rather non-existence of an official policy, to cope with the food supply crisis. Poverty of the lack of purchasing power, therefore, becomes the crucial consideration in attainment of food security. As most of the poor people in developing countries including India dwell in the countryside the policies relating to rural development in its comprehensive form encompassing development of agriculture, health, nutrition, education, literacy, etc. would alone lead to enduring solution to the problem of food insecurity, poverty, unemployment and social tension in the region (Ram, 1996).

Present Status of World Food Security

The world is facing many challenges; prominent among these are sustainable development, environmental degradation, and climate change and food security for growing population. On a global level, food security for all requires that the supply of food be adequate to meet the total demand for food. While this is a necessary condition for the achievement of food security, it is by no means sufficient. Although currently enough food is supplied globally, it is estimated that in 1990-92, some 823.8 million people in the developing countries had inadequate access to food, fundamentally because they lacked the ability to purchase or procure enough, that is, they lacked the means to exert effective demand. This figure, unacceptably high though it is, reflects a substantial degree of progress since the beginning of the 1970s; the number has declined in absolute terms from about 917 million and in relative terms from 35 percent of the population of developing countries to 20 percent, mainly as a result of progress in East Asia (including China) and parts of South Asia, such as India and Pakistan. As per *the State of Food Insecurity in the World, 2008 (FAO Publication)*, FAO estimates that 848 million people suffered from chronic hunger worldwide in 2003-05 (representing an increase of 6 million from the nearly 842 million in 1990-92), in which 832.2 million people were in developing countries. Fact that is more shocking emerged from recent provisional estimates of FAO shows that the number of chronically hungry people in 2007 were 923 million, increased by 75 million over 2003-05, with much of the increase attributed to high food prices. Given the continued and drastic price rises in staple cereals and oil crops well into the first quarter of 2008, the number of people suffering from chronic hunger is likely to have increased further. At 923 million people, the number of undernourished in 2007 was more than 80 million higher than in 1990-92, the base period for the World Food Summit (WFS) hunger reduction target. This makes the task of bringing the number of undernourished to 420 million by 2015 more difficult, especially in an environment of high food prices and uncertain global economic prospects. At the regional level, the largest increases in the number of undernourished people in 2007 occurred in Asia and the Pacific and in sub-Saharan Africa, the two regions that together accounted for 750 million (89 percent) of the hungry people in the world in 2003–05. FAO estimates that rising prices have plunged an additional 41 million people in Asia and the Pacific and 24 million in sub-Saharan Africa into hunger. The estimates presented in Table 2 refer to chronic undernourishment.

TABLE 2

Population Undernourished in the Developing Countries

(percent to total population)

Region	*1969-71*	*1979-81*	*1990-92*	*1996-98*	*2000-02*	*2003-05*
Sub-Saharan Africa	34	37	35	34	33	30
Near East and North Africa	25	9	8	10	10	08
East and South East Asia	43	29	17	13	13	11
South Asia	38	38	26	23	22	21
Latin America and the Caribbean	19	13	13	11	10	8
All developing regions	37	29	20	18	17	16

Source: SOFI, FAO, 2004 and 2008.

It is estimated that the world's population is expected to grow from 6 billion people in 2000 to 7.5 billion people in 2020.

The studies suggest that global agricultural production could be maintained relative to expected baseline levels over the next 100 years with moderate climate change. However, regional effects would be varying widely, and some countries may experience reduced output even if they take measures to adapt. Availability of land for farming is on the decline, and water for agriculture and other uses is increasingly scarce. Together these and other forces will challenge the capacity of the world's food production system (Rosegrant, 2001). Cereals constitute a major of diet of most of the developing countries like India. Cereal grain production kept pace with rising population in some nations, such as India. Many other countries turned increasingly to imports to feed their people, because either domestic production was too low or income rose far faster than population escalating demand for future food and foodgrains. Although developing countries will account for most of the increase in global demand for cereals, growth in their demand is not as rapid as it was earlier. Diversifying diet and slower population growth in developing countries, growth in cereal demand of developing world is projected to decline from 2.3 percent a year in 1974-97 to 1.3 percent in 1997-2020 (see, Table 3). The world demand for meat and poultry is forecast to rise by more than 55 and 40 percent respectively between 1997 and 2020 (for details, see Rosegrant, 2001).

Status of Food Security in India

Improving the food security is an issue of considerable importance for the developing countries like India where millions of people suffer from hunger and malnutrition. Ever since independence, agricultural development policies in India have aimed at reducing hunger, food insecurity, malnourishment and poverty at a rapid rate (Acharya, 2009). Achieving food security has been the overriding goal of agricultural policy in India. Food availability and stability were considered good measures of food security till the seventies and the achievement of self-sufficiency was accorded high priority in the food policies of developing countries, like India. There has been a significant change in the foodgrain scenario from a scarcity to a surplus situation because of the acceleration in the production of foodgrains in the 1980s. More significant,

TABLE 3

All Cereals Production, Demand and Trade Data: 1997 and 2020

Particular	1997				2020			
	Yield	Production	Demand	Net Trade	Yield	Production	Demand	Net Trade
Developed Countries	3377	853996	724980	104334	3976	1024392	822259	202133
United States	5334	337829	244430	76764	6469	424481	305192	119290
EU-15	5540	203900	172599	20042	5970	212527	183038	29489
Former Soviet Union	1448	124264	131287	-2905	1647	144480	136219	8261
Developing Countries	2316	1017055	1118002	-104334	3065	1472835	1674967	-202133
Latin America	2531	124584	138070	-15262	3654	207400	210907	-3507
Sub-Saharan Africa	948	69303	82505	-12374	1380	128528	155872	-27346
West Asia/North Africa	1975	85453	128991	-45080	2574	122474	195585	-73111
South Asia	1814	235477	238325	-3020	2460	331797	353298	-21501
Southeast and East Asia	6395	502204	529448	-27955	8480	682597	758188	-75590
World	2703	1871051	1842983	0	3383	2497227	2497227	0

Note: Yield-kg/ha; For net trade, positive figures indicate exports, negative figures indicate imports.

Source: IFPRI (2001).

foodgrains stocks held by the government have increased beyond the requirements. However, there are indications that the production performance of Indian agriculture during the 1980s has maintained a satisfactory growth rate, but there are indications of falling growth rate during the 1990s. Though India was successful in achieving self-sufficiency by increasing its food production and also improved its capacity to cope with year-to-year fluctuations in food production, it could not solve the problem of chronic household food insecurity.

The concept of food security has undergone considerable changes in recent years. India is one of the few countries, which have experimented with a broad spectrum of programmes for improving food security. It has already made substantial progress in terms of overcoming transient food insecurity by giving priority to self-sufficiency in foodgrains and through procurement and public distribution of foodgrains, employment programmes, etc. Thus, India has solved the problem of food security which is reflected in mounting buffer stocks, but there are millions of food insecure and undernourished people in India. The limitation is not food supply, but its distribution. Despite a significant reduction in the incidence of poverty, chronic food insecurity persists in a large proportion of India's population. The Indian government is more serous on this issue and therefore, the National Development Council (NDC) of India in its 53rd meeting held on 29th May, 2007 adopted a resolution to launch a 'Food Security Mission' comprising rice, wheat and pulses to increase the production of rice by 10 million tonnes, wheat by 8 million tonnes and pulses by 2 million tonnes by the end of the Eleventh Plan (2011-12). Accordingly, A Centrally Sponsored Scheme, *'National Food Security Mission'*, has been launched from 2007-08 to operationalise the above mentioned resolution (http://*agricoop.nic.in*).

TABLE 4

Annual Per Capita Consumption of farm and other products in India

(kg/p/y)

Group	*1983*	*1987*	*1993*	*1999*	*Change in last two decades (%)*
Cereal	140.29	138.67	123.02	120.67	-16.26
Pulses	10.14	10.27	123.02	10.55	3.89
Milk	39.04	48.37	123.02	62.19	37.22
Edible oil	4.1	4.74	123.02	8.71	52.93
V&F	44.27	56.36	123.02	72.92	39.29
MFE	4.69	5.1	123.02	6.19	24.23
Sugar	9.69	9.99	123.02	12.05	19.59
Sugar	31.21	29.81	123.02	32.96	5.31

Note: V&F=Vegetables and fruits; MFE= Meat, fish and eggs.
Source: Mittal (2006).

The single most important implication of India's rapid population growth during the second half of the twentieth century was the threat it posed to national food security. That threat reached dangerous proportions in the mid-1960s, leading to the launching of the Green Revolution, achievement of food self-sufficiency, and subsequently, a growing stock of surplus foodgrains by the mid-1970s. Infact, such a threat no longer exists for the country. Growth of food production has exceeded population growth for each of the past three decades. Statistics present a confusing picture of India's progress on food security. Both per capita foodgrain consumption and total calorific intake have declined slightly in recent years among all levels of the population (Tables 4 and 6). The factors influencing this trend are numerous and complex, however, it can be primarily attributed to, (i) reduction in calorie requirement due to a more sedentary life style among both the rural and urban population. Bicycle and bus travel, mechanized pumps and equipments, access to telephones and newspapers have reduced the physical work to a greater or lesser extent for most Indians, and (ii) diversification of the Indian diet to include a larger intake of fruits, vegetables, dairy products, sugar, oil and pulses, eggs, fish and meat products, thereby reducing the required intake of calories from cereals.

The food policy and agricultural development strategy adopted by India to improve the food security situation paid rich dividends, and the ensuring improvements in food security can be assessed from several angles. The most significant change was the increase in the domestic output of foodgrains, particularly cereals (Table 5). India's achievement since the 1960s and 1970s, of food security with respect to the production and distribution of staple crops, represents one of the most remarkable successes in agricultural development anywhere in the world. With food security now assured, a new set of challenges for these institutions is now emerging, for the green revolution that enabled food security has not brought universal alleviation of poverty in rural India. Nor has it been achieved without significant degrading impact on the bio-physical environment. The use of agrochemicals and irrigation has led to the degradation of land and of water quality on such a scale that levels of productivity have actually started to decline in many areas. The negative impact has also had a deleterious effect on the health of human being—farm workers and consumers alike—as well as on the natural flora and fauna, while the integrity of the landscape ecology as a whole has suffered most especially through its loss of bio-diversity. A key challenge in the face of thus plethora of systemic influences, is to design, develop and manage agri-food systems in India in ways that enable them to be sustainable in terms of the bio-physical environments in which they must operate, and to equitable and inclusive within the socio-cultural environments of the India of today of into the future.

TABLE 5

Production of Foodgrains in India

(million tonnes)

Period	*Cereals*					*Total*
	Rice	*Wheat*	*Coarse*	*Total*	*Pulses*	*foodgrains*
TE 1952-53	21.59	6.71	17.03	45.33	8.67	54.00
TE 1962-63	34.48	11.28	23.86	69.63	12.00	81.63
TE 1972-73	41.51	24.99	26.10	92.60	10.94	103.54
TE 1982-83	51.33	38.85	29.29	119.47	11.33	130.80
TE 1992-93	73.94	56.01	31.76	161.72	13.03	174.75
TE 2002-03	83.38	69.40	30.18	182.96	11.86	194.81
TE 2007-08	93.86	74.52	36.24	204.61	14.24	218.85

Note: TE-Triennium Endings.
Source: GoI (2008).

PHASES OF AGRICULTURAL GROWTH AND SUSTAINABILITY

Indian agriculture has witnessed tremendous changes during the last three decades following the adoption of green revolution technology during late 1960s'. India has made considerable progress in foodgrains production. The green revolution technology was initially adopted on a large scale in the regions well endowed with irrigation. As this technology possessed vast potential for increase in productivity, it led to impressive growth in agricultural output in the regions where it was adopted. Because of the spread of green revolution was highly skewed in favour of certain states and regions, this led to high growth in agricultural output in selected regions while the other regions suffered from stagnancy or poor growth in agricultural output (Chand and Chauhan, 1999). The spread of new technology and then pattern of growth of agriculture has, however brought in its wake uneven development across regions and crops (Deosthali and Nikam, 2004; GoI, 2005) and technological change resulted in widening the regional as well as interpersonal disparities (Bhalla and Alagh, 1979).

Indian agriculture has witnessed significant variations over the last five decades, there wee phases of significant growth and stagnation (Sawant, 1983 and Sawant and Achuthan, 1995). But over years the country has emerged out of the state of chronic hunger and abject dependence on the import, to achieve self-sufficiency in availability of foodgrains. Particularly, this was achieved even under the increasing pressure of population growth at a significant rate. The performance of agriculture growth could be broadly classified in to a few major phases (Deshpande *et al.*, 2004). The first phase covering period up to mid-1960s, widely known as pre-green revolution period, was marked by growth achieved through area expansion. The agricultural production of all crops registered an annual growth of 3.15 per cent with the growth rate in area of 1.58 per cent and productivity of 1.21 per cent (Table 6). Despite major achievement in the initiatives taken by the government, the foodgrain production was not adequate to meet the needs of growing population, particularly from year 1961. The imports of foodgrains increased steeply from 3.5 million tonnes in 1961 to 10.36 million tonnes in 1966. The possibility of increasing production by bringing more additional area under cultivation was limited. Hence, it was felt necessary to look for alternatives to meet the demand of increasing population in the near future. The situation worsened by the droughts in two successive years in mid-sixties. As a response the Green Revolution was ushered in through adoption of high yielding varieties seeds (wheat and rice) and increased use of chemical fertilizers under irrigated conditions. During this phase the country witnessed to a significant growth in foodgrains production. The growth in this periods was characterized by productivity-led growth. Soon the negative externalities of the technological changes began surfacing in various forms (Deshpande, *et al.*, 2004, Bhalla, 2007). The decade of nineties showed mixed performance for the agricultural sector. Initially, the agricultural sector showed

TABLE 6

Compound Growth Rate of Area, Production and Yield of Principle Crops in India

(Base: TE 1981-82=100), percent per annum, A – Area; P – Production; Y – Yield

Crop	1949-50 to 1964-65			1967-68 to 2007-08			1980-81 to 1989-90			1990-91 to 1999-2000			2000-01 to 2007-08		
	A	P	Y	A	P	Y	A	P	Y	A	P	Y	A	P	Y
1	2	3	4	5	6	7	8	9	10	11	12	13	14	15	16
Rice	1.21	3.5	2.25	0.5	2.48	2.01	0.41	3.62	3.19	0.68	2.02	1.34	-0.14	1.87	2
Wheat	2.69	3.98	1.27	1.22	3.75	2.5	0.46	3.57	3.1	1.72	3.57	1.83	1.29	1.36	0.08
Jowar	0.99	2.51	1.49	-1.99	-0.67	1.35	-0.99	0.28	1.29	-3.53	-3.07	0.48	-2.9	0.34	3.37
Bajra	1.08	2.34	1.24	-0.82	1.36	2.2	-1.05	0.03	1.09	-1.46	0.95	2.44	0.31	4.53	4.21
Maize	2.67	3.88	1.18	0.56	2.55	1.97	-0.2	1.89	2.09	0.94	3.28	2.32	3.5	5.84	2.26
Coarse Cereals	0.9	2.25	1.23	-1.41	0.62	1.91	-1.34	0.4	1.62	-2.12	-0.02	1.82	-0.41	3.25	4.25
Total Cereals	1.25	3.21	1.77	-0.07	2.48	2.18	-0.26	3.03	2.9	0.04	-0.02	1.59	0.16	1.95	3.1
Gram	1.64	2.66	1	-0.39	0.35	0.75	-1.41	-0.81	0.61	1.26	2.96	1.68	4.7	5.51	0.77
Tur	0.57	-1.34	-1.9	1.03	1.04	0.01	2.3	2.87	0.56	-0.66	0.89	1.55	0.91	3.66	2.74
Other Pulses	2.06	1.28	-0.77	0	1.02	1.01	0.02	3.05	3.03	-1.61	-1.58	0.04	0.76	1.59	0.82
Total Pulses	1.72	1.41	-0.18	0.02	0.75	0.7	-0.09	1.52	1.61	-0.6	0.59	0.93	1.91	3.42	1.65
Foodgrains	1.35	2.82	1.36	-0.05	2.25	1.99	-0.23	2.85	2.74	-0.07	2.02	1.52	0.48	2.09	2.82
Sugarcane	3.28	4.26	0.95	1.71	2.72	0.99	1.44	2.7	1.24	-0.07	2.73	1.05	1.89	2.2	0.3
Groundnut	4.01	4.34	0.31	-0.25	0.85	1.1	1.67	3.76	2.06	-2.31	-1.25	1.08	-0.23	3.17	3.41
Sesamum	0.14	-0.32	-0.46	-1.08	1.1	2.2	-0.52	3.2	3.74	-5.52	-4.84	0.72	1.03	3.98	2.91

(Contd.)

TABLE 6 *(Contd.)*

1	*2*	*3*	*4*	*5*	*6*	*7*	*8*	*9*	*10*	*11*	*12*	*13*	*14*	*15*	*16*
R & M	2.97	3.35	0.37	2.01	4.47	2.41	1.95	7.28	5.22	0.71	0.78	0.07	6.03	8.17	2.02
Nine Oilseeds	2.53	3.12	0	1.45	3.16	1.67	2.47	5.36	2.49	0.17	1.42	1.42	3.38	7.23	3.7
Total Oilseeds	2.67	3.2	0.3	1.19	3.11	1.63	1.51	5.2	2.43	-0.86	1.63	1.15	2.71	6.69	4.91
Cotton	2.47	4.55	2.04	0.4	2.95	2.54	-1.25	2.8	4.1	2.71	2.29	-0.41	1.45	17.48	15.79
Non Foodgrains	2.44	3.74	0.89	1.26	3.06	1.61	1.12	3.77	2.31	1.18	2.69	1.09	2.46	5.09	3.87
All Crops	1.58	3.15	1.21	0.29	2.56	1.86	0.1	3.19	2.56	0.27	2.29	**1.33**	**1.06**	**3.17**	**3.88**

Source: GoI (2008).

positive signs of growth but soon under the pressure of inter-sectoral growth pulls the investment trends in the agricultural sector showed signs of deceleration. The situation was further impacted by signing of the WTO agreement on agriculture and that placed additional factor in front of the policy planners. A clear picture of intensifying stress in the agriculture sector was emerging and that took very ugly culmination in a few regions.

DECLINING PER CAPITA FOODGRAINS AVAILABILITY IN INDIA

The per capita availability of foodgrains has fallen substantially during the last decade of reforms, and the maximum decline has taken place during the last five years. The population and foodgrains production growth, per capita availability of foodgrains is presented in Table 7. Although there is wide variability from one year to the next, broad trends can still be picked up from this figure showing multi-decadal data. The early years of bounty from the green revolution period were followed by more gradual increases leading up to a peak of 186.2 kg/person/year at national level in 1990-91. Since then, however, food security has steadily declined, throughout what is popularly referred to as the years of liberalization and 'reforms'. As per 2001 data, per capita availability of foodgrains is typical of availability seen in the late 1970s and early 1980s, which was at lower stage of about 152 kg at national level. It is due to the fact that during the last decade, the foodgrains production grew at the rate of 1.60 percent per annum at national level. High growth rate during 1970-71 to 1980-81 was due to the low production base (due to drought). During overall period (1960-61 to 2000-01), the foodgrains production increased at the rate of 2.59 percent per annum at national level.

It can be seen from the above Table 7 that India has made rapid progress in the production of foodgrains during last four decades. India achieved near self-sufficiency in the availability of foodgrains by the mid-seventies. The trend rate of foodgrain production improved from 2.5 per cent during the 1960s to 2.9 per cent in the eighties (Bhalla and Singh, 2001). It is particularly noteworthy that India could build enough buffer stocks to cope with year-to-year variations in foodgrain production. The annual fluctuations in the per capita availability of foodgrain declined in the eighties and nineties when compared to the previous period (Rao and Radhakrishna, 1997). There seems to have been some diversification in food production in the 1980s on account of the impressive growth of output of oilseeds, non-foodgrain and livestock products. The diversification of food production more or less conforms to the growth pattern of domestic demand. The growth of food production slowed down to 2.72 percent per annum in the nineties. Ironically, even at the low growth rate of foodgrain production, the supplies outstripped the effective demand and the nineties has seen a rapid increase in the stock of foodgrain held by the government. Disposal of stocks has become a cause of concern. The domestic supplies are more than adequate to prevent food gaps.

TABLE 7

Net Availability of Foodgrains in India

(kg/person/year)

Years	*Rice*	*Wheat*	*Other Cereals*	*Cereals*	*Gram*	*Pulses*	*Food-grains*
1951	58.0	24.0	40.0	122.0	8.2	22.1	144.1
1961	73.4	28.9	43.6	145.9	11.0	25.2	171.1
1971	70.3	37.8	44.3	152.4	7.3	18.7	171.1
1981	72.2	47.3	32.8	152.3	4.9	13.7	166.0
1991	80.9	60	29.2	171.0	4.9	15.2	186.2
2001	69.5	49.6	20.5	141.0	2.9	10.9	151.9
2005	64.7	56.3	21.7	142.7	3.9	11.5	154.2
2007	71.8	57.0	20.8	149.6	4.3	10.7	160.4

Source: GoI (2008).

HIGH INCIDENCE OF POVERTY AND FOOD SECURITY

India's agricultural growth has been sufficient to move the country from severe food crises of the 1960s to aggregate food surplus today. Despite sizeable national food stocks, widespread poverty and hunger remain because agricultural and national economic growth have not adequately benefited disadvantaged regions and the poor (Kerr, 1996). In the Indian context average farm size is very small, and poverty and food security continue to be preponderant among small holders, and therefore the notion of sustainable agriculture ought to be viewed in the context of need for enhancement of productivity, production and profitability of agriculture and also for the improvement in the economic conditions of the farmers (Kumar, *et al.*, 2006a). The poor agricultural productivity and production, and low level of foodgrain outputs resulting from the low level introduction of agricultural/crop technologies; poor rural infrastructure; high vulnerability of crop production to natural disasters such as floods and droughts; and high rates of unemployment and poverty, are some of the reasons for the high degree of food insecurity (Kumar, 2003). Since sustainable development is expected to produce a favourable impact in terms of reducing inequity and poverty, it would proper to treat it also as an indicator of sustainable development (Nadkarni, 1993).

Poverty is the primary cause of hunger, and of chronic food insecurity. In the mid-1980s, 72 per cent of the world's poor and 66 per cent of the world's extremely poor lived on the Asia-Pacific region. (Swaminathan, 2006). Fostering rapid and sustained agricultural and rural growth and development remain key priorities of the government of India. India made significant advances towards achieving its goals of rapid agricultural growth, improving food security and reducing poverty during the last four decades (World Bank, 2005). Despite self-sufficiency in food production, millions of people in India remain underfed and underemployed. While poverty is multifaceted, manifested in terms of lack of access to food, health, education, shelter, information, quality and other rights and services, we still measure poverty on the basis of consumption expenditure associated with a normative requirement of calorie intake. Economic poverty is an important factor affecting food security at the household level (Acharya, 2007). Poverty is a major cause of food insecurity and sustainable progress in poverty eradication is critical to improve access to food. Over the years, the incidence of poverty, both rural and urban poverty has declined considerably. The percentage of population below poverty line declined from 51.3 per cent in 1977-78 to 38.9 percent in 1987-88 and finally to 26.1 per cent in

1999-2000, which according to some scholars may have been even lower (Bhalla, 2003). However, the absolute number of poor or food-insecure people continues to be sizeable (Table 8).

TABLE 8

Incidence of Poverty in India

Year	*Poverty ratio (%)*			*Number of poor (million)*		
	Rural	*Urban*	*Total*	*Rural*	*Urban*	*Total*
1977-78	53.1	45.2	52.3	264.3	64.6	328.9
1983-84	45.7	40.8	44.5	252.0	70.9	322.9
1987-88	39.1	38.2	38.9	231.9	75.2	307.1
1993-94	37.3	32.4	36.0	244.0	76.3	320.3
1999-00	27.1	23.6	26.1	193.2	67.1	260.3
2007*	21.1	15.1	19.3	170.5	49.6	220.1

Note:*Projected
Source: GoI (2008a).

CROP USE FOR BIOFUEL

As mentioned earlier, the use of foodgrains for manufacturing of bio fuel in US and other countries to meet the energy need of industrial and transportation sector has resulted in diversion of main crop like corn, maize and beans. This has been particularly beneficial for developed countries like the US and EU in more than one way. These countries can give support and subsidies to their producers for producing biofuel crops for domestic use without inviting the ire of other countries or any question at the WTO. The trend towards biofuel production also helps in reducing subsidies and tariff as it leads to higher prices. Substitution of fossil by biofuel is also helpful in meeting the requirements of the Kyoto Protocol on climate change to reduce greenhouse gas emissions. US is looking for energy security and is working hard to reduce its dependence for oil on the Organisation of Petroleum Exporting Countries (OPEC) and other petroleum exporting countries. Liquid biofuel is seen as an important alternative to achieve this goal. No wonder, close to one-fourth of the total corn produced in the US was used for biofuel during 2007-08 as against 11.9 per cent five years back. According to the US Department of Agriculture (USDA), one-third of corn produced in the US would be used for bio-energy during 2008-09 (see, Table 9). As mentioned before, diversion of grain as feedstock to produce bio-energy in the form of ethanol triggered a shift in demand for grains and caused a major surge in their prices over the last two years. The magnitude of the impact of the diversion of grain for biofuel can be seen from the fact that this quantity equals one-third of the global trade in cereals and it can increase cereal availability by 12.4 kg for the entire population of the world. If corn alone, used for biofuel in the US, is made available as food, it would increase the availability of cereals used as food by close to 10 per cent for the whole population of the world (Chand, 2008). With this the question of food security of the increasing population has emerged. In future, the problems of dwindling food security and environmental sustainability will aggravate because the total food production remained constant over the last two decades with growing environmental and socio-economic challenges. Use of bio-fuel may encourage a war between food and fuel. Production of biofuel may lead to decrease in land available for food production creating scarcity of food.

TABLE 9

Use of Corn for Ethanol Production in the US

(in million tonnes)

Particulars	*2002-03*	*2007-08*	*2008-09*
Corn used for ethanol production	27.1	81.6	108.9#
Corn used for ethanol production as % of total corn production in US	11.9	24.6	32.8
Corn used for ethanol prod. as % of Total Global corn production	4.5	11.6	15.4

Note: #. Planned estimate reported by US.

Source: http://www.fas.usda.gov/grain_arc.asp

DEMAND, PRODUCTION AND AVAILABILITY OF CEREALS IN INDIA BY 2020

India's population is still rapidly expanding. The living standards are rising and slated to rise faster than in the past. As they rise, both calorific intake and diversification of diet will increase significantly. Although portion of this increase can and will be obtained from abroad, a fulfilling vision of India 2020 depicts this nation with its conducive and varied climate, the largest irrigated area in the world and a vast farming population, as a major food exporter. Both as a challenge and as an opportunity, India can and must do much more to modernize and diversify its agriculture to meet the increased domestic and international demand for a wide variety of food products. Continued growth of the agriculture sector is particularly important because it plays such a vital role in generating purchasing power among the rural population. However, the challenge of achieving food security for all our people remains a real one even today, and will continue to demand our attention in the coming decades. Food security depends on both availability of food and access to it. Long-term food security requires not only producing sufficient food to meet the market demand, but also ensuring that all citizens have the required purchasing power to obtain the food they need for a nutritious and healthy life. Nearly half of the population still suffers from chronic under-nutrition. The most vulnerable are children, women and the elderly, especially among the lower income groups. In order to pace with growth of population, India needs an agricultural growth rate of 4.0 to 4.5 per cent to reduce poverty and food insecurity significantly (Rao and Radhakrishna, 1997).

In view of changing demand for food by income and population growth, urbanization, food prices and income distribution, India has to take necessary steps towards getting food security as the growth of cereal production barely kept pace with the growth of population and the country continues to be barely self-sufficient in cereal production. Even this self-sufficiency is merely technical, because 20 crore Indians are still not getting enough food for want of purchasing power. It is projected that demand for cereals for the year 2020 range from

223.6 million tonnes to 296.2 million tonnes, however, the estimates of availability of cereals from domestic production range from 222.0 million tonnes to 267.8 million tonnes only (Table 10).

TABLE 10

Demand, Production and Availability of Cereals in India for 2020

(in million tonnes)

Source of Estimate	*Estimated Demand*	*Estimated Production*	*Estimated Availability*
Rosegrant, Mark W., *et. al.* (1995)	237.3	256.2	237.0
Bhall, G.S. (1999)	296.2	251.0	232.2
Kumar, Parduman	254.5	269.9-309.9	249.7-285.9
U.S. Department of Agriculture	267.0	240.0	222.0
Rangi, P.S. *et al.* (for wheat and rice only)	208.92-209.87	188.82-218.54	174.66-202.15
Paroda, R.S.	260-287	-	-
Thamarajakshi	274-287	-	-
Dyson Tim and H. Hanchata	223.6	-	-
Bansal, P.C.	241.35	-	-

Note: Cereals includes wheat, rice and other grains.
Source: Shergill, 2007.

EFFECT OF NATURAL RESOURCE DEGRADATION ON FOODGRAINS PRODUCTION

During last three decades, the issues affecting various aspects of sustainable development have been raised and discussed, both intensively and extensively in the international flora. Since uncontrolled population growth could accelerate the rate of exhaustion of non-renewable resources and thereby make development unsustainable, issues relating to sustainable agricultural development have been at the forefront of discussions. Especially after the green revolution in India in the early 1970s and the achievement of food security for the economy, controversies started since the mid-1980s, as to whether this agricultural development is compatible with environmental sustainability. The rapid population growth and economic development in country are degrading environment through the uncontrolled growth of urbanization and industrialization, expansions and intensification of agriculture, and the destruction of natural habitats. The increasing resource degradation problems such as groundwater depletion, water logging, salinity, and land degradation would add to the challenges. Mainly, food security of the poor will be at risk, as they would face severe resource constraints not only in accessing water, but also in investing in land and water management. Already, regions such as Gujarat, which face groundwater depletion problems, land degradation, and frequent droughts are highly food insecure. On the other hand, in regions like Bihar and Orissa, low agricultural productivity and output, and high poverty rates leave millions, especially those in rural areas, undernourished (Kumar, 2003). In addition to this, weakening agricultural performance during last one decade in a large number of states is a national concern and importantly marked slow-down in growth rates in the traditional green revolution states and breadbaskets of the country, namely, Punjab, Haryana and Utter Pradesh is a major concern (World Bank, 2005). The slowing pace of growth in agricultural output is being further complicated by decreasing per capita availability of arable land. In addition, the climate change risks will have adverse impacts on food production, compounding the challenge of meeting global food demand. Thus, the need to intensify agricultural production from the finite natural resources has assumed greater significance (Awathi, 2007).

Environmental concerns are among the policy priorities in India, particularly degradation of land and water is alarming (Dev, 2009). Environmental impacts of technological change when discussed in the recent past pointed out that the various components of the technology led to certain problems. Among the environmental problems listed out, the prominent are: (i) reduction in soil fertility, (ii) excessive use of fertilizers and imbalances of nutrient content in the soil, (iii) biomass availability of terms of fodder and organic manure, (iv) genetic erosion, (v) water-logging and salination, (vi) depletion of groundwater table, (vii) imbalances in nutrient availability due to changes in the cropping pattern, and (viii) contamination of water bodies and soil with pesticides and fertilizers.

LAND DEGRADATION

Land, a non-renewable resource, is central to all primary production systems. Over the years, the country's landmass has suffered from different types of degradations. Degradation of land is caused by biotic and abiotic pressures. An ever increasing population places enormous demands on land resources. This is particularly acute in India, which has only 2.4 per cent of the world's geographical area but supports over 16 per cent of the world's population. It has 0.5 per cent of the world's grazing area but has over 18 per cent of world's cattle population. These pressures have led to drastic changes in the proportion of land utilized for agricultural activities, urbanization and industrial development. Land degradation has a direct bearing on the productivity of soil, its vulnerability to rainfall variations, scarcity of drinking water, fodder and fuel wood. Given the interlinkages of crop production, livestock economy and environment, land degradation has a major impact on the livelihoods of the people, especially in rural areas (GoI, 2002b).

Land degradation by deforestation, erosion and waterlogging are the gravest problems of Indian agriculture (Nadkarni, 1993). Land degradation could indeed be a potentially serious threat to food production and rural livelihoods by the year 2020, particularly densely populated pockets of rural poverty. It can be difficult to assess the actual extent and impact of land degradation. Farmers often mask the effects of degradation by converting their land to less demanding uses or increasing levels of compensating inputs, for example, applying more fertilizer just to maintain stable yield. Several studies have estimated degraded land area in India. As per the guidelines of the Global Assessment of Soil Degradation and by using data from various sources such as remote sensing data, soil maps of India, Sehgal and Abrol (1994) estimated the national figures and effect of land degradation on crop yields. They estimated that about 187.7 million hectares land is degraded by various sources (Table 11), which is quite large, even after adjusting the figures cover only agricultural land. The impact of degradation on yield ranges from 4.7 percent to 10 percent. Also the continued spread of degradation could have debilitating effect on food output growth and if the current level of degradation were reduced through investments to improve soils conditions, then presumably yields could rise. As per *Centre Water Commission of India (2004)*, nearly 173.64 million hectares of land is degraded (see, Table 14) and problem of land degradation is most severe in Rajasthan, followed by Madhya Pradesh, Maharashtra and Uttar Pradesh.

TABLE 11

Extent of Soil Degradation Severity in India and Yield Implication of Soil Degradation

Type of degradation	*Severity of degradation (million hectares)*				*Total Area*
	Low	*Medium*	*High*	*Very High*	
Water erosion	5.0	24.3	107.2	12.4	148.9
Wind Erosion (loss of top soil, due to terrain deformation/due to over-blowing)	0	0	10.8	2.7	13.5
Chemical deterioration (Loss of nutrients and Salination)	2.8	2	9	0	13.8
Physical deterioration (Water logging)	6.4	5.2	0	0	11.6
Total Area	14.2	31.5	127.0	15.1	187.7
Yield Implications (loss in %)*	up to 15%	15-33 %	33-67 %	uneconomical unmanageable and to use	

Notes: *Negligible loss (up to 15%), early manageable, Moderate loss (15-33%), soils can be managed at farm level, Significant loss (33-67%), affected area not economical to cultivate, could have other uses such as agro-forestry, Unmanageable and uneconomical to use.

Source: Sehgal and Abrol, 1994

Another ecological process that is supposed to have eroded the sustainability of agriculture is the soil fatigue caused by this monoculture. The continuous cultivation of wheat, rice, sugarcane monoculture over the last four decades, it is asserted, has resulted in a serious deficiency of micro-nutrients in the soil and has adversely affected its fertility. Among the other reasons, the virtual stagnation of these crops yields in recent years is attributed to the decline in soil fertility caused by this monoculture.

DEPLETION OF GROUNDWATER

Irrigation is the largest user of water in India. Irrigation would continue to play an unquestionable role in achieving food self-sufficiency, creating grain surpluses, stabilizing food prices, sustaining agricultural growth, absorbing labour force in rural areas, and alleviating rural poverty; all of which are vital for food security (Kumar, 2003). Many researchers have argued that increasing water shortage would be a major challenge to achieving global food security (Leisinger, 1996). Groundwater accounts for more than 50 percent of the net irrigated area, and nearly 80 percent of the agricultural production from irrigated areas in the country. Its contribution to the nation's food basket is quite significant. Over and above, groundwater is a decentralised and democratic resource. This is unlike canal irrigation wherein investment is mainly from the State, and access is restricted by topographic constraints. By virtue of this unique characteristic of groundwater, its contribution to local food security is great. In arid and semi-arid areas, the increased demand for water for agriculture and other uses is being met by excessive withdrawal of groundwater, leading to its depletion and quality deterioration. One is the fast depletion of groundwater resources said to be caused by wheat, rice and sugarcane cultivation on a large area, which cannot be sustained if the groundwater table continues to fall at the current rate. Given India's unique food security policy, there is a growing need to manage water for agriculture.

Over exploitation of ground water is leading to falling water levels in many areas especially, the hard rock areas (GoI, 2002). Recent research by many scholars and institutions have shown that the future water supplies are going to fall short of the demand from different sectors, with a differential negative impact on agriculture, if India continues to follow the same trajectory of water resource development and water use as in the past. Given the political economy of growth based on urbanization and industrialization, there will be a greater pressure to allocate an increasing quantum of water for industrial and municipal uses. This will pose a threat to food security at the aggregate level. The problems would be acute in semi-arid Gujarat, Tamil Nadu, Rajasthan and Maharashtra, which also experience ever increasing demand for water in all sectors.

TABLE 12

Critical and Over Exploited Blocks/Mandals/Talukas in Groundwater in India

States	*Total No. of Assessed Units*	*Critical*		*Overexploited*	
		Nos.	*%*	*Nos.*	*%*
Andhra Pradesh	1231	77	6	219	18
Gujarat*	223	12	5	31	14
Haryana	113	111	10	55	49
Karnataka	175	3	2	65	37
Punjab	137	5	4	103	75
Rajasthan*	237	50	21	140	59
Tamil Nadu*	385	33	9	142	37
Uttar Pradesh	803	13	2	37	5
Total (including UTs)	5723	226	4	839	15

Notes: *Rest blocks are saline, UT—Union Territories.
Source: CGWB (2006) (http://cgwb.gov.in).

The rapid development of ground water has led to over exploitation of ground water in the country. In 15 percent of the blocks the annual extraction of ground water exceeds annual recharge and in 4 percent of blocks it is more than 90 percent of recharge. As the ground water recedes wells have to be deepened and more energy has to be used to pump water. The status of ground water use in the country shows two challenges: how to restrain ground water use to sustainable level in over exploited regions and the second to develop the large untapped ground water potential in Eastern India (GoI, 2008b). It can be seen from Table 12 that the out of 5723 numbers of assessment administrative units (blocks/taluks/mandals/watershed), 15 percent units are overexploited, 4 percent units are critical, 10 percent are semi-critical, 71 percent are safe and 30 units are saline (http://wrmin.nic.in). Highly intensive development of ground water in certain areas in the country has resulted in over exploitation leading to decline in the levels of ground water and sea water intrusion in coastal areas.

PROBLEMS OF WATER-LOGGING AND SALINITY

In addition to above, the problems of water-logging and salinity pose a serious threat to sustainability of agriculture in command areas. Intensive agricultural practices that rely heavily on water, chemical fertilizers and pesticides have caused waterlogging and salinity in many parts of the country. As per *Central Water Commission of India (2004)*, nearly 8.53 million hectares of land is affected by waterlogging and 7.62 million hectares land is salt affected (www.cwc.nic.in). This trend is caused by excessive irrigation from canal water and under-utilization of groundwater. The underlying cause is the incredibly low water rates and the poor control over water delivery. The problem of waterlogging is most severe in Haryana, followed by Punjab (Table 13). Waterlogging leads to salinity of groundwater and soils, causing permanent degradation of land and sharp productivity declines. Yield declines are reported from the canal-irrigated areas of Punjab, Uttar Pradesh and Haryana.

NEED OF SUSTAINABLE AGRICULTURE

As discussed above, many traditional and most conventional farm practices are not ecologically sustainable as they overuse natural resources, reducing soil fertility, causing soil erosion, and contributing to global climatic change. Sustainable agriculture has several major advantages over both traditional and conventional practices. A continuous fall in soil fertility is a major problem in many parts of India. Sustainable agriculture improves fertility and soil structure and prevents erosion, so would be an answer to this problem. Irrigation is the biggest consumer of fresh water, and fertilizer and pesticides

TABLE 13

Area Affected by Waterlogging and Salinity and other Reasons in Indian States

(Area in lakh ha)

Name of the State	*Water Erosion*	*Wind Erosion*	*Water logged*	*Salt affected*	*Ravines*	*Shifting cultivation*	*Degraded forests*	*Special problems*	*Total degraded land*
A.P.	103.54	-	3.39	2.4	-	1.5	11.48	-	122.31
Bihar	32.39	-	7.07	0.04	6.0	0.85	10.21	9.0	65.52
Gujarat	94.62	7.04	4.84	10.42	4.0	-	4.84	0.10	125.86
Haryana	15.35	14.0	6.2	5.2	-	-	0.56	0.25	41.62
Karnataka	102.25	-	0.1	4.04	-	-	7.64	-	114.03
M. P.	155.1	-	0.57	2.42	6.83	1.25	41.0	-	207.17
Maharashtra	175.89	-	1.11	5.34	0.2	-	15.92	-	198.46
Orissa	27.71	-	0.6	4.04	1.13	26.48	18.07	2.95	78.03
Punjab	9.14	-	10.9	7.18	1.2	-	0.93	-	32.3
Rajasthan	188.41	156.92	3.48	10.0	4.52	-	10.61	-	373.94
Tamil Nadu	32.42	-	0.18	1.04	0.6	-	3.98	-	38.22
U. P.	58.98	-	19.8	12.95	12.3	-	12.12	15.00	131.15
West Bengal	7.64	-	21.6	9.86	1.04	-	2.69	-	43.03
India	1071.26	177.96	85.26	76.1	39.75	49.16	194.94	27.3	1721.75

Source: CWC (2004), www.cwc.nic.in

contaminate both surface and groundwater. Sustainable agriculture increases the organic matter content of the topsoil, so raising its ability to retain and store water that falls as rain. Sustainable agricultural practices frequently involve mixed cropping, so increasing the diversity of crops produced and raising the diversity of insects and other animals and plants in and around fields. Pesticides are hazardous to human health as well as to the local ecology. Incorrect handling, storage and use of pesticides lead to health and pollution problems. Sustainable agriculture reduces or eliminates the use of hazardous chemicals; instead it controls pests with a variety of biological and agronomic measures and the use of natural substances. Agriculture and forestry clothe the rural landscape.

Inappropriate use causes erosion, landslides and flooding, clogs irrigation channels, and reduces the ability of the land to support the local population. Impoverished rural people flock into the cities in search of jobs, forming unsightly, insanitary slums that further destroy the landscape. Rehabilitating ecologically damaged areas needs huge investments that few countries can afford. Sustainable agriculture avoids these problems by improving productivity, conserving the soil, avoiding the expansion of farming into unsuitable areas, and preserving rural jobs. The way agriculture is practiced contributes significantly to global climatic change. Conventional agriculture contributes to the production of greenhouse gases in various ways: by reducing the amount of carbon stored in the soil and in vegetation, through the production of methane in irrigated field and through energy intensive activities such as production of artificial fertilisers. Adopting sustainable agriculture would reduce these impacts significantly.

NEED OF PRODUCTIVITY GROWTH FOR FOOD SECURITY

Low production and productivity is the core of problems of Indian agriculture. Low productivity keeps the farmers impecunious and resource starved resulting into a vicious circle of low productivity and poverty in this prime sector of the economy. Despite substantial increase in the use of modern inputs, the agricultural productivity in India has remained low over a long period of time and even today (Table 14). The need to feed teeming millions propelled country to increase to use of fertilizers and adopt better agricultural practices, which have multifarious problems in India. The persistently growing use of external nutrients enormously raised the cost of farming and led the agriculture become an un-remunerative occupation. Secondly, excessive use of chemical fertilizers has increased the amount of alkalinity and salinity in soil causing long-term hazards to soil fertility and sustainable growth of agriculture. Third, growing demand of fertilizers has increased its prices, thus emerges the need of subsidy on domestic and imported budget deficit and adverse balance of payment.

As the increase in food production through area expansion is limited, therefore future increases in the food demand will

TABLE 14

Productivity of Major Crops in India and World

(kg/ha.)

Crop	*India*	*World*	*Highest Productivity (Country)*	*World Crop yield (% higher than India)*
Paddy	3124	4112	10598 (Egypt)	31.63
Wheat	2619	2804	8039 (U.K.)	7.06
Maize	1938	4815	9360 (Turkey)	148.45
Cereals	2453	3261	6973 (Netherland)	32.94
Pulses	603	835	4540 (Netherland)	38.47
Soybean	1063	2343	3969 (Turkey)	120.41
Groundnut	859	2149	20804 (Indonesia)	150.17
Sugarcane	66945	68257	129887 (Egypt)	1.96

Source: GoI (2008) and FAI (2008).

have to be essentially achieved through increase in yield per hectare. There is enormous scope for accelerating growth in agriculture, through improved soil nutrition and pest management, diversification into higher value-added crops, expansion and more efficient use of irrigation potential, rainwater harvesting, and infrastructure development for agro-processing industries. India's productivity on major crops ranks far below the world average. This low productivity contributes to low farm incomes and wages, lower on-farm employment generation, and relatively high food prices for all Indians. Infact some progressive farmers in India have achieved yields comparable to their foreign counterparts till recently; but these high achievers are a rare exception. Progressive farming must become the rule and the standard. Raising the productivity of our soil and water resources is an effective way to increase the profit margins of farmers, while at the same time reducing the cost of farm produce, so that it is more affordable to the masses. A minimum target should be to double or triple the average yields of major commercial crops. This will reduce pressure on scarce land and water resources as well as enable the country to utilize less fertile areas for other purposes.

Tapping the full potential of Indian agriculture to meet the rising domestic demand and to take advantage of the liberalization of international trade will require, first and foremost, the recognition of the vital role that agriculture can continue to play in national development. The other necessary conditions are: (i) greater public investment in research, (ii) expansion and development of rural infrastructure including roads, storage capacity and organized markets, (iii) improved farmer education, (iv) effective involvement of the private sector to provide technology, investment and organizational expertise for commercialization, and (v) modification of land regulations to achieve greater production efficiency. A suitable land use pattern will also need to be implemented, based on the principle that each region would focus on crops best suited to their agro-climatic characteristics, soil types and water resources. Strong measures will also be needed to address the problem of land degradation that affects an estimated 45 per cent of total land area. India's objective for 2020 must not only be to produce the food its population requires but also to fully exploit the comparative advantages it possesses agro-climatic variety, irrigation, scientific capabilities and low labour cost to become a low cost, high profit producer for the world market. In order to ensure food security on a sustainable basis, three concerns need to be addressed; (i) the adequate supply of irrigation water to sustain the growth in agricultural production at the national level, (ii) the water security for poor farmers to grow food for subsistence, and (iii) the adequate economic incentives for farmers to maximise their production from the available land and water with least environmental consequences (Kumar, 2003).

PUBLIC DISTRIBUTION SYSTEM (PDS)

The most important component of the food security system is public distribution of foodgrains through a net work of fair price shops. As on March 2004, there existed nearly 4 lakh shops, 3.05 lakh in rural and 0.94 lakh in urban areas. One fair price shop covers a population of about 2000 (Bhalla, 2007). The food management system instituted subsequent to the Committee's proposals consists of procurement, storage and public distribution of foodgrains. The main objective is to give price insurance to farmers to encourage them to increase food production and to provide food to consumers at reasonable prices. India has a large programme of public food distribution through fair price shops, accounting for a significant part of the government's budgetary subsidies. It was then mainly confined to urban and food deficit areas with its emphasis primarily on price stabilisation till the late seventies. The welfare dimension of the PDS has gained importance since the early eighties and its coverage has been extended to rural areas in some states as well as to areas with a high incidence of poverty. The food subsidy of the Central Government, at Rs. 17,612 crores, accounted for 0.89 per cent of GDP in 2001-02. In the wake of economic reforms, the PDS is perceived to be the main safety net to protect the poor from potential short-run price-induced adverse effects of economic reforms.

Till 1997, the public distribution system in India was universal in character. PDS has been criticized for its failure to serve the population below the poverty line, its urban bias, limited coverage in the states with high concentration of rural poor and lack of transparent and accountable arrangement of delivery. Therefore, targeted public distribution system (TPDS) was introduced in 1998. PDS supplies of wheat and rice have increased rapidly since the mid-sixties: the annual average supply increased from 7.82 mn tonnes in 1970-71 to 13.01 mn tonnes in 1980-81 and 19.10 mn tonnes in 1990-91. It remained around 17 to 10 mn tonnes during 1990-91 to 1999-2000. However, the off-take of rice and wheat collapsed after institution of TPDS and was low as 12.04 mn tonnes in 2000-01. It only revived in 2002-03 and reached a level of 29.57 mn tonnes in 2004-05. A noteworthy feature of these trends is the response of government supply to fluctuations in production; it is higher in drought years than in normal ones. For instance, in 1979-80 and 1987-88 the years associated with low foodgrain production the government supplies were substantially higher than in normal years. In both the years, the government increased the supplies through both PDS and employment generation programmes to prevent famine, though the procurement levels were lower than in normal years. It is noteworthy in this context that there were only a few instances of deaths due to starvation.

Many empirical studies have shown severe biases in the inter-regional distributions of the PDS supplies states with the high incidence of poverty such as Bihar, Orissa and Madhya Pradesh received a lower share. Further, with few exceptions, the PDS remained an untargeted programme. In comparison with other anti-poverty programmes, PDS has been found to be the costliest. In terms of cost of per rupee income transferred, PDS has also been found to be inferior to employment programmes. Therefore, re-focusing of PDS should be a priority task. However, fresh challenges to PDS may come from price volatility in the world market. Price stabilization will soon emerge as a major function of food management.

WTO AND FOOD SECURITY

The beginning of the 1990s saw the initiation of far reaching changes in the economic policy framework of India. A recent study by National Council of Applied Economic Research (NCAER) has calculated that free trade is likely to benefit India immensely since it is competitive in wheat, rice, cotton, and soybeans, but non-competitive in groundnut and rapeseed, mustard and near parity price in maize and sorghum (Bhalla, 2006). However, while advocating for bringing more flexibility in trade in agriculture, the need for maintaining a policy of self-sufficiency in foodgrains production need more emphasis/ attention. The implementation of Agreement on Agriculture (AoA) under WTO has raised concerns in India about the possibility of its destroying food security. These are justified because agriculture provides a lot of employment and food accounts for a major share of the expenditure of the poor (Dev, 2003). While the world trading environment has become more liberal, transparent and rule bound than before, it would have become even more favourable had the developed countries adhered strictly to the Uruguay Round agreement and permitted better access to imports from developing countries. In fact, India does not have to change her food policies relating to minimum support price, buffer stock and the public distribution system. The actual tariffs for most of the commodities in India are much lower than the Uruguay Round bound rates. As such, it can easily check edible oil imports by raising its tariff.

India seems to be a victim of thirty years of agricultural policy with an exclusive focus on spreading HYV seed fertilizer technology in a few potential regions for achieving food self-sufficiency. Consequent to the adoption of this strategy, India achieved self-sufficiency in foodgrains by the mid-seventies and is currently facing the problem of disposing off huge foodgrains stocks. It is observed that self-sufficiency in foodgrains is partly due to the weak purchasing power of the poor. As a remedial measure it is suggested that India should diversify its agriculture and get a foothold in the world food market. The diversified and accelerated agricultural growth would enhance the food security by improving the purchasing power of the poor. However, even after the establishment of WTO, the agricultural trade did not improve much during the transition period since agricultural prices have sharply declined in the world markets and there has been no reduction in the degree of protection by the developed countries. The protectionist measures are coming in the form of non-tariff measures and preventing the entry of agricultural commodities from developing countries by resorting to anti-dumping restrictions in one form or another. Some concessions under the Green and Blue Boxes do not favour developing countries. Some of these concerns should figure in future negotiations. It is argued that if India is to benefit from the emerging opportunities opened up by liberalized agricultural trade, major reforms have to be undertaken on the domestic front. It is recognized that cereal prices in the world market which have declined during the nineties are unlikely to rise on account of reforms in the developed countries. Fresh challenges also have come from the sharp fall in the international price of some commercial crops. As domestic food economy gets integrated with the world market, it will experience price volatility. India should depend on cost-reducing technology through domestic reforms, promote agricultural diversification and put pressure on the developed countries to open up their markets for value-added agricultural products prices which are more volatile than domestic prices.

CONCLUSION

The global food security is in question today with ever increasing food prices resulting from adverse climatic effects on agricultural production, increasing resource degradation, rise in oil prices, increasing use of grains for biofuels, and reduction in public spending on agricultural sector over the last three decades. The world food situation is currently being rapidly redefined by new driving forces. The influence of the private sector in the world food system, especially the leverage of food retailers, is also rapidly increasing. The world has experienced an unprecedented increase in population during the past century, with a billion people added every decade during the last three decades alone and global food prices witnessed a very sharp increase in 2007 and they are continuing to rise which is causing worldwide concern. Importance of food management and maintaining food security the world over has been abundantly recognized since long. The world food situation is currently being rapidly redefined by new driving forces. Income growth, climate change, high energy prices, globalization, and urbanization are transforming food consumption, production and markets. The need for food security arises primarily due to the fluctuations in food production and non-availability of sufficient food from domestic sources. Large proportion of the world's underfed population starves not because of general food shortage but because of the insufficient access to food supplies or insufficient income to purchase good. The slowing pace of growth in agricultural output is being further complicated by decreasing per capita availability of arable land. Also the climate change risks will have adverse impacts on food production, compounding the challenge of meeting global food demand. The world's population is expected to grow from 6 billion people in 2000 to 7.5 billion people in 2020. Availability of land for farming is on the decline, and water for agriculture and other uses is increasingly scarce. Together these and other forces will challenge the capacity of the world's food production system.

Achieving food security has been the overriding goal of agricultural policy in India. Indian agriculture has witnessed tremendous changes during the last three decades following the adoption of green revolution technology during late 1960s'.

However, per capita per day availability of foodgrains is almost stagnant. Despite the impressive growth and development, India is home to more than 230 million undernourished people, which is 21 percent of the national population. With about 251 million below the poverty line, India accounts for about one-fifth of the world poor. Though India was successful in achieving self-sufficiency by increasing its food production and also improved its capacity to cope with year-to-year fluctuations in food production, it could not solve the problem of chronic household food insecurity. India has solved the problem of food security which is reflected in mounting buffer stocks, but there are millions of food insecure and undernourished people in India. Thus, limitation is not food supply, but its distribution. The latest report on '*State of Food Insecurity in Rural India*' released by the World Food Programme and the M.S. Swaminathan Research Foundation (MSSRF) warns that high economic growth rates have failed to improve food security in India leaving the country facing a crisis in its rural economy. Slowing growth in food production, rising unemployment and declining purchasing power of the poor in India are combining to weaken the rural economy. The per capita availability of foodgrains has fallen substantially during the last decade of reforms, and the maximum decline has taken place during the last five years. In order to pace with growth of population, India needs an agricultural growth rate of 4.0 to 4.5 percent to reduce poverty and food insecurity significantly (GoI, 2002a). In view of changing demand for food by income and population growth, urbanization, food prices and income distribution, India has to make necessary steps towards getting food security. India's productivity on major crops ranks far below the world average and it has to increase at par. In the Indian context, average farm size is very small, and poverty and food security continue to be preponderant among small holders, the notion of sustainable agriculture ought to be viewed in the context of need for enhancement of productivity, production and profitability of agriculture and also for the improvement in the economic conditions of the farmers. The poor agricultural productivity and production, and low level of foodgrain outputs resulting from the low level introduction of agricultural/crop technologies; poor rural infrastructure; high vulnerability of crop production to natural disasters such as floods and droughts; and high rates of unemployment and poverty, are some of the reasons for the high degree of food insecurity. India has a large programme of public food distribution through fair price shops, accounting for a significant part of the government's budgetary subsidies. It was then mainly confined to urban and food deficit areas with its emphasis primarily on price stabilization till the late seventies. The welfare dimension of the PDS has gained importance since the early eighties and its coverage has been extended to rural areas in some states as well as to areas with a high incidence of poverty. However, fresh challenges to PDS may come from price volatility in the world market. Price stabilization will soon emerge as a major function of food management. The implementation of Agreement on Agriculture (AoA) under WTO has raised concerns in India about the possibility of its destroying food security. These are justified because agriculture provides a lot of employment and food accounts for a major share of the expenditure of the poor. In fact, India does not have to change her food policies relating to minimum support price, buffer stock and the public distribution system. The actual tariffs for most of the commodities in India are much lower than the Uruguay Round bound rates. As such, it can easily check edible oil imports by raising its tariff. In order to ensure food security on a sustainable basis, three concerns need to be addressed, viz., (i) the adequate supply of irrigation water to sustain the growth in agricultural production at the national level, (ii) the water security for poor farmers to grow food for subsistence, and (iii) and the adequate economic incentives for farmers to maximize their production from the available land and water with least environmental consequences. The challenge to food security comes mainly from the slow growth of purchasing power of the people in the rain-fed eco-systems. Efforts must be made to help them by developing drought resistant seeds, cost-effective dry-land farming techniques. In addition, rain water harvesting techniques, moisture conservation, inter-cropping are imperative to stabilize and improve the production in the dry-land areas. To promote sustainable agricultural growth, a regionally differentiated strategy-based agro-climatic conditions and land and water resource availability is needed.

References

Acharya, Shabd S. (2007), "National Food Polices Impacting on Food Security: The Experience of a Large Populated Country—India", in Basudeo Guha-Khasnosis, Shabd S. Acharya and Benjamin Davis (Eds) Food Insecurity, Vulnerability and Human Rights Failure, Studies in Development Economics and Policy, United Nation University, World Institute for Development Economics Research.

Acharya, Shabd S. (2009), "Food Security and Indian Agriculture: Polices, Production Performance and Marketing Environment", *Agricultural Economics Research Review*, Vol. 22, No. 1, pp. 1-20.

Awasthi, U.S. (2007), "Food Security and Fertilizer—A Global Perspective", IFFCO, New Delhi.

Bhalla G.S. (2007): 'Indian Agriculture since Independence', National Book Trust of India, New Delhi.

Bhalla, G.S. and Y.K. Alagh (1979), Performance of Indian Agriculture: A District-wise Study, Sterling Publisher, New Delhi.

Bhalla, G.S. and Gurmail Singh (2001), Indian Agriculture: Four Decades of Development, Sage Publications, N. Delhi.

Bhalla, G.S., Peter Hazell and John Kerr (1999), Prospects for India's Cereal Supply and Demand to 2020, International Food Policy Research Institute, Washington, Discussion Paper 29, November.

Bhalla, S.S. (2003), "Recounting the Poor: Poverty in India, 1983-99", *Economic and Political Weekly*, Vol. 38, No. 4, pp. 338-49.

Bhall, G.S. (2007), Globalization and Indian Agriculture, State of Indian Farmers—A Millennium Study, Vol. 19, Department of Agriculture and Cooperation, Ministry of Agriculture, Government of India, New Delhi.

Bhatia, M.S. (2006), "Sustainability and Trends in Profitability of Indian Agriculture", *Agricultural Economics Research Review*, Vol. 19, Conference Number, pp. 9-100.

Bose, M.L. and M.M. Dey (2005), "Food and Nutritional Security in Bangladesh: Going beyond Carbohydrates Counts", *Agricultural Economics Research Review*, Vol. 20, No 2, July December, pp. 203-25.

Braun, Jochim Von (2007), The World Food Situation: New Driving Forces and Required Action, International Food Policy Research Institute (IFPRI), Washington, D.C.

CGWB (2006), Dynamic Ground Water Resources of India (as on March 2004), Central Ground Water Board, Ministry of Water Resources, Government of India, Faridabad.

Chand, Ramesh (2008), "The Global Food Crisis: Causes, Severity and Outlook, *Economic and Political Weekly*, Vol. 43, No.26-27, June 28, 2008, pp. 115-23.

Chand, Ramesh and Sonia Chauhan (1999), Are Disparities in Indian Agriculture Growing, Policy Brief No. 8, National Centre for Agricultural Economics and Policy Research, New Delhi, October.

Chopra, Kanchan (1993), "Sustainability of Agriculture", *Indian Journal of Agricultural Economics*, Vol. XLVIII, No. 3, July-September, pp. 527-35.

CWC (2004), Water and Related Statistics, Information Systems Organisation,

Water Resource Information System Directorate, Water Planning and Projects Wing, Central Water Commission, New Delhi.

Deosthali, Vrishali and Chandrashekahr M. Nikam (2004), "Rice Region-wise Growth Trends in Maharashtra", *Economic and Political Weekly*, Vol. XXXIX, No. 3, January 17, pp. 240-42.

Deshpande R.S. and Prabhu Nagesh (2005)' Farmer Distress: Proof Beyond Doubt', *Economic and Political Weekly*, Vol. 40, Nos. 40 and 45, Oct. 29-Nov. 4, Mumbai.

Deshpande R.S., Bhende M.J., Thippaiah P. and Vivekananda M. (2004), "Crops and Cultivation", State of Indian Farmer: A Millennium Study, Vol. 9, Academic Foundation and Ministry of Agriculture, GoI, New Delhi.

Dev, Mahendra S. (2009), "Challenges for Revival of Indian Agriculture", *Agricultural Economics Research Review*, Vol. 22, No. 1, January-June, pp. 21-46.

Dev, Mahendra S. (2003), "World Trade Organisation and Food Security", in Towards a Food Secure India: Issues and Policies (Eds) by S. Mahendra Dev, K.P. Kannan and Nita Ramachandran, Institute for Human Development, Centre for Economic and Social Studies.

FAI (2008), Fertilizer Statistics, 2007-08, The Fertilizer Association of India, New Delhi.

FAO (2004, 2008), The State of Food Insecurity in the World, 2008, Food and Agriculture Organization.

Ferro-Luzzi, A. (2002), Individual Food Intake Survey Methods, Keynote paper presented at the International Scientific Symposium on Measurement and Assessment of Food Deprivation and Under-nutrition, 26-28 June, Rome, FAO.

George, P.S. (2006), "Some Reflections on Food Security in India", in N.A. Mujumdar and Uma Kapila (Eds) Indian Agriculture in the New Millennium—Changing Perceptions and Development Policy, Academic Foundations, New Delhi, pp. 194-226.

Gill, G.J., J. Farrington. E. Anderson, C. Luttrell, T. Conway, N.C. Saxena, and R. Slater (2003), Food Security and the Millennium Development Goal on Hunger in Asia, Working Paper 231, Overseas Development Institute, UK.

GoI (2001), Report of the Task Force on Greening India for Livelihood Security and Sustainable Development, Planning Commission, Government of India, July.

GoI (2002), National Water Policy, 2002, Ministry of Water Resources, Government of India, New Delhi, April.

GoI (2002a), Report of the Committee on India Vision 2020, Chairman, Dr. S.P. Gupta, Planning Commission, Government of India, New Delhi, December.

GoI (2002b), Development of Wastelands and Degraded Lands, Tenth Five Year Plan: 2002-2007, Vol. II, Planning Commission, Government of India, New Delhi.

GoI (2005, 2008a), Economic Survey of India, Ministry of Finance and Company Affairs, Economic Division, New Delhi.

GoI (2008), Agricultural Statistics at a Glance, Directorate of Economics and Statistics, Ministry of Agriculture, Government of India, New Delhi.

GoI (2008b), Agriculture, Rural Development, Industry, Services, and Physical Infrastructure, Vol. III, Eleventh Five Year Plan, 2007-12, Planning Commission, Government of India, New Delhi..

Goyal, P. 2002. Food Security in India, *The Hindu*, Jan 10.

Goyal, S.K. and J.P. Singh (2002), "Demand *versus* Supply of Foodgrains in India: Implications to Food Security", Paper presented at the 13th International Farm Management Congress, Wageningen, The Netherlands, July 7-12.

IFPRI (2001), IMPACT Projection, June (www. http://www.ifpri.org/pubs/books/gfp/gfp_apxd.pdf).

Jodha, N.S. (1991), "Sustainable Agriculture in Fragile Resource Zones: Technological Imperatives, *Economic and Political Weekly*, Vol. 26, No. 13, March 30, pp. A15-26.

Kalamkar, S.S. (2008), "Food Security in India in Global Perspective", Agricultural Situation in India, Vol. LXV, No. 5, Special Issue, August 2008, pp. 291-302.

Kerr, John (1996), Sustainable Development of Rainfed Agriculture in India, EPTD Discussion Paper No. 20, Environment and Production Technology Division, International Food Policy Research Institute, Washington, D.C., USA.

Kumar, M. Dinesh (2003), "Food Security and Sustainable Agriculture in India: The Water Management Challenge", Working Paper No. 60, International Water Management Institute, Colombo, Srilanka.

Kumar, Praduman (1996), "Agricultural Productivity and Food Security in India: Implications for Policy", *Agricultural Economics Research Review*, Vol. 9, No. 2, pp. 128-41.

Kumar, Praduman (2001), "Agricultural Performance and Productivity", in S.S. Acharya and D.P. Chaudhary (Eds) Indian Agricultural Policy at the Cross Road, Rawat, Jaipur.

Kumar, Praduman (2005), "Empowering the Small Farmers Towards a Food Secure India", in (Eds.) India's Agricultural Challenges: Reflections on Policy, Technology and other Issues, Centad Publications, New Delhi, pp. 197-225.

Kumar, Praduman and Surabhi Mittal (2006), "Agricultural Productivity Trends in India: Sustainability Issues", *Agricultural Economics Research Review*, Vol. 19, Conference Number, pp. 71-88.

Kumar, Praduman, N.P. Singh and V.C. Mathur (2006a), "Sustainable Agriculture and Rural Livelihoods: A Synthesis", *Agricultural Economics Research Review*, Vol. 19, Conference Number, pp. 1-22.

Leisinger, K.M., 1996, Food Security for a Growing World Population. Paper presented at the Saguf Symposium, "How will the Future World Feed Itself?", October 9-10.

Mittal, Surabhi (2006), Structural Shift in Demand for Food: Projections for 2020, Indian Council for Research on International Economic Relations (ICRIER), New Delhi.

Nadkarni, M.V. (1993), "Sustainable Development: Concept and issues with

Special reference to Agriculture", *Indian Journal of Agricultural economics*, Vol. XLVIII, No. 3, July September, pp. 5516-526.

Narayanamoorthy, A. (2006a), "Relief Package for Farmers: Can it Stop Suicides?", *Economic and Political Weekly*, Vol. 41, No. 31, August 5, pp. 3353-55.

Narayanamoorthy, A. (2006b), "State of India's Farmers", *Economic and Political Weekly*, Vol. 41, No. 6, February 11, pp. 471-73.

Narayanamoorthy, A. and S.S. Kalamkar (2005), "Indebtedness of Farmer Households across States: Recent Trends, Status and Determinants", *Indian Journal of Agricultural Economics*, Vol. 60, No. 3, July-September, pp. 290-301.

NSSO (2005a), Situation Assessment Survey of Farmers: Indebtedness of Farmer Households, Report No. 498, 59th Round (January-December, 2003), National Sample Survey Organization, Ministry of Statistics and Programme Implementation, Government of India, New Delhi, May.

NSSO (2005b), Situation Assessment Survey of Farmers: Some Aspects of Farming, Report No. 496, 59th Round (January-December, 2003), National Sample Survey Organization, Ministry of Statistics and Programme Implementation, Government of India, New Delhi, July.

Paroda, R.S. and Praduman Kumar (2000), "Food Production and Demand Situation in South Asia", *Agricultural Economics Research Review*, Vol. 13, No. 1,

Radhakrishna and C. Ravi (1990), Food Demand Projections for India, Centre for Economic and Social Studies, Hyderabad.

Radhakrishna, R. and K. Venkata Reddy (2002), Food Security and Nutrition: Vision 2020.

Ram, G.S. (1996), "Food Security System, Poverty and Rural Development", Presidential Address, *Agricultural Economics Research Review*, Vol. 9, No. 2, 121-27.

Rosergrant, Mark W., Michael S. Paisner, Siet Meijer and Julie Witcover (2001), 2020 Global Food Outlook—Trends, Alternatives, and Choices, International Food Policy Research Institute, Washington, D.C., August.

Sawant, S.D. and C.V. Achutan (1995): 'Agricultural Growth Across Crops and Regions: Emerging Trends and Patterns', *Economic and Political Weekly*, XXX (12).

Sawant, Shashikala (1983), "Investigation of Hypothesis of Deceleration in Indian Agriculture", *Indian Journal of Agricultural Economics*, Vol. 38(4), p. 475.

Sehgal, J. and I.P. Abrol (1994), Soil Degradation in India: Status and Impact, Oxford and IBH, New Delhi.

Shergill, H.S. (2007), "Sustainability of Wheat and Rice Production in Punjab", *Economic and Political Weekly*, Vol. 42, No. 52, December, pp. 81-85.

Singh, N.B. and J.P. Mishra (2008), "Towards Sustainable Foodgrain Production for National Food Security", Agricultural Situation in India, Vol. LXV, No. 5, Special Issue, August 2008, pp. 267-80.

Swaminathan, M.S. (2006), "Science and Technology for Sustainable Food Security", in N.A. Mujumdar and Uma Kapila (Eds.) Indian Agriculture in the New Millennium—Changing Perceptions and Development Policy, Academic Foundations, New Delhi, pp. 169-92.

Swaminathan, M.S. (2009), "Strengthening Food Security Based on Home Grown

Foods", *Indian Journal of Agricultural Economics*, Vol. 64, No. 2, April-June, pp. 177-86.

World Bank (2005), India Re-Emerging the Agricultural Sector to Sustain Growth and Reduce Poverty, Agriculture and Rural Development Unit, South Asia Region, The World Bank, Oxford University Press, New Delhi.

World Food Summit (1996), Rome Declaration on World Food Security.

14

Genetically Modified Crops: The Essence of Second Green Revolution and Food Security

S.M. Jawed Akhtar, Md. Imdadul Haque, Mohd. Sharif and Md. Shabbir Alam

Agriculture in India faces serious challenges from population growth and climatic changes. The four decade older Green Revolution needs to be revamped and revitalised. GM crops as a tool of an addition to conventional plant breeding could revive and spread the growth in yields of agricultural produce.

I. INTRODUCTION

Agriculture is very old form of human technology over the millennia, the interaction of agriculture with population growth and dispersion has been core of human culture and economic progress. For as long as ten thousand years, human beings have been purposely choosing the genetic make up of the crops they grow. Genetic selection for features such as faster growth, larger seeds, or sweeter fruits has dramatically changed domestic plant species compared with their wild relatives.

Indeed, many of our modern crops were developed before modern scientific understanding of plant breeding (Byrne, Pat, Sarah, Harrington, and Fuller, 2004).[1] Despite such improvement (agricultural improvement) concerns have arisen many times and in numerous places regarding the growth of population and the food available to feed them.

In the late of 19th to early 20th century, a series of unprecedented technological revolutions transformed agriculture, first, in industrialized countries and then more broadly worldwide, although not universally. The grain reaper and cotton gin, and later the tractor and thrasher, pushed the mechanical revolution of the 1890s forward, in increasing the amount of seeds that could be planted and the amount of land that could be usefully framed with the same amount of labour. Then, shortly after the turn of 19th century, the Haber-Bosch made possible the economical production of nitrogen fertilizer, whose spreading application in United States and Western Europe introduced a chemical revolution that further increased the yield a farmer could produce from the same amount of seed and land. The first half of the 20th century brought a third set of sweeping changes. Hybrid crop breeding, first done with corn in the United States, created new strains that with increased application of chemical fertilizers substantially boosted production per acre. This hybrid revolution actually extended to many other crops in many other countries.

These agricultural revolutions from technological innovations in industrialized countries primarily affected the farmers and consumers in those countries. The second half of the 20th century produced a different kind of agricultural transformation, one concentrated in less developed countries with traditional agriculture. This is so called 'Green Revolution' brought the rapid spread of hybrid wheat and rice, then other hybrid crops, first in Mexico and then in various Asian nations. Production per hectare dramatically increased when the crop was appropriately fertilized and irrigated.

Surging costs, population growth, drought and other setbacks linked to global climate change are pressuring world food supplies, while soaring prices on the street have triggered riots and raised the number of people going hungry to more than 923 million, according to UN estimates (CheckBiotech, 2008).[2]

These problems can be minimized and met only by providing required amount of food at affordable price with embracing the new technology. The engineered technology for the future with promises that it will solve the problem of world hunger as it revolutionizes agriculture, facilitates sustainability and improves food security and profitability (Nuffield Foundation, 1999 and Nuffield Council on Bioethics, 2003).[3,4] Keeping in view of the above facts this paper aims to analyze the area, production and yield of Bt cotton, both state-wise and for India as a whole.

II. THE IMPORTANCE OF GENETIC MODIFICATION

The motivations for the use of GM technology are basically rooted in the belief that given the imminent increase in population and decrease in areas and resources available for cultivation, technological solutions to meet future demand needs to be welcomed. GM technology is also being used to create crops resistant to abiotic stresses such as drought, soil acidity, and salinity. Possibilities for modifications such as improved storage stability, delayed ripening, and other changes to increase flexibility in distribution and/or facilitate juicing or other processing for greater economic benefits are being explored. Advances in resistance to abiotic pressures will allow crops to be grown in marginal, low productivity areas most commonly the domain of the poor, whereas increased storage stability and delayed ripening will benefit those with few resources to invest in refrigeration and other equipment to increase the shelf-life of agricultural produce (J.E. Thies and M.H. Devare, 2007).[5] The issue of sustainability of agricultural growth is often raised due to the growing scarcities of land and water and negative externalities of high input intensive agriculture (Acharya, S.S. and Chaudhri, D.P., 2001).[6] The message of the GM proponents, including bureaucrats and scientists working with the Government, and various private players engaged in genetic research, is that in the coming millennium we will have no other option than producing more food and agricultural commodities from diminishing per capita land and water resources.

Over three billion people, mostly in the world's poorest countries, are currently troubled with micronutrient malnutrition, while almost two-thirds of childhood mortality is associated with nutritional deficiencies. Micronutrient-enriched staple crops developed through genetic modification target the most vulnerable—resource-poor women and children. For instance, vitamin A deficiency causes partial or complete blindness in half a million of the poorest children each year. By engineering rice, a staple food for half the world's population, to overproduce beta-carotene—a precursor to vitamin A—biotechnologists expects to reduce these numbers significantly. Rice is also an excellent choice of cereal grain to target iron deficiency, which causes anemia, and has been identified as a contributing factor in over 20 per cent of post-partum maternal deaths in Asia and Africa. A study, conducted by Qaim, M., Stein, A.J. (2008),[7] shows that if genetically modified rice known as GR (Golden Rice) were to be consumed widely, the disease burden of VAD (Vitamin A Defeciency) could be reduced by 60 percent, while under more pessimistic assumptions the reduction would be around 10 percent. When valued in dollar terms, these positive health effects also translate into large economic benefits. Regardless of the underlying assumptions, GR is likely to be more cost-effective than alternative vitamin A interventions, such as food supplementation or fortification. Therefore, it should be considered seriously as a complementary intervention to fight VAD in rice-eating populations.

Genetically modified crops during 1996-2006 has contributed enough energy (in kcal terms—kilo-calories) to feed 467 million people for one year (equal to 40 percent of the energy requirement of India's population). The contribution of additional protein and fat was enough to meet the requirements of 1.3 billion and 449 million people respectively. As a significant proportion of these crops and their derivatives are used for industrial or animal feed purposes, the more likely contribution of the additional production arising from biotech crops to meeting global food requirements, since 1996, has been to provide sufficient energy to meet the requirements of about 310 million people for a year (similar to the annual requirement of the combined populations of Indonesia and Vietnam). The more likely contribution of additional protein and fat has been enough to meet the requirements of 920 million and 390 million people respectively. In 2006, biotech crops have contributed enough energy, protein and fat to meet the requirements of about 67 million (similar to the population of Thailand), 207 million and 124 million people respectively (PG Economics Limited, 2008).[8] The story of Bt cotton in India is remarkable. In six years, from 2002 to 2007, the productivity of cotton almost doubled, insecticides use reduced to half and the country was transformed from a cotton importer to a significant exporter. India has recognized the importance of using biotechnology to make the country self-sufficient in foodgrains with the first biotech food crop, biotech eggplant, brinjal, expected to be approved in the near-term. (IndiaPRwire.com, 2008).[9] It is important to note that there has been a positive impact of Bt cotton on cottonneseed oil production in India over the years. The Cotton Advisory Board (CAB) indicated that Bt cotton has been a major contributing factor for increasing cottonneseed oil production by 22 percent or more than 1.1 million tonnes in 2007-08, from 0.9 million tonnes in 2006-07. The Solvent Extractors' Association of India (SEA) estimated that the recovery of cottonneseed oil, particularly from Bt cotton hybrid seeds is higher, which has helped to increase the production of cottonneseed oil. This may be attributed to availability and widespread use of good quality cotton hybrids. Interestingly, cottonneseed oil is generally consumed as such or blended with other vegetable oils in India as a cheaper alternative to most other edible oils and is gaining popularity among consumers (Mayee, 2008; SEA, 2007).[10,11]

III. REVIEW OF LITERATURE

There are a large number and different varieties of genetically modified (GM) crops being planted in the world. Broadly, the varieties may be grouped in two parts; the first is insects resistance, and second herbicides tolerance of genetically modified crops. Since the present study is concerned with India's genetically modified crops where only Bt cotton as biotech crop was approved by the government, therefore, only review of literature of insect resistant cotton, that is, Bt cotton, has been analyzed along with South Africa, China and Argentina.

Many authorities such as WHO (1995)[12] and FAO (1996)[13] reveal that nutritional safety assessment of any new GM crop requires a thoroughly investigations case-by-case approach and the substantial equivalence represent an important component in the safety assessment of GM plants intended for nutritional consumption. This concept recommended a scientific approach in which the newly produced GM plant must be compared to its conventional counterpart.

Taylor (1997)[14] is of the view that the genetic modification of the food and feed crops result in the introduction of new proteins into the food and feed plant. Therefore, the safety of the newly introduced proteins must be assessed and the assessment of the allergenicity of the newly introduced protein should focus on the source of the gene.

Fernandez-Cornejo and Koltz-Ingram (1998)[15] as well as Gianessi and Carpenter (1999)[16] argue that higher yields , lower levels of labour and pesticides use for crops such as cotton, soybean, and corn varieties can be achieved if biotechnology is adopted.

Safety issues associated with the DNA in animal feed derived form GM crops area reviewed by Beever and Kemp (2000).[17] They argue that there is a growing body of scientifically valid information available that indicates no significant risk associated with the consumption of DNA or the resulting proteins from GM crops. Further, based on the safety analysis of each new crop, consumption of milk, meat and eggs produced from animal fed GM crops should be considered to be safe as traditional practices.

Pray , Ma, Huang and Qiao (2001)[18] focus that genetically modified (GM) plants are the centre of a heated debate on the value of agricultural biotechnology. Large biotechnology companies such as Monsanto and the biotechnology industry organizations, see agricultural biotechnology as a tool that can help alleviate serious problems of hunger and excessive pesticides use.

Ismail , Bennette and Morse (2001)[19] are of the view that an effective use of this technology can provide a way to lessen poverty in developing countries.

Altieri, and Rosset (2001)[20] examine the adoption of Bt cotton and has expressed concerns including the fear of damage to the environment, the development of pest resistance to Bt, reduction of biodiversity, increased profit for multinational companies and improvement of small farmers in developing countries, they argue that GM crops have limited value for the less developed world as they have resulted in small yield gains.

In South Africa, a study was conducted by Ismail, Bennette and Morse (2002)[21] indicating to some advantages from growing Bt cotton in terms of either yield or pesticide costs. They found that farmers who grew Bt cotton had both higher yields and lower pesticide costs than those who did not, outweighing the higher seed costs. They estimated the difference in gross margins at 11percent in 1998-99 and 77 percent in 1999-2000.

Huang, Hu, Rozelle, Qiao and Pray (2002)[22] develop their most complete analysis with three years of survey data and expanded sample coverage, a damage control production function, and an attempt to correct for the potential bias from growing of pesticide use and farmers' decision to grow Bt cotton varieties. Applying more advanced methods, they conclude that growing Bt cotton varieties:

(i) does have a positive effect on crop yield and not just damage abatement;
(ii) Bt cotton also reduces yield losses through abated damage;
(iii) pesticide use on non-Bt cotton varieties only decreases damage;
(iv) benefits from Bt cotton vary across provinces, and are lowest in Henan and Jiangsu; and
(v) farmers overuse pesticides, even when they grow Bt cotton.

Orphal (2005)[23] indicated that yield differences do not necessarily translate into differences of profit. A major yield factor is irrigation, therefore, the potential advantage of Bt cotton can only be realized if access to water is assured. Such favourable conditions apply to less than one-third of India's cotton area. Based on the results of this study the productivity of Bt cotton under rainfed conditions in Karnataka was not better or was even below that of local varieties. This shows that the economic performance of a cotton crop is not only determined by its genetic make-up but also by the agro-ecological conditions under which it is grown. A large degree of misinformation among farmers with regards to the true biological traits of Bt cotton was found. This could lead to a negative image of this new technology. Hence, there is a need for more farmer education. Overall, this study also underlines that one must be careful not to draw far reaching conclusions about the prospects of Bt cotton in India too quickly, because 2002 was the first season of commercial use. Nevertheless, the results presented in this study can serve as a starting point for further evaluation. Due to the high diversity of cotton growing in India more location-specific information is required. Thus, the benefits of conducting more economic studies in other areas would be significant.

Bennett, Kambhapati, Morse and Ismael (2006)[24] studied a production function that introduces use of Bt hybrids as a shift and interaction variable, with a large sample of pooled cross-sectional and time-series data recorded at the plot level, collected by company extension agents. Their analysis confirmed the spatial and temporal variation in partial productivity of Bt cotton. In some areas, they found that farmers did not benefit at all. They advocated a production function analysis to compare the performance of Bt cotton and non-Bt cotton farmers' plots in Maharashtra. The study shows a significant and positive impact of Bt technology on the average yield and on the economic performance of cotton growers.

IV. DATA SOURCES AND METHODOLOGY USED

The study is exclusively based on the secondary data. The relevant data have been collected from the publication of Cotton Advisory Board (CAB), Centre for Indian Cotton Research (CICR), and Indian Council of Agricultural Research. The data of states-wise cultivation area and production of cotton in India in the same period are collected from India Coordinated Cotton Improvement Project, Annual Report, 2004-05.

As far as the methodology is concerned, the statistical tools such as t-test and ANOVA are used to test whether there is any significant difference between the means of various samples. t-test has been used to check the hypothesis as to whether there is any significant difference in the ratio of area under plain cotton and Bt cotton. ANOVA is used to check the hypothesis that the yield, production, and area has been same across all the periods 1950-60, 1960-70, 1970-80, 1980-90, 1990-2000, and 2000-07. ANOVA is also used to check the hypothesis that there is no significant difference in cotton production between various countries. Annual growth rates have been calculated for selected states for the period 1996-97 to 2006-07. In this study the CAGR has been calculated for area, production, and yield over a time series data covering period 1950-51 to 2006-07. For calculating CAGR the years have been coded as 1, 2, 3 and so on. The natural log of area, production and yield is taken and then regression is done. The coded years have been taken as the independent variable and the area, production and yield have been taken as the dependent variables, case-wise and the regression coefficient has been obtained. Then, Inv and Ln are taken which is then subtracted by 1 and then multiplied by 100, which finally yields the value of CAGR.

V. DISCUSSION

GM crops as a tool of an addition to conventional plant breeding, could revive, stabilise and spread the growth in yields of food staples and of other crops growth by poor people. Seventy per cent of the world's poor live in rural areas and depend mainly upon agriculture for their livelihood. Despite increasing urbanization, over half of them will remain there in 2035 (FAO, 2002).[25] The role of agriculture in reducing poverty is therefore crucial; its rapid growth can lower and stabilize the cost of food to poor consumers living in rural and urban environments. Due to the sharper increase in the proportion of people, countries are facing water shortage. In almost all of Asia and most of Africa, expansion into marginal lands is unprofitable and increases environmental hazards. Moreover, the quality of soil in many places is poor or actually decreasing, due to erosion, salination, loss of micronutrients and accumulation of heavy metals (Bhattacharya, 2003).[26] Agricultural progress therefore has to depend on increased yields. To safeguard the environment from degradation, it is increasingly important to achieve higher and more conservative use of water and land already devoted to farming. GM technology may well have a significant contribution to make towards such progress by producing plants that are more resistant to moisture stress or higher salty soils.

Many genetically modified crops are now planted around

the world. The most common are GM soybean followed by GM corn, cotton, and canola. Others are GM tomatoes, potatoes, papayas, chicory, melons, rice, squash, and sugar beets (plants with swollen root: a plant with a large swollen root. Some types are eaten cooked, others are fed to animals, and one type yields sugar and wheat). One of the most common and important purpose of GM crops today is to confer tolerance to herbicides that are sprayed on farmland to control weeds. Herbicide-tolerance crops include transgenes providing tolerance to the herbicide glyphosate or glufosinste ammonium. These herbicides are broad spectrum; meaning that they kill nearly all kinds of plants except those that have the tolerance gene. Thus, a farmer can apply a single herbicide to his fields of herbicide effectively at most crop growth stages as needed. Another important benefit is that class of herbicides break down quickly in the soil, eliminating residue carry over problems and reducing adverse environmental impacts.

Another common purpose of genetic modification of crops is to confer protection against insects and pests. Importantly, this crop's trait could substantially improve yields in developing countries where pest damage is rampant and/or reduce the use of chemical pesticides. The soil bacterium bacillus thuringiensis in Bt corn and Bt cotton produce crystal protein that are toxic to certain insects but genetically harmless to vertebrates and non-lepidopteran insects. The genetic insertion of the bacterial gene into the plant genome (set of chromosomes: the full complement of genetic information that an individual organism inherits from its parents, especially the set of chromosomes and the genes they carry) enables the plant to produce its own pesticide. Depending on the sub-species of the bacterium from which the gene is taken, the pesticide is toxic to insects of the orders lepidoptera (which includes the common corn pests, European corn borer, South western borer, and corn earworm).

Other purpose of modification in current and past GM crops include changing the fat and acid composition of the crop (canola and soybeans), conferring male sterility (chicory), conferring resistance to vital infection (papaya), and delaying time to ripeness to allow for longer transportation time and shelf life (tomatoes). Some GM may be able to grow in conditions that have been unsuited for agriculture. For example, scientists have developed and may soon be marketing a type of genetically modified tomato that is able to grow in salty soil. This type of modified tomato is particularly useful in areas where crops could not be grown previously because of soil salinity. The tomato itself channels the excess salt into its leaves so that the fruit retains its normal flaver (Zhang and Blumwald, 2001).[27] Thus, farmers could be able to grow crops in otherwise difficult conditions, these crops, if affordable, could be an attractive option for farmers in areas with poor agricultural lands.

(i) Bt Cotton in India

While the total cotton area has increased from 87,30,000 hectares in 2002 to 94,00,000 hectares in 2007, total Bt cotton area increased from 29,000 hectares to 62,00,000 hectares during the same period (Table 1). The number of Bt cotton farmers increased from 20,000 in 2002 to 38,00,000 in 2007.

TABLE I

Area under Cotton Production

Year	*Total cotton area*	*Bt cotton area (in hectares)*	*No. of Bt cotton farmers (in hectares)*
2002	87,30,000	29,000	20,000
2003	76,70,000	86,000	75,000
2004	76,30,000	5,53,00	3,50,000
2005	89,20,000	12,67,000	10,00,000
2006	91,58,000	38,00,000	23,00,000
2007	94,00,000	62,00,000	38,00,000
CAGR	3.06	225.64	192.40

Source: Manjunath,T.M. ,"Bt-Cotton in India: Remarkable Adoption and Benefits" FBAE (Foundation for Biotechnology Awareness and Education), http:www.fabe.org/index.html.

Genetically modified crop, Bt cotton is being planted since 2002 in India and the area for the crop has been rising and it has reached to 6.2 million hectares in 2007. It is to be seen here whether production of cotton, area and yield in India has increased or not (Table 2).

TABLE 2

Area, Production and Yield of Cotton Production

Year	*Area (lakh hectares)*	*Production (lakh bales of 170 kgs)*	*Yield (kgs per hectare)*
1950-51	56.48	30.62	92
1660-61	76.78	56.41	124
1970-71	76.05	47.63	106
1980-81	78.24	78.6	170
1990-91	74.39	117	260
1991-92	76.93	119	263
1992-93	75.41	138	311
1993-94	74.4	121.5	278
1994-95	78.61	138.5	300
1995-96	90.63	170.2	319
1996-97	91.66	177.9	330
1997-98	89.04	158	302
1998-99	92.87	165	302
1999-00	87.31	156	304
2000-01	85.76	140	278
2001-02	87.3	158	308
2002-03	76.67	136	302
2003-04	76.3	179	399
2004-05	87.86	234	470
2005-06	86.77	244	478
2006-07	91.44	280	501
2007-08	95.55	315	560
2008-09	92.6	322	591

Source: Cotton Advisory Board, Central Institute for Cotton Research, Nagpur, (Maharashtra), India, Advance Estimates as on 04.04.2007, http://www.cicr.org.in/

Note: The yield rates given above have been worked out on the basis of production and area figures taken in '000 units

Now we assume, null hypothesis, that there is no difference between the area under cotton production during 1990-91 to 1999-2000 and 2000-01 to 2008-09 and alternate hypothesis is that there is a significant difference between the area under cotton production during 1990-91 to 1999-2000 and 2000-01 to 2008-09. After analyzing it we find that p value (0.322) is greater than á (0.05), null hypothesis is accepted (Appendix-1). It is clear that area of cotton after 2000-01 has increased.

Now another hypothesis regarding the production of cotton in terms of bales (1 bale=170 kg cotton) the null hypothesis is, there is no difference between the production of cotton during 1990-91 to 1999-2000 and 2000-01 to 2008-09 and alternate hypothesis, there is significant difference between the production of cotton during 1990-91 to 1999-2000 and 2000-01 to 2008-09. The result shows that p value (0.005) is lesser than á (0.05), null hypothesis is rejected (Appendix-2).

We make another hypothesis regarding yield of cotton per hectare in the two specific durations, that is, null hypothesis, there is no difference between the yields of cotton during 1990-91 to 1999-2000 and 2000-01 to 2008-09 and alternate hypothesis, there is significant difference between the yields of cotton during 1990-91 to 1999-2000 and 2000-01 to 2008-09. Since the p value (0.002) which is less than á (0.05), null hypothesis is rejected (Appendix-3).

(ii) State-wise Analysis

So far as production of cotton in different states of India is concerned, question arises that whether production has improved after 2002-03 or declined in different states in terms of annual growth of production. In Rajasthan, there are only two years, 1997-98 and 1998-99 for which annual growth rate (AGR) of production is positive and for remaining periods before 2002-03 we noticed negative annual growth rate. After that period there are only two periods, 2003-04 and 2004-05 where we found improvement. In other words, so far as annual growth rate of production of cotton in Rajasthan is concerned, very slight enhancement was perceived. Gujarat is one of the major states of growing cotton in India where illegal genetically modified crops were being planted since 2001 supplied by Navbharat company, seeds producers company in Gujarat. The annual growth rate of production of cotton cultivation has been positive after 2002-03. It is obvious that growth of cotton production in Gujarat is steadily boosted by the farmers tending towards cotton production. In Maharashtra, before 2002-03, high fluctuations in increment of cotton production were remarked. The annual growth rate of cotton production was negative during 1997-98,

2000-01, and 2002-03. And after 2002-03 there was only one period, that is, 2005-06 in which annual growth of production in Maharashtra was negative. It is meant that production in cultivation of cotton has swelled up steadily after 2002 period. There was higher fluctuation in cotton production recognized in Madhya Pradesh across the period of eleven years. In Andhra Pradesh, the production of cotton has multiplied better after 2002-03 than that of previous periods. The cotton production of Karnataka has been more up and down than other cotton growing states of India. In Tamil Nadu, it is noticed that annual growth rate of cotton production has become steadier and enhanced after 2002-03 in comparison to previous periods. In Punjab, before 2001-02, there were three years, 1997-98, 1998-99, and 2001-02 in which annual growth rate of yield was negative. After 2002-03, no year has shown negative results. It is meant that the growth rate of yield has been stable. For it, two reasons are considered responsible. First, adoption of genetically modified crops by the farmers has multiplied in the State, and second, irrigation facility in Punjab which is about 100 percent. Haryana is the state which is situated in Northern India. The irrigation facility is also found better in the State. Annual growth of yield of the State remained more steady and high after 2002-03 than that of the previous periods. In Rajasthan, there was one year, 2003-04 where annual growth rate of yield per hectare was positive otherwise remaining years have pointed out negative growth rate. One of the main reasons of decline of cotton production in Rajasthan is the lack of water facility. Annual growth of cotton yield in Gujarat is more stable and constant during 2001-02 to 2005-06 than that of 1997-98 and 2000-01. There are number of factors that are contributing in this scenario. But three of them are important, first, genetically modified corps is creating more interest among the farmers; second, soil of the state is more suitable for the cultivation of the crops and third, the farmers are planting more illegal seeds of genetically modified crops which may be dangerous for both farmers and environment. Thus, it is found that the production of most states which are planting cotton in India has enlarged and come into cultivation of the cash crops. If we see annual growth of sum of the states it indicates that production of the states has been better after 2002-03 than that of previous periods.

In Maharashtra, the annual growth rate of yield per hectare of cotton is not higher and stable than that of Gujarat, but it remained substantially higher and steady during 2001-02 to 2006-07 in comparison to that of 1996-97 to 1999-00. After Gujarat, Maharashtra is the state where genetically modified crops are being grown higher than other states. In Madhya Pradesh and Andhra Pradesh, the rate of yield was slightly improved or remained the same. The main reasons are, drought season in few years and lack of knowledge about the new technology as well as lack of irrigation facilities. In Karnataka, the production-wise annual growth rate shows that the production has not increased. In other words, production of cotton in Karnataka, on average remained the same but annual growth of yield per hectare was perceived more stable than that of Madhya Pradesh, Andhra Pradesh, and Tamil Nadu. It is also clear that the steady growth rate in yield was observed after 2002-03. In Karnataka, even though the farmers did not increase their cultivation of cotton but they have embraced new technology, that is, Bt cotton. In comparison of two periods in Tamil Nadu, 19997-98 to 2001-02 and 2002-03 to 2006-07, it reveals that latter period is more stable and prosperous than the former in terms of annual growth rate of cotton production and yield. The annual growth rate of area has been increasing since 2002 in Punjab. In Haryana, the farmers have realized slightly improvement in AGR in area during 2001-02 to 2006-07 than other years. In Rajasthan, annual growth rate of area remained the same across the whole years. Annual growth rate of cotton production, productivity and area in Gujarat was more stable than other states of cotton growing in India after 2000-01. In Maharashtra and Tamil Nadu, farmers are enjoying substantial and steadier annual growth rate during 2002-03 to 2006-07 than that of other years. The remaining states are showing slight improvement in the growth rate of productivity of cotton per hectare in India. It is clear that there are five states including Gujarat, Maharashtra, Haryana, Punjab, and Karnataka that have contributed large in the total production of cotton in India.

As far as the impact on state-wise area, production and yield of cotton is concerned, for this purpose, state-wise areas (million hectares) from 1994 to 2006-08 have been taken (Appendix-4). For this we assume, null hypothesis, that there is

TABLE 3

State-wise Area, Production and Productivity of Cotton

Year	*Punjab*	*Haryana*	*Rajasthan*	*Gujarat*	*Maharashtra*	*Madhya Pradesh*	*Andhra Pradesh*	*Karnataka*	*Tamil Nadu*	*Total of the States*
State-wise Cotton Production (Lakh Bales)										
1996-97	16	13.5	14	34.3	33	18.8	26.5	9	5.5	170.5
1997-98	7.25	9	11	42	21.5	22.5	25.5	7.5	5	149.9956
1998-99	5	7	11.5	47.5	26.5	18.8	25	8.8	5.5	155.333
1999-00	7.85	10.7	1300	27.5	38	15.5	22.5	7	5.5	1547.125
2000-01	9.5	10	10.8	23.8	18.3	19.3	25.3	7.8	5.5	128.9623
2001-02	9.25	5.5	7	32.5	34.3	20	26.8	7	5	147.6612
2002-03	7.5	8.75	5	30.5	26	18	19.8	5	3	122.5519
2003-04	10.4	11.5	9.15	50	31	19.7	27.4	4.2	3.8	169.6445
2004-05	16.5	15.5	11	73	52	16	32.5	8	5.5	232.757
2005-06	21	14	11	89	36	18	30	6.5	5.5	230.9048
2006-07	26	17	8	93	52	18	32	6	5	257.6524
State-wise Cotton Yield (Kg/Hectare)										
1996-97	367	354	364	382	182	605	447	229	360	3290
1997-98	170	240	290	470	116	740	483	246	344	3098.178
1998-99	151	204	303	502	141	636	333	245	385	2899.612
1999-00	281	332	379	304	199	502	368	220	505	3091.537
2000-01	341	306	358	250	101	647	420	235	484	3141.904
2001-02	262	153	343	328	195	546	454	201	425	2907.225

2002-03	284	287	220	317	158	561	418	216	600	3061.396
2003-04	389	372	452	516	191	565	557	228	619	3891.949
2004-05	551	424	427	651	311	472	469	261	725	4292.195
2005-06	610	379	397	794	213	494	527	268	668	4350.032
2006-07	752	542	389	662	283	486	565	276	639	4594.89
State-wise Cotton Area (Lakh Hectare)										
1996-97	7.42	6.49	6.54	15.2	30.9	5.27	10.1	6.7	2.6	91.16
1997-98	7.27	6.38	6.45	15.2	31.4	5.17	8.98	5.2	2.5	87.9765
1998-99	5.62	8.82	6.45	16.1	32	5.01	12.8	6.1	2.4	96.00658
1999-00	4.75	5.46	5.83	15.4	32.5	5.25	10.4	5.4	1.9	85.69928
2000-01	4.74	5.55	5.1	16.2	30.8	5.06	10.2	5.6	1.9	85.03056
2001-02	6	6.1	3.47	16.9	29.8	6.23	10	5.9	2	86.75875
2002-03	4.49	5.19	3.86	16.3	28	5.45	8.03	3.9	0.9	74.35711
2003-04	4.52	5.26	3.44	16.5	27.7	5.91	8.37	3.1	1	75.78009
2004-05	5.09	6.21	4.38	19.1	28.4	5.76	11.8	5.2	1.3	88.97767
2005-06	5.57	5.83	4.71	19.1	28.8	6.2	10.3	4.1	1.4	85.87785
2006-07	5.88	5.33	3.5	23.9	31.2	6.3	9.62	3.7	1.3	90.63472

Source: Cotton Advisory Board, www.agribusinessdwd.com/Cotton/Cotton%20statistic.pdf.

no significant difference between the state-wise cotton areas and the alternate hypothesis, there is significant difference between state-wise cotton areas.

Further in the inter-state analysis the next hypothesis aims at studying the inter-state production pattern. The null hypothesis is that there is no significant difference between the state-wise cotton production, and the alternate hypothesis is that there is significant difference between the state-wise cotton productions. The calculated result (Appendix-5) shows that the p value is less than 0.05 we reject the null hypothesis and accept the alternate hypothesis. It is meant that production of cotton has significantly changed in different states over the period by introducing the new technology. It also indicates that in Maharashtra, Gujarat, and Andhra Pradesh, Bt Cotton is extensively used.

The last hypothesis to be tested is regarding state-wise productivity of cotton (Appendix-6). In this case the null hypothesis is that there is no significant difference between the state-wise cotton productivity and alternate hypothesis is that there is significant difference between the state-wise cotton productivity. The findings of the hypotheses that are tested show the p-value is less than 0.05 we reject the null hypothesis and accept the alternate hypothesis. This means that the productivity of cotton per hectare has increased significantly in the state where the use of Bt cotton is rising. Thus, due to the adoption of new technology, there has been impressive increase in the productivity of cotton. Bt cotton area has increased only after 2002-03. So far as productivity of cotton is concerned, over all India, it increased to 69.15 percent during 2002 to 2007 and 74.83 percent during 1994 to 2006-07.

VI. CONCLUSION

It is very crucial that agricultural production keeps pace with the growing population. The population has already exceeded 1.0 billion and our country is projected to be the most populous country in the world with 1.5 billion by 2050. Arable land is diminishing every year as it is diverted for industrial, residential, recreational and other human needs. Other resources like water, fertilizers and labour are also becoming scarce and costly. Our crop yields are lost due to biotic factors like pests, diseases and weeds despite spending heavily on chemical pesticides. Similarly, crop losses due to abiotic stresses like drought, cold, heat and salinity are high and unpredictable. Huge losses of fruits, vegetables and flowers also occur during storage and transport. The yield growth rates of most crops are declining.

During the Green Revolution, because of inadequate understanding and monitoring, different problems have been faced by the farmers such as soil erosion and water contamination. Therefore, there is need of potential benefits of crops such as improving crop productivity on existing land and water resources, increasing production stability, thereby reducing the impact on farmers of biotic and abiotic stresses, preventing or even reversing soil and water degradation through reduced pesticide applications by use of herbicides and pest-resistant varieties and improving human health through reduced pesticides use and crops engineered for improved nutritional content or vaccine delivery. One of the greatest achievements of India since mid-sixties has been the phenomenal increase of research-based agricultural productivity that has fed millions and served as the basis of economic transformation in India. However, much remains to be done despite this gain. Poverty continues to limit access to food, leaving more than 200 million people undernourished. In addition, increased population, income growth and urbanization will rotate sustained growth in food demand. Thus, India is facing real challenges with a multitude of problems like poverty, hunger, food and water shortages, exploding population, and serious concerns about its water and food quality. Tackling these problems is closely-related to agricultural growth.

Therefore, the challenge before the agricultural scientists today is to 'produce more from less', i.e., more nutritious food from less land, water and other resources. Another challenge is to protect what we produce. These can be completed only through new technologies as the existing technologies do not seem to be adequate. Recent advances made in biotechnology offer exciting opportunities to address some of these challenges. GM technology in crops is one of the most powerful methods and has already made some breakthrough in this field. As the average yield and production of Bt cotton was highest during the period 2000-07, which happened to be the period when Bt cotton was initiated in India, hence resorting to GM crops cultivations can be used to have a higher yield and greater production. This will positively affect the livelihood of the millions of small farmers by improving their net incomes. The state-wise study shows that the production of cotton in Gujarat, Maharashtra, and Andhra Pradesh was higher than other states where the use of Bt cotton has been impressive. Huge inter-state disparities are a very common phenomenon in the Indian scenario. Removing this disparity and concentrating on the poor performing states can work wonders.

Notes and References

1. Byrne, Pat, Sarah Ward, Judy Harrington, and Lucy Fuller, (2004), "Transgenic Crops: An Introduction and Resource Guide," Department of Soil and Crop Sciences, Colorado State University.
2. CheckBiotech (2008), "World Goes For GM Crops To Tackle Food Crisis", Commodity Online India, Monday, December 15.
3. Nuffield Council on Bioethics (1999), "Genetically Modified Crops: The Ethical and Social Issues", Nuffield Council on Bioethics, London.
4. Nuffield Council on Bioethics (2003), "The Use of Genetically Modified Crops in Developing Countries", Nuffield Council on Bioethics, London.
5. Thies, Janice E. and Devare, Medha H., (2007), "An Ecological Assessment of Transgenic Crops", *Journal of Development Studies*, 43:1.
6. Acharya, S.S. and Chaudhri, D.P. (2001.), "Emerging Issues in Indian Agriculture", in Acharya, S.S. and Chaudhri, D.P. (eds.), Indian Agricultural Policy at the Crossroads, Rawat Publications, Jaipur and New Delhi, pp. 3-13.
7. Stein, A.J., Sachdev, H.P.S., Qaim, M. (2008). "Genetic Engineering for The Poor: Golden Rice and Public Health in India", *Journal World Development*, Canada, Vol. 36, No. 1, pp. 144-18.
8. PG Economics Limited (2008) "Biotech Crops: The Real Impacts 1996-2006— Yields", PG Economics Limited, Wessex Barn Frampton Dorchester Dorset DT2 9NB UK.
9. IndiaPRwire.com (2008), Biotech Crops Experience Remarkable Dozen Years of Double—Digit Growth, New Delhi, 18 Feb.
10. Mayee, C.D. (2008), Agricultural Scientists Recruitment Board (ASRB), Ministry of Agriculture, Personal Communication—Choudhary, B. and Gaur, K. (2009), "The Development and Regulation of Bt Brinjal in India (Eggplant/Aubergine)", ISAAA Brief No. 38, ISAAA: Ithaca, NY. ISBN: 978-1-892456-43-5.
11. Solvent Extractors' Association of India (2007), Report on Cotton and Cottonneseed oil Production, August 10, SEA.

12. WHO (1995), "Application of the Principle of Substantial Equivalence to the Safety Evaluation of Foods or Food Components from Plants Derived by Modern Biotechnology", Report of a WHO Workshop. World Health Organization, Geneva.
13. FAO (1996), "Biotechnology and Food Safety, Report Of A Joint FAO/WHO Consultation", FAO Food and Nutrition Paper 61, Food and Agriculture Organisation of the United Nations, Rome
14. Taylor, S.L. (1997), "Food From Genetically Modified Organisms and Potential For Food. Allergy", *Environ Toxicol Pharmacol*, 4: pp. 121-26.
15. Fernandez-Cornejo, J. and Klotz-Ingram, C. (1998), "Economic, Environmental And Policy Impact Using Genetically Modified Crops For Pest Management". Select Presented Paper at the 1998 NEREA Meetings. Ithaca, NY 22-23 June.
16. Gianessi, L. and Carpenter, J. (1999), "Agricultural biotechnology: Insect control benefits." Washington, DC: National Center for Food and Agricultral Policy.
17. Beever, D., and Kepm, C. (2000), "Safety Issues Associated with the DNA in Animal Feed Derived from Genetically Modified Crops: A Review of the Scientific and Regulatory Procedures", Nutritional Abstracts and Review, Series B(NARB): *Livestock Feeds and Feeding*, 70: pp. 175-82.
18. Pray, C., Ma D., Huang J., and Qiao, F. (2001), "Impact of Bt Cotton in China", World Development 29(5): pp. 813-25.
19. Ismail, Y, Bennette, R. and Morse, S. (2001), "Biotechnology in Africa: The Adoption and Economic Impacts of Bt Cotton in the Makhatini Flats", Biotechnology Conference Sub-Saharan Africa. Johannesburg, South Africa.
20. Altieri, M. and Rosset, P. (2001), Ten Reasons Why Biotechnology Will Not Ensure Food Security, Protect the Environment and Reduce Poverty in the Developing World, http://agbioforum.org/volno34/altieri.htm
21. Ismael, Y. Bennett, R. and Morse, S. (2002), "Farm-level economic impact of biotechnology: smallholder Bt cotton farmers in South Africa", *Outlook on Agriculture*, 31(2): pp. 107-11.
22. Huang, J., Hu, R.,. Rozelle, S., Qiao. F., and Pray, C. (2002), "Transgenic Varieties and Productivity of Smallholder Cotton Farmers in China", *Australian Journal of Agricultural and Resource Economics*, 46(3): pp. 367-87.
23. Orphal, J. (2005), "Comparative Analysis of the Economics of Bt and Non-Bt Cotton Production", Pesticide Policy Project Publication Series Special Issue No. 8, January, Institute of Economics in Horticulture Faculty of Business Administration and Economics Universität Hannover, Germany with Food and Agricultural Organization of the United Nations (FAO), Rome, Italy.
24. Bennett, R., Kambhampati, U., Morse, S., and Ismael, Y. (2006), "Farm-Level Economic Performance of Genetically Modified Cotton in Maharashtra, India", *Review of Agricultural Economics*, 28(1), pp. 59-71.
25. FAO, (2002), The State of Food and Agriculture, FAO, Rome.
26. Bhattacharya, S. (2003), "GM Crops Boost Yields More in Poor Countries", New Scientist.com News Service Feb. 6.
27. Zhang, Hong-Xia, and Eduardo, Blumwald (2001) "Transgenic Salt-Tolerant Tomato Plants Accumulate Aalt in Foliage but Not in Fruit," *Nature Biotechnology*, Vol. 19, No. 8, pp. 765-68

Appendix I

Area Analysis (Lakh Hectares)

t-Test: Two-Sample Assuming Equal Variances

Area in lakh hectares

Variable 1	Variable 2	
Mean	83.36454545	86.81125
Variance	55.36600727	49.42464107
Observations	11	8
Pooled Variance	52.91956237	
Hypothesized Mean Difference	0	
Df	17	
t Stat	-1.019671945	
P(T<=t) one-tail	0.161088414	
t Critical one-tail	1.739606716	
P(T<=t) two-tail	0.322176828	
t Critical two-tail	2.109815559	

Null Hypothesis: There is no difference between the area under cotton production between 1990-91 to 1999-2000 and 2000-01 to 2008-09.

Alternate Hypothesis: There is a significant difference between the area under cotton production between 1990-91 to 1999-2000 and 2000-01 to 2008-09.

p-value (0.322) is greater than á(0.05), Null hypothesis is accepted.

Appendix 2

Production Analysis

t-Test: Two-Sample Assuming Equal Variances
Production in lakh bales of 170 kgs

Variable 1	Variable 2	
Mean	146.11	223.1111111
Variance	499.8476667	5336.861111
Observations	10	9
Pooled Variance	2776.089288	
Hypothesized Mean Difference	0	
Df	17	
t Stat	-3.180714811	
P(T<=t) one-tail	0.002734902	
t Critical one-tail	1.739606716	
P(T<=t) two-tail	0.005469805	
t Critical two-tail	2.109815559	

Null Hypothesis: There is no difference between the production of cotton between 1990-91 to 1999-2000 and 2000-01 to 2008-09.

Alternate Hypothesis: There is significant difference between the production of cotton between 1990-91 to 1999-2000 and 2000-01 to 2008-09.

p-value (0.005) is lesser than á(0.05), Null hypothesis is rejected.

APPENDIX 3

Yield Analysis

t-Test: Two-Sample Assuming Equal Variances
Yield kgs per hectare

Variable 1	Variable 2	
Mean	296.9	431.8888889
Variance	529.2111111	13383.36111
Observations	10	9
Pooled Variance	6578.222876	
Hypothesized Mean Difference	0	
Df	17	
t Stat	-3.622331437	
P(T<=t) one-tail	0.001052193	
t Critical one-tail	1.739606716	
P(T<=t) two-tail	0.002104387	
t Critical two-tail	2.109815559	

Null Hypothesis: There is no difference between the yields of cotton between 1990-91 to 1999-2000 and 2000-01 to 2008-09.

Alternate Hypothesis: There is significant difference between the yields of cotton between 1990-91 to 1999-2000 and 2000-01 to 2008-09.

p-value (0.002) is lesser than á(0.05), Null hypothesis is rejected.

APPENDIX 4

Yield Analysis

State-wise cotton area
Anova: Single Factor

SUMMARY

Groups	*Count*	*Sum*	*Average*	*Variance*
Maharashtra	14	421.23	30.08786	2.84794
Gujarat	14	244.09	17.435	12.62727
Andhra Pradesh	14	138.91	9.92214	2.11351
Punjab	14	81.58	5.82714	1.11368
Haryana	14	80.35	5.73929	0.28204
Madhya Pradesh	14	79.59	5.685	0.29218
Karnataka	14	70.82	5.05857	1.36403
Rajasthan	14	67.91	4.85071	1.45398
Tamil Nadu	14	25.79	1.84214	0.42957
Others	14	8.79	0.62786	0.02386

ANOVA

Source of Variation	*SS*	*df*	*MS*	*F*	*P-value*	*F crit*
Between Groups	9822.53689	9	1091.392990	484.02949	0	1.95261
Within Groups	293.12489	130	2.25481			
Total	10115.66177	139				

Null Hypothesis: There is no significant difference between the state-wise cotton area.

Alternate Hypothesis: There is significant difference between the state-wise cotton area. Since the p-value is less than 0.05 we reject the null hypothesis and accept the alternate hypothesis.

States have been arranged in the summary table as per descending areas.

APPENDIX 5

Cotton Production Analysis State-wise Data in India

State-wise cotton production
Anova: Single Factor

SUMMARY

Groups	*Count*	*Sum*	*Average*	*Variance*
Gujarat	14	718.89	51.34929	870.96962
Maharashtra	14	472.19	33.72786	173.79933
Andhra Pradesh	14	394.31	28.165	32.80700
Madhya Pradesh	14	256.05	18.28929	5.48468
Punjab	14	189.3	13.52143	43.06720
Haryana	14	160.29	11.44929	10.74678
Rajasthan	14	144.62	10.33	6.49283
Karnataka	14	103.5	7.39286	2.48802
Tamil Nadu	14	71.25	5.08929	0.63084
Others	14	15.5	1.10714	0.09341

ANOVA

Source of Variation	*SS*	*df*	*MS*	*F*	*P-value*	*F crit*
Between Groups	30090.17906	9	3343.35323	29.15936	0.00	1.95261
Within Groups	14905.5361	130	114.65797			
Total	44995.71516	139				

Null Hypothesis: There is no significant difference between the state-wise cotton production.

Alternate Hypothesis: There is significant difference between the state-wise cotton production. Since the p-value is less than 0.05 we reject the null hypothesis and accept the alternate hypothesis.

States have been arranged in the summary table as per descending production.

APPENDIX 6

Cotton Productivity Analysis State-wise Data in India

Cotton Productivity
Anova: Single Factor

SUMMARY

Groups	*Count*	*Sum*	*Average*	*Variance*
Madhya Pradesh	14	7609	543.5	7326.73
Tamil Nadu	14	7193	513.786	21921.6
Andhra Pradesh	14	6865	490.357	10657
Gujarat	14	6651	475.071	32867.8
Punjab	14	5488	392	30665.8
Rajasthan	14	5017	358.357	3022.25
Haryana	14	4763	340.214	12348.8
Karnataka	14	3469	247.786	1704.18
Maharashtra	14	2672	190.857	5237.05
All India	14	5146	367.571	9375.19

ANOVA

Source of Variation	*SS*	*df*	*MS*	*F*	*P-value*	*F crit*
Between Groups	1680358	9	186706	13.8172	0	1.95261
Within Groups	1756643	130	13512.6			
Total	3437001	139				

Null Hypothesis: There is no significant difference between the state-wise cotton productivity,

Alternate Hypothesis: There is significant difference between the state-wise cotton productivity. Since the p-value is less than 0.05 we reject the null hypothesis. States have been arranged in the summary table as per descending productivity.

15

Cohort Induced Reforms in Food Front: The Case of Indian Agriculture

BIPUL MALAKAR AND SUDIP JANA

INTRODUCTION

Improved supply of foodgrain continued to be significant objective in many third world countries. India is attaching relatively less importance to food sector. The nation is having a buffer stock of cereals to cover up short supply. However, the republic does not deny the existence of a sizeable number of persons below the poverty level—unable to afford a square meal for dearth of purchasing power. Polity is striving to improve the situation. Demand of foodgrain would necessarily increase even with one percent meaningful decline in the percentage of people below the poverty line. The major portion of increased purchasing power of one million people (one percent of 111 million populations) will be for food. Increased demand for foodgrain is inevitable. However, we may expect that extend of demand for foodgrain will also be influenced by recent observed change in food habit of Indian. Richer sections of people are showing increased preference for non-cereals. This tendency obviously would have a compensating effect on demand of cereals. Increased supply of non-cereal would necessarily influence the cropping pattern in favour of non-cereals.

On the other hand, success in population front has already changed the population cohort, percentage of dependable population is on the increasing slope. Over aged population accounts for nearly 9 per cent of total population. A sizeable portion of them are not involved with productive activity. We should not also forget to take account of persons in the lower bottom of population cohort. They jointly constitute the dependent population The ratio is increasing. This dependent population is net consumer. India has to cope with the challenge of providing them with basic necessities. On the food front, improving land productivity is inevitable. The present essay deliberates on this issue.

Trend in Food Production and Food Security

The most conservative statement seems to be that India has partially been successful in arresting population explosion. Nevertheless, we have no room for complacency. Population growth rate is though declining but net yearly addition is quite large due to population size of our country—yearly addition to population is around 17 million during the recent years.

The cause of concern lies with change in population cohort. The phenomenon of population aging—proportion of persons aged 60 and above—is increasing. At the same time favourable performance in the health sector is also slowly inflating the proportion of children population—persons aged below fifteen year. Both are contributing towards increase in proportion of dependable persons; children are not expected to earn their bread on the other hand over aged persons normally retire from the productive activities. The society need be more concerned about population aging.

Population aging is a long drawn process. Associated economic and social phenomena are only coming to surface recently. Sociologists and demographers have addressed various aspects of aging. Economists are late to visualize the consequences of changing population cohort. A sizeable portion of the over aged group of persons will be net consumer. They had to be provided with necessities—home, food and nutrition. Would the present tempo of foodgrain production be sufficient to cope with the changing situation?

Domestic supply of food or self-sufficiency in food front continued to be a desired objective of most of the developing countries including India. We have attained recognizable success in food front. Food supply in the country is increasing. At the same time food habits of Indian is undergoing a mutative changes—demand for non-cereal food items is increasing. Recent economic reform is posing a threat to our traditional underpinning that the significance of the agriculture sector primarily lies with supply of wage goods. Indeed crop diversification—cropping pattern—in Indian agriculture, is started favouring nonfood crops—in particular export-oriented crops.

Significance of agriculture sector stems from its obvious connection with food security and human nutrition—an issue of national priority since planned economic development began in India in the 1950s. The economy is still heavily dependent on its agricultural and farming sector. This dependence is not so much in terms of the share of agriculture in the gross domestic product (GDP)—currently 25 percent. Agriculture still accounts for around 65 percent of all employment in the economy (Jha, 2004).

FOOD ECONOMY AND FOOD POLICY

Republic of India was born with food scarcity. Inward looking five year planning in India started with relatively greater stress on industrial front. Tacitly it was assumed that wage good sector would develop by exploiting market forces. Public endeavor was at minimum level until the severe food crisis occurred due to natural calamities in sixty decade. India had to bow to the external pressure to modify her economic process. Substantially devaluing our currency in 1966 and reorienting our planning process restored the sustainability and continuation of our planning process. Agriculture and food sector came in the forefront. The word sustainable development was not in practice in those days but the underpinning was sectoral balance or consistency.

India opted for long-term sustainability of her economy by emphasizing improved food supply. Changed orientation and strategy was rewarding and forty years after mending, we are now expecting to be globally competitive.

India since the decade 1970 has more or less been successful in tackling the food supply by introducing and adopting bio-chemical technology and mechanization. Indeed, India boasts of buffer stock for climatic failures. Localized draught is no longer a threat to administration. Criticism centers on inefficiency to tackle the localized crop failure. However, many of us subscribe to the argument that India would fail in the food front if the purchasing power of people below the poverty line increases (Rao, CH). According to official estimate, around one-fourth of Indians or over 260 million people are below poverty line. Lack of purchasing power of this section of people cannot be denied. This phenomenon exhorts a downward pressure on demand for food. Nevertheless, supply side performance of our polity attracted international attention. Republic of India could successfully surpass the international pressure.

FOODGRAIN PRODUCTION TREND

Foodgrain production in India at the onset of our planning process was around 51 million tonnes. The nation had to import about 4 million tonnes foodgrain—slightly less than 10 per cent of net availability of 52 million tonnes. Indian administration did not hesitate to import foodgrain to the best of her ability to improve the supply of foodgrain.

Foodgrain production in India, more or less steadily improved. One might ignore the yearly fluctuations that can largely be attributed to climatic factors (Figure 1).

Deficit continued. India eventually became self-sufficient in food front (however, with people surviving below poverty line) after introduction of biochemical technology in the late sixties. Dependence on external world for foodgrain supply (better read net availability of foodgrain} during the sixties and early years of seventy, i.e. after the introduction of new agricultural technology can be attributed to low level of production. It seems more appropriate to relate import of foodgrain in post-green revolution period to crop failure. India emerged as a net importing nation since the last decade of the last century (Table 1).

FIGURE I

Foodgrain Production in India

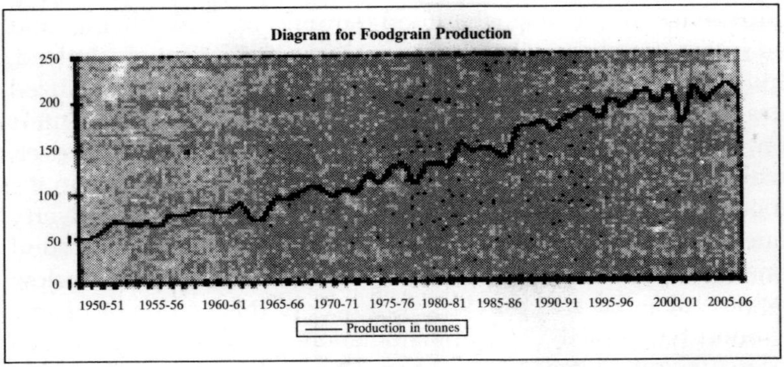

TABLE I

Production and Per Capita Availability of Foodgrain in India

(units: million tonnes)

Year	*Total production*	*Net production*	*Net Import*	*Net availability*	*per capita availability (grams per day)*
1950-51	50.82	48.10	4.80	52.40	394.90
1950-55	59.97	55.22	2.28	57.62	418.76
1955-60	70.97	63.78	3.44	66.82	446.94
1960-65	82.98	72.64	5.08	77.86	461.10
!965-70	87.03	76.18	6.42	81.86	433.96
1970-75	103.02	90.06	4.58	93.14	442.64
1975-80	120.04	105.04	0.40	104.26	441.76
1980-85	138.06	120.80	2.15	119.76	456.12
1985-90	155.03	135.66	1.55	138.28	473.86
1990-95	180.00	157.58	1.55	155.68	481.92
1995-2000	197.11	172.48	- 1.98	167.36	469.08
2000-2001	196.81	172.20	- 2.90	157.00	416.20
2005-06	208.30	182.50	-2.30	181.70	444.50
2002-06	201.50	176.38	- 5.40	179.08	452.38

Source: Economic Survey, GoI.

Adoption of new agriculture technology from fourth five-year plan was beneficial to the nation so far one concentrates on net production level. From the beginning of the plan period to mid-sixties—better be characterized by severe imbalances between the demand and domestic supply—net production was less than net availability—nation was net importer . The picture started improving from early seventy. Total foodgrain production crossed 100 million tonnes. Inconsequence net availability could be pushed forward with reduced quantum of foodgrain import . During the census year 1971, total production was around 105 million tonnes and without any import of foodgrain nation successfully pushed up the net availability to above 96 million tonnes. However nation had to wait till the second half of decade seventy for experiencing net availability above 100 million tonnes.

During the second half of 1970, net product crossed the hundred million tonnes and was nearly two-fold compared to our inherited level of less than fifty million production. External supply of foodgrain continued. Favourable increasing production trend resulted in reduction of external dependence. In the census year 1981, total production crossed 130 million mark with net production and net availability around 116 million tonnes. Ironically official estimate suggests import of 1.6 million tonnes of foodgrain. Foodgrain import could only be discontinued from second half of eighty decade.

Acceleration in growth of foodgrain production cannot be denied. Inconsequence, Indian Republic could push up net availability more or less depending on domestic production.

Increased quantum of food supply was more than imperative for population growth. About 159 million tonnes of net availability of foodgrain in 1991 was seen to be almost five million tonnes less than net domestic production (appox. 154 mt), without any dependence on external world as reflected in the negative sign of net import of foodgrain—(-0.6 mt}. This had been possible by releasing government stock . It may be resolved that the economy has been successful in scaling down external dependence on food front—external dependence in the form of import—if not nil, negligible—was the common experience from the census year 1991 (Figure 2).

The favourable food production trend since early seventy

FIGURE 2

Production, Import and Net Availability of Foodgrain in India

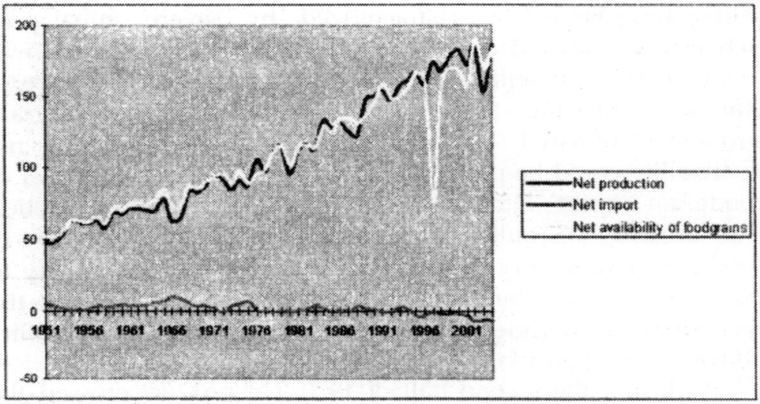

decade accompanied by increased fluctuation—may be attributed to climatic sensitivity of new yield augmenting technology.

Despite some years of exceptional crop failure, the qualitative changes in food economy of the nation after 1991 census, can not evade our attention. Net domestic production of foodgrain with some few exceptional years of climatic failure is greater than net availability. India eventually emerged as a food exporting nation since the decade nineties. Foodgrain output from the beginning of the present century continued to be well above 200 million tonnes. Unfortunately net availability started experiencing increased level of fluctuation .Net availability of foodgrain jumped to all time highest figure of around 190 million tonnes in the year 2001-02 from about 157 million in 2000-01 but scaled down in subsequent year 2002-03 by about 20 million tonnes to about 171 million tonnes . The fluctuating trend is continuing. Net availability in 2005-06 is about 182 million tonnes. Production performance however failed to influence per capita per day availability of foodgrain.

Per Capita Availability

The trend of foodgrain production from the angle of food security may be welcomed. At the same time India started experiencing a favourable reduction in population growth rate. However , our complacency is thwarted by the fact that the yearly foodgrain production since the 1980 started experiencing violent fluctuation which rolled over to per capita net availability (Table 1). On the other hand, growth of food production has yet to be greater than population growth rate. No less significant is the fact that the decline in the percentage of persons below the poverty line—not the absolute number of persons. We may further expect that Indian polity would emphasize on distributive justice or inclusive growth process. The demand for food would invariably increase.

Per capita per day, availability in India has only moderately improved. Change seems to be far below expectation. Increase in foodgrain production or net availability is grossly inadequate to influence the situation.

During the transfer of power, per capita per day food availability appears to be less than 400 gram. Availability as expected has increased but much below expected level. Prior to introduction of new agricultural technology during late sixties despite crisis in food front, polity could successfully push up the per capita availability around 450 grams per day. It appears there has not been any mentionable improvement in per capita availability after the adoption of new technology. Green revolution has however been successful to retain the level. On the other hand, we should be more concerned about increased level of fluctuation starting with the eighty decade. One observes violent fluctuation in availability during the nineties as well as during the present century (Figure 3).

Partial explanation obviously lies with population explosion. It would be unjustified to ignore the success in population front—India has entered the fourth stage of population growth.

The situation might further deteriorate in consequence of change in population cohort. Percentage of dependent population—children below 15 years and persons above sixty—is increasing.

Improved supply of foodgrain is more than imperative. Possibilities lie with expansion of gross cropped area, extension of irrigation facility and productivity.

FIGURE 3

Daily Availability of Foodgrain Per Person in India

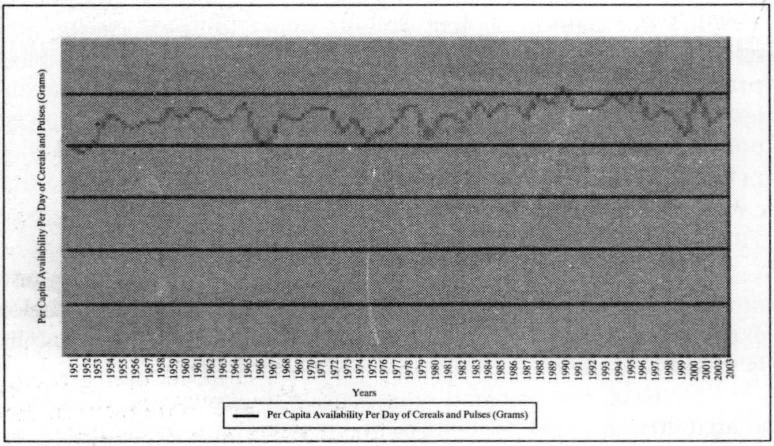

TABLE 2

Foodgrain: Area, Irrigation and Yield Rate

Period	*Area (m. hectares)*	*Irrigated Area (m. hectares)*	*Production (m. tonnes)*	*Yield rate (kg/hectre)*
1950-55	102.66	23.67	59.97	582
1955-60	112.35	26.94	70.97	631
1960-65	116.42	29.26	82.98	708
1965-70	119.16	33.85	87.03	728
1970-75	122.77	40.57	103.02	839
1975-80	126.86	46.10	120.04	946
1980-85	127.75	52.27	138.06	1080
1985-90	125.53	57.81	155.03	1231
1990-95	123.89	66.91	180.00	1453
1995-2000	123.34	77.04	197.11	1598
2000-05	120.24	78.58	199.20	1655

Source: Compiled from Agriculture Census.

Possibility of Furthering Food Production: Growth Component

Ecological balance and sustainability obviously restrict us from influencing the net cropped area. Multiple cropping is the way out which demands extension of irrigation facilities and better water management.

In general about 200 m. hectare land area is annually cropped in India. Major cropped area is accounted by food crops. Over time area under food crops increased from around 103 during the 1950 to above 125 m hectare in recent period. Gross food cropped area during the recent years is varying between 120 to 130 m. hectare (Table 2). About seventy percent of gross cropped areas is devoted to foodgrain crops. Increase in cropped area has obviously been possible due to extension of irrigation possibility. Further extension of food cropped area is possibly only by extending irrigated area.

Irrigation facility in the country is increasing. Food crop area irrigated during the recent period is about 45 percent of total cropped area. However, estimate suggests area irrigated has experienced nearly three-fold, increase from around 24 m. hectares during the early fifty to above 75 m. hectares during the recent period. It seems implausible to expect any dramatic change in irrigated area under food crop. Thus, supply of foodgrain might not be sufficient for the reason stated above. However, some experts are hopeful that foodgrain availability would not pose a threat to the nation.

Rice is the major food crops—accounting for nearly one-fourth of cropped area and approximately one third of foodgrain area. Rice continues to hold the key to sustained food security in the country. It has been resolved that for food security 'future rice production targets must be achieved exclusively through yield improvement.' Improved yield requirement for other food crops is also essential.

Food crop yield per hectare of cultivated land in the Indian economy was a major cause of concern during the sixties. Land productivity after the introduction of biochemical technology during the early seventies started improving slowly. With spatial diffusion and better adoption across the crops, land productivity at the national level started gradually increasing and could cross the 1000 kg per hectare level during the early half of eighty.

Available estimate suggests that by the end of the last century land productivity was well above one thousand five hundred kilogram. Achievement is good. Present level of yield rate is nearly two-fold in comparison to less than 850 kg during the initial period after the introduction of new agriculture technology during 1970-75. One expects acceleration for complacency. However , it is not difficult to observe that nearly two fold increase in food production in India during the period 1975 to 2005 from around 100 m. to 200 m. tonnes has largely been contributed by land productivity. The fact that during the period, area under food crop declined by about 2 million hectare or 2 per cent further reflects the beneficial effect of green revolution in the food front. Indeed productivity increase could compensate the reduction in gross cropped area due to joint effect of change in cropping pattern in favour of non-food crops and reduction in net cropped area. However, one should not ignore the contribution of (incremental) area in pushing up the production level. Extension of irrigation facility influenced gross cropped area during the early years. Area increase accounted for more than one-fifth of total production—during the period 1960 to 1971 while yield rate contributed nearly seventy percent (Table 3).

The contribution of biochemical revolution during the fourth five year plan has truly been reflected by the contributions of productivity in subsequent decades. During the decade eighties yield rate accounted for marginally less than ninety percent of 47 million tonnes increment in foodgrain production, share of incremental area is merely 2.42. Explanation possibly lies with diversion of cultivable area to non-food crop, area under food crop improved by less than one million hectare despite favourable trend in irrigated area . The tendency of diversion continued, during the decade nineties food cropped area declined by more than five percent. Indeed, since decade ninety, onwards it cannot possibly be denied that area under food crop remained almost stagnant, if not reduced. Consequently, it became entire responsibility of land productivity to improve the level of foodgrain production. Estimation suggests that yield rate improvement could compensate for reduction in area under food crop.

Our future is endangered in the field of improving per

TABLE 3

Increasing Production of Foodgrain: Contribution of Area and Productivity

Period	Production Increase		Contribution (in per cent)		
	Total (m. tonnes)	Percentage	Area	Yield	Interaction
1960-61	26.41	32.19	7.35	22.82	1.73
1970-71			(22.91)	(71.13)	(5.39)
1970-71	21.16	19.56	1.93	17.32	0.14
1980-81			(9.95)	(89.32)	(0.72)
1980-81	46.80	36.11	0.87	34.89	0.3
1990-91			(2.42)	(96.89)	(0.94)
1990-91	4.03	2.27	-5.32	8.04	-0.43
1995-96			(-232.31)	(351.09)	(-18.78)
1995-96	16.39	9.08	.03	9.05	0.00
2000-01			(0.33)	(99.67)	(.03)
1970-75	96.18	93.36	-2.06	97.26	-1.84
2000-05					

Note: Figures in parentheses indicate percentage contribution in total change.

capita availability of foodgrain which has almost become stagnant around 450 grams. It would be difficult to improve the production level if the present trend continues. With the increase in the number of dependent people, labour intensive cultivation, which we have already abated, is difficult.

Suitable measures have to be undertaken immediately to influence land productivity Thus, for future sustainability it becomes more than imperative to go for further mechanization and eco-friendly irrigation and cultivation practices. Relative contributions of area and productivity did not reflect any substantial change (Table 3). Given many under and unexploited crop production technologies, sustainable productivity can be accomplished. Sustainability demands another Green Revolution.

REFERENCES

Bhardwaj, K. (1974), Production Conditions in India Agriculture, OUP.

Bhattacharya, B.B. and C.H. Hanumantha Rao (1986), Agriculture Industry

Interrelations: Issues of Relative Prices and Growth in the context of Public investment, Paper Presented at the Eighth World Economic Congress, New Delhi.

C.H. Hanumantha Rao, Agriculture, Food Security, Poverty and Environment. Essays on post-reform India, OUP.

Census of India 1971, India Series I, Paper 3 of 1977, Age Tables, New Delhi: Registrar General and census Commissioner of India , pp. 56-62.

Chand, S.K. and A. Jaeger, 1996, Aging Populations and public pension schemes. Occasional Paper no. 147. International Monetary Fund.

Chesnais, J.C., 1992. The Demographic Transition. Oxford: OUP.

Desai Bhupat, M. and N.V. Namboodiri (1997), "Determinants of Total Factor Productivity in Indian Agriculture" (mimeo), Ahmedabad, India: Indian Institute of Management.

Dev, Mahendra S., C. Ravi, Brinda Viswanathan and Ashok Gulati (2003), "Economic Liberalization, Targeted Programmes and Household Food Security: A Case Study of India", CESS-IFPRI Report, IFPRI, Washington, D.C.

Dutta and Sundaram, Indian Economy, Chapter 4, Volume 1.

Economic Survey, 2006-07.

Evandrou, M., and J. Falkingham, 2000, Looking back to look forward: lessons from four birth Cohorts for aging in the 21st century, *Population Trends* 99: 27-36.

Gee, E.M. and G.M. Gutman, 2000, The overselling of population aging: Apocalyptic demography, intergenerational challenges and social policy, New York: OUP.

Riley, J.C., 2001, Rising Life Expectancy: A Global History, OUP.

16

Food Security and Structural Reforms in India

Indu Upadhyay

INTRODUCTION

Three fundamental basic needs of humanity are: food, shelter and clothing. Rightly does the Indian Constitution provides that every man, woman and child has right to food, to work and to enjoy the basic necessities like education, medical aid and employment facilities. Unfortunately even after 62 years of independence the problem of food has remain unsolved. It has been estimated that every third person in Asia suffers from hunger and a much larger people suffer from malnutrition.

India is no exception to this observation. It should however be pointed out that Rome Declaration on World Food Security defines access to food as "Physical and Economic access, at all times, to sufficient, safe and nutritious food (for people) to meet their dietary needs and food preferences for an active and healthy life." In other words, food security refers to security which requires access to adequate quantity and satisfactory quality of food. India has miserably failed in ensuring access to food to all our people. It should be noted that according to the

National Family Health Survey, conducted in 1998-99 at all India level 45.5 percent of the children between the age of 6 and 36 months were stunted (undernourished on the basis of height), 47 percent were under nourished, 74.3 percent of children of the same age group had anemia and 51.8 percent of all women surveyed were anemic.

Further in this regard National Nutrition Monitoring Bureau Reports similar findings, Body Mass Index (BMI) is taken as an indicator of under nutrition in a study of eight States in 1991-92 wherein it was estimated that 46 percent of men and women adults were energy deficient.

It needs no emphasis that India adopted New Economic Reforms in the year 1991. These includes the structural changes which deregulates liberalizes, decontrols various of sectors economy. The process of decontrol leads to a change from Nehruvian socialism towards a new market economy. This standardized package of neo-liberal economic policy included devaluation of currency, privatization of efficient public enterprise, reduction of various subsides and liberalization of trade. No doubt, it has brought about improvements in budgetary and fiscal conditions in some of years—Nevertheless, such macroeconomic changes on certain sectors such as agriculture were negative. It should however be pointed out that the present paper is an attempt to look into the effects of 'New Economic Reforms' on agriculture.

Objectives of Study

1. To study about the requirement of food security in Indian economy; and
2. To examine whether the supply is equal to the demand for agricultural commodities.

The study is based on the secondary source of information. The data have been collected from Reserve Bank of India Bulletin, Currency and Finance Report, Reports of Planning Commission, Economic Survey, etc. Further, the study is divided into three sections: First section deals with the requirement of food subsidy in Indian economy while, the second section deals with the balance between demand and supply for agricultural commodities in the country. Last section deals with conclusion of the study.

I

HISTORICAL EVOLUTION OF THE FOOD PROBLEM

Malnutrition starvation and occasional famines have been more or less endemic under Indian conditions "During the last 300 years, India has experienced 26 major famines: during the last 700 years there have been 17 very severe food disasters and during the historical time of the 34 great famines of the world 18 have occurred in India. The frequency and cyclical order show the peculiar susceptibility of this country to crop failures and recurrent shortage of food supply."

It needs no emphasis that in the earlier part of the nineteenth century India was a self-sufficient country in matters of food production, but in 1880, the Famine Commission sounded a note of warning that the pressure of population was increasing on land. It pointed out that the country taken as a whole was definitely surplus in food. But the minority numbers opined that the alleged surplus (of 5 million tonnes) was greatly over estimated. It should however be pointed out that food was not a problem for India at that time. Even in the years 1896-97 and 1899-1900 when there was at famine, India exported 1.5m and 2.2 million tonnes of foodgrains, respectively. Even in the year 1921 when population started rising rapidly balance between demand and supply was maintained by increasing production of foodgrains.

The position deteriorated further after the separation of Burma in 1937 which was further aggravated with outbreak of Second World War as is clear from the following Table (Table 1).

The Table 1 shows net production, imports and availability of foodgrains in India. In the year 1951 Net Production was worth 48.1 million tonnes which was less than the requirement of the Indian economy. Therefore, 4.8 million tonnes had to be imported from various countries. The net production increased by 67.5 million tonnes in 1960 but still imports of foodgrains were worth 5.1 million tonnes. The point to be noted is that even the imported foodgrain was not equal to

TABLE I

Net Production, Imports and Availability of Foodgrains

(million tonnes)

Year	*Net Production*	*Imports*	*Availability of Foodgrains*
1951	48.1	4.8	52.4
1955	61.9	0.5	63.2
1960	67.5	5.1	71.2
1965	78.2	7.4	84.6
1970	87.1	3.6	89.5
1975	87.4	7.5	89.3
1980	96.0	-0.3	101.4
1985	127.4	-0.4	124.3
1990	149.7	1.3	144.8
1995	167.6	0.4	169.8
1996	157.9	-1.2	165.2
1997	174.4	1.0	177.2
2000	182.8	-1.4	155.8
2001	171.8	-2.9	146.5

Source: Economic Survey, 2001-02.

the required quantity to satisfy the hunger. In this regard Agricultural team (1959) observed "An immediate and drastic increase in food production is India's primary problem of next 7 years. Without enough food India's hope for improving human welfare achieving social justice and securing democracy will become almost impossible of attainment".

The team estimated that 28 million tonnes food was short than country's demand but only 10.3 million tonnes could be imported. It needs no emphasis that supply of foodgrains could not be increased while demand was increasing on account of increasing population, rise income and defence expenditure. This caused a wide gap which had to be filled up by larger imports, intensification of internal procurement, taking over greater responsibility for distribution of available supplies by extension of rationing and opening of fair price shops and launching emergency food, production drive to encourage production of foodgrains. The Imports rose sharply to 7.5 million in 1975. In 1980 the import of foodgrains was less than exports, by -0.3 million tonnes. Further in the year 1990 it was 1.3 million tonnes. Finally in the year 2001 it became -2.9 million tonnes.

There is no denying of the fact that foodgrains production has increased substantially in India. As a result in normal condition there in no need of import of foodgrains still there are food deficit areas in India where supply of foodgrains do not match its demand. Therefore providing minimum nutritional support to the poor through subsidized foodgrains and ensuring price stability in different states are the twin objectives of the food security system.

II

It should however be pointed out that poverty in any State

TABLE 2

Trends in Poverty: 1973-74 to 1998, All India

Year	*Datt's Estimates*		*S.P. Gupta's Estimates*		
	Rural	*Urban*	*Rural*	*Urban*	*Total*
1973-74	55.72	47.96	-	-	-
1977-78	50.60	40.50	-	-	-
1983	45.31	35.65	45.65	40.79	44.48
1986-87	38.81	34.29	-	-	-
1988-89	39.06	36.60	-	-	-
1989-90	34.30	33.40	33.70	36.00	34.28
1990-91	36.43	32.76	35.04	35.29	35.11
1991	37.42	33.23	-	-	-
1992	43.47	33.73	41.70	37.80	40.70
1993-99	36.66	30.51	37.27	32.36	35.07
1994-95	41.02	33.50	38.03	34.24	36.98
1995-96	37.15	28.04	38.29	30.05	36.08
1997	3578	29.99	38.46	33.97	37.23
1998 (Six months)	-	-	45.25	34.58	43.01

Source: Estimates based on NSS data on consumer expenditure.

can be regarded as an indicator of need towards food security in that particular State.

Table 1 shows that the poverty was 55.72 percent and

47.96 percent in 1973-74 in rural and urban areas respectively. In the year 1983 poverty stood at 45.31 and 35.65 percent. Further is 1989-90 it was 39.06 and 36.60 respectively. In 1992 it stood at 43.47 and 33.73 percent respectively. In 1997 it was 35.78 and 29.99 percent according to Datta's estimates and S.P. Gupta's estimates show the same trend and in the year 1998 43.01 percent people lived under poverty line of which 45.25 percent were from rural areas while 34.58 percent are from urban areas. That means about 40 percent of the people are not able to fulfil even their basic requirements even after nearly two decades of adoption of economic reforms in India. Therefore, it is the responsibility of Indian Government to provide them with the minimum nutritional standard which is not only important for their livelihood but also for efficient working of any economy. Therefore, food security is essentially required by any underdeveloped economy.

Now the question arises as to whether Indian Government should continue to give food security or should gradually phase it out, as it is against the philosophy of Globalization. It should however be pointed out that since India had adopted New Economic Reforms in 1991 and since then the growth rate of food subsidy has be uneven. This can be shown by Table 3.

TABLE 3

Growth of Food Subsidy in India (other than Sugar)

Year	*Food Subsidy (Rs. Crores)*	*Annual (Growth percent)*
1997-98	7500	45.2
1998-99	8700	16.0
1999-2000	9200	5.8
2000-01	12010	30.5
2001-02	17494	45.7
2002-03	24176	38.2
2003-04	25160	4.1
2004-05	25746	2.3
2005-06	23071	-10.4
2006-07	23828	3.3
2007-08 (B.E)	25425	6.7

Source: Economic Survey, 2007-08, Government of India, Ministry of Finance, Economic Division.

Provision of minimum nutritional support to the poor through subsidized foodgrains and ensuring price stability in different States have been the twin objectives of the food security system in India. To fulfil the obligation towards distributive justice the Government incurs food subsidy Table 3 shows that food subsidy was Rs. 7500 crores in 1997-98 when average annual growth rate of food subsidy stood at 45.2 percent. The quantum of food subsidy increased to 12,010 crores while the annual growth was 30.5 percent respectively in 2000-01. Further in the year 2003-04 the food subsidy increased in absolute terms and stood at Rs. 25,160 crores but annual growth rate of subsidy declined to 4.1 percent. In the year 2004-05 food subsidy declined to 23,071 crores and annual growth rate of subsidy became negative by -10.4 percent. Finally, in the year 2007-08 the food subsidy was Rs. 25,425 crores while the growth rate of food subsidy stood at 6.7 percent. Food subsidy showed an annual increase of 30 percent during each of the three years: 2000-01, 2001-02 and 2002-03 but has been relatively stable since 2003-04. It should however be pointed out that in a country where nearly 40 percent people are not able to live with minimum nutritional standards required for living, it is the responsibility of Government to look after them. Therefore, food security is required to be continued.

It should however be pointed out that food subsidy being the difference between the economic cost of wheat and rice and their issue price, the quantum of food subsidy for different groups of beneficiaries is to be linked to the increase in economic cost and the issue prices. However, the economic cost of wheat has gone up due to an increase in MSP, the issue price has been kept unchanged since July 2002 as can be shown by Table 4.

Table 1 shows that the Minimum Support Price (MSP) has continued to rise since 2002. It was Rs. 620 for wheat and Rs. 550 for Paddy while the issue price was Rs. 610, 415, 200 for wheat and Rs. 795, 565, 300 for rice for APL, BPL and AAY, respectively in the year 2002-03. Further in the year 2005-06 the MSP of wheat increased to Rs. 640 while the issue price remained the same at Rs. 610, 415, 200 for APL, BPL and AAY, respectively. Similarly in 2007-08, MSP of wheat increased and stood at Rs. 850 while the issue price remained the same at Rs. 610, 415 and 200 respectively. The point to be noted is that in

TABLE 4

MSP and Issue Price for Wheat and Rice under TPDS

Marketing Season	*Minimum Support Price*		*Central Issue Price*					
	Wheat	*Paddy*	*Wheat*			*Rice*		
			APL	*BPL*	*AAY*	*APL*	*BPL*	*AAY*
2002-03	620	550	610	415	200	795	565	300
2003-04	630	550	610	415	200	795	565	300
2004-05	630	560	610	415	200	795	565	300
2005-06	640	570	610	415	200	795	565	300
2006-07	700	620	610	415	200	795	565	300
2007-08	850	745	610	415	200	795	565	300
2008-09	1000							

From 1 April, 2002 to 30 June, 2002 issue price for APL for both wheat and rice was reduced by Rs. 100 per quintal.

MSP and CIP (for APL families) for Paddy/rice are for common grade.

Source: Government of India, Ministry of Finance, Economic Survey 2007-08, p. 179.

order to maintain a minimum standard of nutrition, Government of India has kept issue price as it is since 2002-03 which has resulted into an increase in burden of food subsidy for the Government. It needs no emphasis that the issue price is different for the three segments issue price for Below Poverty Line (BPL), Above Poverty Line (APL) and Antyodaya Anna Yojana (AAY). People who are above poverty line do not require food subsidy as they are able to pay for what they consume but the point to be noted is that the Minimum Support Price, at which the foodgrains are available in the open market is always more than issue price for the same category of people for the same commodity leading to increased burden of food subsidy.

While the total amount of subsidy has continued to rise in absolute terms, State-wise allocation of subsidies is not related to poverty levels. The ratio of the percentage allocation of subsidies do not seems to correspond to poverty levels. The ratio of percentage allocation of subsidies as given by the off-take of foodgrains under TPDS and the proportion of people below poverty line is less than one for many of the poorer States as shown in Table 5.

TABLE 5

Allocation of Subsidies and Population Below Poverty Line

State	*Food Subsidy for TPDS*		*Average*	*% of total food Subsidy*	*% of people below poverty line*	*Ratio of % of subsi-dies/ % persons of below poverty line*
	2005-06	*2006-07*				
Bihar	975.1	625.1	800.1	3.5	12.2	0.3
Punjab	119.2	49.6	84.4	0.4	0.7	0.5
Jharkhand	678.1	429.4	553.7	2.4	3.9	0.6
Rajasthan	882.4	388.5	635.4	2.8	4.5	0.6
Madhya Pradesh	1571.4	949.0	1260.2	5.5	8.3	0.7
Uttar Pradesh	4024.3	2766.3	3395.3	14.8	19.6	0.8
Maharashtra	2183.5	1499.6	1841.6	8.0	10.5	0.8
Haryana	275.0	139.1	207.1	0.9	1.1	0.9
Orissa	1111.8	1130.9	1121.4	4.9	5.9	0.8
Gujarat	744.4	438.7	591.6	2.6	3.0	0.9
Goa	18.6	18.3	13.5	0.1	0.1	1.0
Chhattisgarh	787.9	663.4	725.7	3.2	3.0	1.1
West Bengal	1903.2	1593.4	1748.3	7.6	6.9	1.1
Karnataka	1611.9	1409.0	1510.5	6.6	4.6	1.4
Delhi	373.0	239.4	306.2	1.3	0.8	1.8
Kerala	821.6	674.7	748.1	3.3	1.6	2.0
Tamil Nadu	2636.1	2595.2	2615.7	11.4	4.8	2.4
Andhra Pradesh	2415.3	2243.0	2329.1	10.2	4.2	2.4
Total of all States	25813	19945.5	22.8	79.3	100	

Note:
1. Subsidies have been calculated in the basis off-take and difference between economic cost and issue price.
2. Share of BPL population is per planning Commission, 2004-05.
3. Total Covers all the States and UT's including the ones not specifically mentioned.

Source: Government of India, Ministry of Finance, Economic Survey, 2007-08, p. 180.

Table 5 shows that Uttar Pradesh, the most populous State of India, where 19.6 percent people are not able to fulfil their bare necessities, only 0.8 percent people of the State are benefited by the food security. Second, in the ladder is Bihar where 12.2 percent people live under poverty line but only 0.7 percent people enjoy the benefits of food security. Third, in the ladder is Maharashtra where 10.5 percent people live below poverty live while only 0.8 percent people get its benefits. Fourth one is Madhya Pradesh where 8.3 percent people live under poverty line of which only 0.7 percent enjoy the benefits of food subsidy.

Now let us take a glance of the relatively better-off States like Goa, where only 0.1 percent people live under poverty line but 1.1 percent people avail the benefits of public distribution system. The next richer State is Delhi where only 0.8 percent people live below poverty line while 1.8 percent people avail the benefits of PDS. Third in order is Punjab where 0.7 percent people live below poverty line while 0.5 percent people enjoy the benefits of food security. It should however be pointed out that the people who are not able to fulfil even their basic requirements Government should spend for them. However, the situation here appears to be quite different because the States having lower per capita income, where relatively more people live below poverty line as compared to the richer States still they avail relatively less benefits of cheaper foodgrains being provided under Public Distribution System (PDS). On the other hand, the richer States where per capita income is higher as compared to their underdeveloped counterparts take the benefits of food security more even though their citizens can bear the entire cost, i.e. MSP. One of the cause of this may be lack of foodgrains in the buffer stock available with the States. It is for this reason that in view of the declining stock position of in the Central pool, the Central Government has taken several steps to mitigate the shortage of wheat, such as rationalization of allocation of wheat for APL category under the TPDS and imports of wheat. The allocation of wheat under TPDS for APL category has been rationalized from June 2006 based on each State's average off-take during the earlier three years or last years off-take, whichever was lower. A 25 percent cut was imposed on rice consuming States. However, there has been no change in the overall allocation/entitlements for BPL and AAY category. The Department of Food and Public Distribution has released about 1 lakh tonnes of wheat under APL category for all the States/UT's every month from September 2006 to July 2007 and further from September 2007 to March 2008. Similarly keeping in view the stock position of rice in Central Pool, allocation of rice made for the APL category under the TPDS has been rationalized from April 2007 for all the States/UT's on the basis of their off-take during 2003-04, 2004-05 and 2005-06. While the allocation for AAY and BPL categories are made at 35 kgs/ family per month. While allocation for per APL category are made depending upon the availability of Stocks on central pool.

III

CONCLUSION

It has been proved by researches that India had abundance of food for its citizen but after 1937 the food crisis started and in order to maintain the minimum nutritional requirement food subsidy was started. It should however be pointed out that efforts have been made by Government of India to increase the net production of foodgrains since the planning started. No doubt the production has increased by more than 4 times since the inception of the plan. Now the question arises whether the balance between the demand and supply of foodgrains been secured. It appears that the Government has tried its best by importing foodgrains, maintaining buffer stock of foodgrains, providing foodgrains at lower prices, to the people belonging to BPL and APL, etc. However, Table 2 shows some what different facts. According to S.P. Gupta's (1998) estimates still 45.25 percent people in rural areas and 34.58 percent people in urban areas and total of 43.01 percent people live below poverty line. That means near about half of the population of India is not able to provide itself with minimum nutritional standards.

There is no denying of the fact that India, adopted the philosophy of 'Globalization' in the year 1991 and were supposed to reduce subsidies of all kinds. Table 3 shows that Indian has given food subsidy to the extent of Rs. 25,425 crores in 2007-08 which grew to Rs. 23,825 crores in 2006-07. No doubt the subsidy has increased in absolute terms but the food subsidy which was 45.2 percent in 1997-98 declined to 6.7 percent in

2007-08. It is clear that India's expenditure or food subsidy bill has more than doubled from the year from 1997 to 2008 but it should be noted that in a country where near about half of the population is not able to satisfy its hunger, it is but natural that Government should support these people (BPL people) through food subsidy.

It should however be pointed out that the Minimum Support Price of wheat was Rs. 620 in 2002-03 which increased Rs. 850 in 2007-08 while the issue price remained at Rs. 610, 415 and 200 for APL, BPL, AAY, respectively during the same period. Same is the case with rice where the MSP was Rs. 550 in 2002-03 which increased Rs. 745 in 2007-08 for paddy while the issue price remained at Rs. 795, Rs. 565 and 300 during the same period for APL, BPL and AAY respectively. This is one of the causes regarding the increase in Government's burden of food subsidy in absolute terms.

Now the question arises whether the food subsidy really helped in reducing the hunger of people below poverty line. Table 5 shows that in Uttar Pradesh 19.6 people live below poverty line while only 0.8 percent people were covered by food security system. Next in terms of poverty ratio in Bihar, where 12.2 percent people were below poverty line while only 0.3 percent people were benefited by Public Distribution System (PDS). If we take the example of the richer States like Goa, 0.1 percent people were below poverty line and 1.0 percent people availed the benefits of food subsidy. In the case of Delhi, where 0.8 percent people were below poverty line, 1.8 percent people enjoyed the food subsidy. That means in relatively poorer States, the Public Distribution System has failed to achieve its objectives because relatively lesser number of people are able to avail of the benefits of Public Distribution System. There can be many reasons for this. This could be either because of institutional barriers, such as need to prove residence and buy ration entitlement once a fortnight. Migrant households do not satisfy the first requirement while the poorest households do not have enough saving to buy in bulk. Apart from inadequate access to the PDS there is the huge cost of providing subsidies to the poor through PDS. Indeed many researches show that it costs more than a rupee of subsidy to the target families.[8]

It should however be pointed out that mere providing

foodgrains like wheat and rice is not sufficient for the poorer section of the society. There is no denying of the fact that a balanced diet is required which includes not only carbohydrates but also proteins, minerals, vitamins in the balanced quantity for healthy body and mind, etc. However, in an economy where prices are sky rocketing it is very difficult for the consumer, especially for those of below poverty line to have balanced diet. Therefore, it is the duty of the State to provide other articles of consumption which are necessities as well.

TABLE 6

Comparative Analysis of Prices of Necessities

Name of Genes	*Prices (Per kg/lit)*	
	2004 (Rs.)	*2009*
Wheat Normal	8.50	11
Flour	9.00	13
Gram	20	32
Channa Dal	25	40
Arhar Dal	30	90
Rice	10	20-22
Mustard oil	55	65
Vanaspati Ghee	50	60
Desi Ghee	160	220-240
Besan	25	40-42
Sugar	18	28
Gur	16	28
Salt	6	12
Red Chilly	65	70
Turmeric	40	100

Source: Reported in *Hindustan*, 17 July 2009.

As can be seen from Table 6 it is very difficult for a poorer family to take protein which is found in pulses which are Rs. 40 kg (Channa Dal) and Rs. 90 kg (Arhar Dal), respectively. It seems, oil, sugar, which are the basic necessities are also out of their reach due to increasing price. Therefore, the other commodities which are not part of balanced diet at least necessities for the people should be provided through Public Distribution System at reasonable prices.

Even if the right to food is restricted to just foodgrains alone, the delivery mechanism will pose one of the biggest challenge to the Government. The Public Distribution System has become something like a sacred cow and many people assert that PDS is the only option before the Government. However, this view completely ignores the shortcomings of the PDS as shown above.

An alternative to PDS is the system of food stamps. Under this scheme, the Government issues coupons to the target families. These coupons can then be redeemed at any shop—private or public for specified quantities of foodgrains at stipulated prices. Obviously, the Government will have to pay private retailer the difference between the stipulated price and market price.

The PDS and the system of food stamps can have the same level of leakages due to the targeting costs—the identification of BPL families must precede both systems. So, the effectiveness of food stamps obliviously depends on how efficient it is in delivering foodgrains to consumers as compared to PDS. By its very nature, food stamps do not have some of the costs associated with PDS, for instance there cannot be any chance of illegally diverting grains to the open market. Procurement and storage costs are also higher in PDS.

On the other hand, private retailers may demand excessive profit margins in order to enter the remote areas. So, the superiority of one system *versus* another is an empirical issue. This suggests that the sensible option is to allow both systems to co-exist so as to enable the costs associated with the system get evaluated.

References

Bhalla, G.S. 2001, "Demand and Supply of Food and Foodgrains by 2020" in Towards Hunger Free India (eds) M.D. Asthana and P. Medrano, New Delhi; Manohar.

Chand, R., 2001, "Wheat Exports Little Gain", *Economic and Political Weekly*, 36, 35, June 23.

Damodaran, H., 2002, "Foodgrains Off-Take Surges by 55 percent", *Business Line*, Jan. 21.

George, P.S., 1979, Public Distribution of Foodgrains in Kerala, Income Distribution, Implications and Effectiveness IFPRI, Research Report, 7 March.

Government of India (1997a), "Focus on Poor", Ministry of Civil Supplies, Consumers Affairs and Public Distribution, New Delhi.

Government of India (1997b), "Ministry of Rural Areas and Employment, Department of Rural Employment and Poverty Alleviation, Letter No. M-28012/16/91-IRD.III", New Delhi (April 1997).

Kriesel, S. and S. Zaidi, 1999, "The Targeted Public Distribution System in Uttar Pradesh, India—A Evaluation", Draft Paper, The World Bank, Washington, August.

Krishna Kumar, 2000 "Public Distribution System: A system in Peril", *Frontline*, 17 (19) Sept. 16-29.

Madura Swaminathan, "Excluding the Needy: The Public Provisioning of Food in India", *Social Scientist*, Vol. 30, Nos. 3-4, March-April 2002.

S.S. Chauhan, "The Food Problem", 1958.

Report of the Famine Commission, 1880.

Census of India Report, Pt. I-A., p. 164.

Late Dr. C.B. Mamoria and Dr. Badri Bishal Tripathi, "Agricultural Problems of India".

Economic Survey, Government of India, Ministry of Finance, 2007-08.

17

Trends in Public Expenditure in Livestock Sector of India during the Period of Economic Reforms

K. Elumalai

I. BACKGROUND

Agricultural sector plays an important role in the Indian economy despite its share in the total GDP has declined to 17.8 per cent in 2007-08. Agriculture provides employment to about 52 per cent of labour force in India. Among the sub-sectors such as livestock, horticulture, forestry and fishery, livestock contributes about 4.7 per cent to total GDP and 24.9 per cent to GDP from total agricultural and allied activities (Government of India, 2006). Besides its traditional role in providing employment, cash liquidity, nutrition through milk, meat and eggs, livestock plays a paramount role in sustaining the livelihoods of poor in marginal areas. According to Planning Commission (2007), livestock contribute about 70 per cent of total agricultural income in the arid regions and over 40 per cent in the semi-arid regions. Further, it acts as insurance against extreme events like drought in these regions.

Livestock sector has registered growth rate of over 4 per cent per annum during the last two decades. India possesses the largest livestock population in the world. According to Livestock Census 2003, there are about 485 million livestock, which comprises 283 million bovines, 186 million ovines (sheet and goat) and 489 million poultry birds. However, for the first time since 1951 that growth in livestock population between two inter-census periods of 1997-2003 was negative with 0.01 per cent. Though deceleration in growth rate is marginal, it has serious implications for livelihood and nutrition security, crop production and ecological sustainability. Livestock produces annually about 800 millions tonnes of manure, most of which are used for crop production (Planning Commission, 2007). Further, even with increasing mechanisation, livestock is still being used as a source of draught power in several parts of the country.

Despite importance of livestock in the rural economy, this sector has suffered due to lack of proper policy attention to improve output and productivity. Public investment, in particular has not increased in commensuration with value of output generated from the sector. Falling investment was observed not only in livestock sector, but also across other sub-sectors of agriculture since 1980s. In fact, Gross Fixed Capital Formation in agriculture as percentage of GDP has declined from 3.4 per cent in 1980-81 to 2.3 per cent in 1990-91 and then to 1.6 per cent in 2001-02 (Government of India, 2003). The decline in gross capital formation was sharp during 1980s and it had further decelerated in 1990s due to contraction in public spending as a result of introduction of structural reforms in response to fiscal crises. Since public investment has crowding-in effect, the private investment has also decelerated over time.

However, in India past research studies have generally focused on the impact of public investment in crop sector growth only or in overall agricultural growth and productivity (Rath, 1989; Dhawan, 1996; Jairath and Purohit, 1996; Dhawan and Yadav, 1997; Fan *et al,* 1999; Chand, 2001). Little research attention has been given to study public investment in sub-sectors of agriculture. Thus, the present study makes a modest attempt to analyse the trends in public spending in livestock sector since the beginning of economic reforms in India. The paper is organised in six sections. The second section presents data sources and the third section analyses expenditure pattern in animal husbandry and dairy development by plan periods. Trends in public spending and the share of public spending in total value of output are discussed respectively in the fourth and fifth sections. Concluding remarks are made in the final section.

II. DATA SOURCES

The data on government expenditure were compiled from annual State Finance Accounts published by Comptroller and Auditor General of India (CAGI). The government accounts are given in six-tier arrangements namely sectors and sub-sectors, major heads, sub-major heads, minor heads, sub-heads, and object heads. The Finance Accounts by State present the transaction up to the level of minor heads, which identify the programmes undertaken to achieve objectives given in the major heads. The revenue (current) expenditure and capital expenditure have been utilized for estimating total public spending in livestock sector for the period 1990-91 to 2004-05. All the expenditures were deflated into 1993-94 prices using the Gross State Domestic Product (GSDP) deflator. Data on value of output from livestock sector were obtained from Basic Animal Husbandry Statistics published by Ministry of Agriculture.

III. EXPENDITURE BY FIVE YEAR PLANS

The Planning Commission, Government of India allocates Central Government funds for development of animal husbandry and dairy sectors through central and centrally sponsored schemes. Except during the Sixth Plan period, total outlay had increased in absolute terms across all the Five-Year Plan periods (Table 1). However, the share of allocation of funds for animal husbandry and dairy development has declined from 1.1 per cent in the First Plan to 0.4 per cent in the Sixth Plan and then to 0.3 per cent in the subsequent plan periods. This is in sharp contrast to the fact that the livestock sector has shown a high rate of growth of 4.0 per cent per annum during the last two decade and an increasing contribution to agricultural GDP.

Animal husbandry accounted for a large share of total outlay in the livestock (animal husbandry plus dairy

TABLE I

Expenditure on Animal Husbandry and Dairy Development by Five-Year Plan

(Rs. Crore)

Plan	*Animal Husbandry*	*Dairy Development*	*Total*	*% AH&D to total outlay*
First Plan (1950-55)	14.2	7.8	22.0	1.1
Second Plan (1955-60)	38.5	17.4	55.9	1.2
Third Plan (1960-65)	54.4	36.1	90.5	1.1
Fourth Plan (1967-72)	94.1	139.0	233.1	1.5
Fifth Plan (1975-80)	-	-	437.5	1.1
Sixth Plan (1980-85)	60.5	336.1	396.6	0.4
Seventh Plan (1985-90)	165.2	302.8	467.9	0.3
Eighth Plan (1992-97)	400.0	900.0	1300.0	0.3
Ninth Plan (1997-2002)	1076.1	469.5	1545.6	0.3
Tenth Plan (2002-07)	1384.0	361.0	1745.0	-

Source: Government of India (2006).

development) sector until the Third Plan. However, the initiation of the Operation Flood Programme in the Fourth Plan attracted substantial amount of funds for the provision of marketing infrastructures for dairy development. The dairy sector received relatively high priority in fund allocation until the middle of the Eighth Plan during which the third phase of the Operation Flood Programme came to an end. With the completion of the Operation Flood Programme, the outlay in the dairy sector has slowed down and the priority in fund allocation has again shifted towards animal husbandry. During the Ninth and Tenth Plans Animal Husbandry received Rs. 1076.1 crore and Rs. 1384.0 crore, respectively.

IV. TRENDS IN PUBLIC EXPENDITURE IN LIVESTOCK SECTOR

Trend in public spending at current and constant prices in animal husbandry and dairy sector of India is presented in Table 2. The public spending in animal husbandry at current prices showed fluctuating trend during 1990-91 to 2004-05. Though it had showed increasing trend between 1996-97 and 2000-01, but slowed down during the last two years of the study period. In dairy sector, public expenditure at current prices showed by and large, increasing trend.

Public spending in animal husbandry at 1993-94 prices ranged between Rs. 5909 million and Rs. 11308 million during 1990-91 to 2004-05. It had, by and large showed declining trend during the last fifteen years. The declining public spending was relatively sharp during 2003-04 and 2004-05. However, public expenditure in dairy development continued to rise until 1995-96 and thereafter declined to recover in 1998-99 and then in 2002-03. At constant prices, public spending in dairy sector ranged between Rs. 10872 million and Rs. 13915 million during 1990-91 to 2004-05.

TABLE 2

Public Expenditure in Animal Husbandry and Dairy at Current and Constant Prices

(Rs. million)

Year	*Current Prices*		*Constant (1993-94) Prices*	
	Husbandry	*Development*	*Husbandry*	*Development*
1990-91	7079	8326	9599	11290
1991-92	6854	9125	8166	10872
1992-93	8628	10464	9455	11468
1993-94	11308	11912	11308	11912
1994-95	11068	13619	10114	12445
1995-96	8403	14974	7043	12550
1996-97	11418	14802	8907	11547
1997-98	12332	16082	9018	11760
1998-99	12585	19003	8526	12875
1999-00	13682	22225	8918	14486
2000-01	14122	19969	8895	12577
2001-02	13844	20506	8433	12492
2002-03	15128	21690	8845	12681
2003-04	12784	22649	7258	12859
2004-05	10936	25752	5909	13915

Source: Finance Accounts, CAGI.

As total expenditure includes both current and capital expenditure, an attempt has also been made to analyse trends in capital expenditure separately. Capital expenditure, i.e. investment in animal husbandry and dairy development at current prices has showed erratic trends during 1990-91 to 2004-05 (Table 3). After a marginal recovery in 1992-93, the real investment in Animal Husbandry has declined from Rs. 326 million to Rs. 265 million in 1995-96. The real investment has reached the peak of Rs. 462 million in 1996-97. But, it has slid down continuously thereafter and recorded Rs. 125 million during 2004-05. In dairy sector, real investment trend has showed secular decline from 1990-91 to 2004-05. It was Rs. 230 million in 1991-92 and declined to Rs. 59 million in 2004-05. Capital expenditure constituted only a smaller share in total

TABLE 3

Percent Share of Major Agricultural and Allied Sectors in Total Public Expenditure in Agriculture at 1993-94 Prices

Year	*Crop*	*Animal Husbandry*	*Dairy Husbandry*	*Fisheries Development*	*Forestry and Wild Life*	*Others**
1990-91	25.1	10.5	8.8	2.4	19.3	33.9
1991-92	27.8	10.2	7.2	2.4	19.7	32.7
1992-93	31.9	9.1	7.5	2.3	17.8	31.4
1993-94	30.3	10.2	9.4	2.6	18.0	29.5
1994-95	29.1	10.2	9.2	2.6	21.0	27.9
1995-96	25.2	12.1	6.1	2.8	22.1	31.8
1996-97	24.6	10.1	7.4	2.7	21.6	33.6
1997-98	25.9	11.0	8.3	2.8	23.1	28.9
1998-99	24.6	10.9	7.2	2.6	23.3	31.4
1999-00	26.8	10.7	6.9	2.7	22.0	30.9
2000-01	24.9	12.0	7.9	2.6	21.8	30.8
2001-02	28.8	12.1	7.6	2.6	22.5	26.3
2002-03	29.0	12.9	6.6	2.7	23.3	25.5
2003-04	28.8	13.5	6.6	2.7	23.5	24.9
2004-05	23.7	11.7	4.5	2.3	19.6	38.2

* include soil and water conservation, plantation, food storage and warehousing, agricultural research and cooperation.

Source: Finance Accounts, CAGI.

public expenditure. In Animal Husbandry, the share of capital expenditure hovered from 2 to 5 per cent only. For dairy development, the share of capital expenditure was little over one per cent only until 1996-97 and even it has declined thereafter.

Meanwhile, the agriculture sector as a whole had witnessed slump in public spending during 1990s. This had resulted in the contraction of allocation of resources among sub-sectors. Within agriculture, the pattern of public spending has varied depending on the priorities of the central and state governments. The per cent share of total public spending in animal husbandry and dairy sector relative to other major sub-sectors of agriculture like crop husbandry, fisheries and forestry and wild life is presented in Table 4. Crop husbandry accounted for a little over a quarter of total expenditure in agriculture and allied sectors during 1990-91 to 2004-05. The share of animal husbandry varied from 10-13 per cent during the last fifteen years. Though the expenditure in this sector showed accelerating mode from 2000-01, it declined during the recent year. In case of dairy development, the share of public spending declined sharply since 1995-96. The falling share was drastic during the recent years: from 7.7 per cent in 2000-01 to 4.5 per cent in 2004-05.

The public spending in fisheries remained constant at about 3.0 per cent during 1990-91 to 2004-05. The forestry and wild life sector also witnessed stagnation in public investment during most of the years and it even declined in the recent years. Others comprised soil and water conservation, plantation, food storage and warehousing, agricultural research and education and cooperation. The other categories accounted for a little over one-third of total public investment.

The pattern of public investment in animal husbandry and dairy development in selected years at constant prices by states is given in Table 5. The pattern of expenditure has varied between animal husbandry and dairy development across the states. Animal husbandry accounted for the largest share, but in Maharashtra and West Bengal the spending in dairy development was considerable. The public investment in animal husbandry has been increasing in Jammu and Kashmir, Karnataka, Kerala, Madhya Pradesh, Maharashtra, Manipur, Meghalaya, Sikkim and Uttar Pradesh. In 2004-05 it was the highest in Maharashtra (Rs. 10078.2 million) followed by

TABLE 4

Public Expenditure in Animal Husbandry and Dairy Development in Major States at 1993-94 Prices

(Rs. Million)

States	*1990-91*		*1994-95*		*1998-99*		*2004-05*	
	Animal Husbandry	*Dairy Development*	*Animal Husbandry*	*Dairy Development*	*Animal Husbandry*	*Dairy Development*	*Animal Husbandry*	*Dairy Development*
Andhra Pradesh	647.1	17.3	445.3	1.8	689.5	54.2	1559.0	0.0
Arunachal Pradesh	79.0	2.8	159.8	6.3	85.7	2.8	163.2	4.7
Assam	623.6	76.5	535.2	64.4	930.1	87.1	743.2	84.2
Bihar	908.5	64.1	2659.3	27.5	930.2	61.1	737.4	104.5
Goa	42.5	1.8	50.5	3.2	77.2	4.0	71.4	9.8
Gujarat	236.7	4.5	442.4	44.2	740.2	11.1	558.8	8.4
Haryana	229.7	29.3	364.7	16.8	853.6	38.2	745.4	12.8
Himachal Pradesh	123.6	9.3	215.6	21.0	447.7	41.2	420.2	37.1
Jammu and Kashmir	268.5	8.9	385.1	9.1	693.6	10.6	721.3	0.0
Kerala	171.2	21.1	328.4	75.4	581.7	117.0	678.5	84.5
Madhya Pradesh	395.3	60.3	602.4	124.8	1200.7	146.6	3013.8	0.0
Maharashtra	3097.9	2772.2	4702.0	4195.4	6264.4	5566.0	10078.2	7733.6
Manipur	55.0	3.6	55.9	3.1	83.7	2.6	271.0	9.1
Meghalaya	44.3	7.2	58.9	10.4	121.0	16.8	291.8	56.3
Mizoram	94.4	10.0	58.8	7.1	65.2	7.1	200.0	10.3
Nagaland	162.1	10.0	103.0	1.7	82.8	7.0	214.3	7.1
Orissa	333.2	16.4	611.9	62.1	1167.7	61.6	674.0	36.2
Punjab	453.1	80.5	525.0	27.2	1243.9	60.5	805.3	33.7
Rajasthan	410.6	32.9	634.2	52.5	1159.0	0.3	846.1	6.0
Sikkim	33.8	2.4	60.8	15.2	89.6	3.4	101.2	28.2
Tamil Nadu	507.4	32.6	841.1	56.2	1570.9	158.1	802.4	69.8
Tripura	57.2	5.3	102.2	18.4	162.7	7.0	145.9	5.4
Uttar Pradesh	518.8	78.8	844.3	148.3	1215.5	74.8	1443.3	17 8.6
West Bengal	641.4	360.0	843.3	516.4	1672.1	848.6	1195.4	480.1

Source: Finance Accounts, CAGI.

Madhya Pradesh (Rs. 3013.8 million) and Andhra Pradesh (Rs. 1559.0 million). However, in the major states like Gujarat, Haryana, Orissa, Rajasthan, Tamil Nadu, West Bengal, it has declined during recent years. The declining public investment in animal husbandry is a major concern for maintaining higher growth rate in this sector.

After the third phase of Operation Flood Programme, most of the states pruned expenditure on dairy development. This had led to reduction in capital expenditure across the states. The falling investment in dairy sector is evident since mid-nineties in most of the Indian states. Public spending in dairying in West Bengal continued to rise although it has been reduced in 2004-05. However, Maharashtra continued to maintain a high level of spending on the dairy sector, amounting to Rs. 7733.6 million in 2004-05.

An important point to note is that higher public spending does not necessarily result in productivity growth. A rise in public spending might be the result of subsidies that state governments provide in the form of supply of milk to consumers at cheaper prices, supply of breeding services like artificial insemination at a nominal rate or supply of fodder seeds and cuttings at subsidized rates, etc.

V. SHARE OF PUBLIC EXPENDITURE IN VALUE OF OUTPUT

Figure 1 shows the public investment as proportion of value of output from India's livestock sector. The percentage of

FIGURE 1

Public Investment as Percentage of Value of Output from Livestock

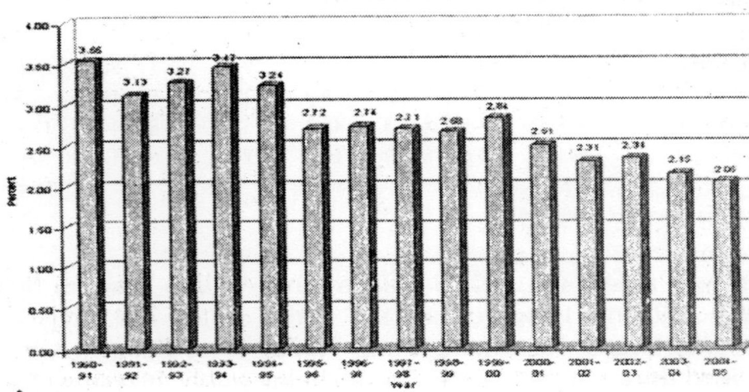

TABLE 5

Per cent Share of Public Expenditure in Total Value of Output at 1993-94 Prices

States	*TE 1992-93*	*TE 1995-96*	*TE 1998-99*	*TE 2002-03*
Andhra Pradesh	1.16	1.08	1.46	1.37
Arunachal Pradesh	9.49	19.60	13.68	18.71
Assam	4.61	3.62	5.26	4.23
Bihar	1.87	3.20	1.03	1.26
Goa	7.91	5.95	7.07	8.61
Gujarat	1.10	1.44	1.30	1.38
Haryana	0.80	1.08	1.36	1.54
Himachal Pradesh	2.82	4.16	5.01	5.89
Jammu and Kashmir	4.55	3.94	4.06	4.19
Karnataka	1.25	1.37	1.90	1.76
Kerala	1.23	1.60	2.36	2.86
Madhya Pradesh	1.13	1.23	2.12	2.60
Maharashtra	7.23	11.93	9.77	13.22
Manipur	5.34	6.34	10.56	7.83
Meghalaya	4.85	5.88	7.88	8.41
Mizoram	12.99	12.40	13.93	16.55
Nagaland	8.54	10.46	10.83	7.63
Orissa	2.84	4.98	7.00	4.71
Punjab	0.69	0.79	1.35	1.53
Rajasthan	1.20	1.04	1.39	1.37
Sikkim	17.67	30.80	23.62	32.71
Tamil Nadu	1.62	2.44	2.85	2.68
Tripura	6.26	8.03	7.76	9.02
Uttar Pradesh	0.89	0.98	1.29	0.81
West Bengal	2.07	1.66	2.95	4.04

Source: Finance Accounts, CAGI.

public investment in total value of output has continued to decline during the last fifteen years. The share of public investment in total value of output was 3.55 per cent in 1990-91 and has declined during subsequent years and recovered marginally in 1993-94. However, the deceleration momentum continued thereafter. The falling share was dramatic from mid-1990s. During 2004-05, the public spending as the proportion of value of output was 2.06 per cent.

VI. CONCLUDING REMARKS

Public spending in agriculture sector has declined during nineties. The structural reforms have affected the level of investment in across sub-sectors of agriculture. The limited availability of resources led to competing allocation among different sub-sectors like crop husbandry, animal husbandry, dairy development, fisheries and forestry and wildlife. Livestock sector suffered stagnation in investment throughout nineties. The proportion of public investment in Gross Domestic Product from livestock has declined continuously from 5.0 per cent in 1990-91 to 3 per cent in 2004-05. Similarly, its share in value of output has declined from 3.55 per cent in 1990-91 to 2.06 per cent in 2004-05.

Declining public investment is the cause of the concern among the policy-makers and development planners as it has implications for accelerating growth in livestock production and capacity of the sector to meet to the future demand emanating from domestic and global markets. There is a need to reverse this falling trend in public spending in order to promote sustainable growth in livestock production on which millions of people depend on for their livelihood.

References

Chand, Ramesh (2001). "Emerging Trends and Issues in Public and Private Investments in Indian Agriculture", *Indian Journal of Agricultural Economics*, 56(2): 161-184, April-June.

Dhawan B.D. and S.S. Yadav (1997). "Public Investments in Indian Agriculture: Trends and Determinants", *Economic and Political Weekly*, 32(14): 710-14, April 5.

Dhawan, B.D. (1996). "Trends and Determinants of Capital Investment in Agriculture", *Indian Journal of Agricultural Economics*, 54(4), October-December.

Fan, Shenggen, Peter Hazell, Sukhadeo Thorat (1999). "Linkages between Government Spending, Growth and Poverty in Rural India", Research Report 110, International Food Policy Research Institute (IFPRI), Washington, D.C.

Government of India (2003). Report of the Committee on Capital Formation in Agriculture, Ministry of Agriculture, Government of India, New Delhi.

Government of India (2006). Basic Animal Husbandry Statistics 2006, Ministry of Agriculture, Government of India, New Delhi.

Jairath, M.S. and Brijesh C. Purohit (1996). "Trends in Capital Formation in Agriculture—A Case of Arid India", *Indian Journal of Agricultural Economics*, 51(4), October-December.

Rath, Nilakantha (1989). "Agricultural Growth and Investment in India", *Journal of Indian School of Political Economy*, 1(1), January-June.

18

Impact of WTO on Indian Agriculture with Special Reference to Livestock Sector

RAJENDER KUMAR

With the signing of agreement and attaining the membership of WTO, the international trade restrictions and regulations are gradually melting away. The traditional livestock and livestock sector, which had been under high level of government interventions and regulations has now moved to a situation, where there are commonly acceptable trade barriers, export subsidies restraints and minimum market access provisions that are sure to put the industry on new gears. The combined effect of both the macroeconomic reforms and WTO commitments may enter into the new environment in which the livestock industry will operate. The liberalization of trade in livestock and livestock products under the agreement on agriculture (AOA) would bring significant changes in the production, marketing and stock of various livestock products. It would provide unlimited opportunities to the developing countries like India and devise the ways and means to increase the production of livestock and livestock products. The livestock industry is showing structural changes in the trade pattern.

This development at the domestic and global level indicates that Indian livestock industry has to compete and face the world market. In view of this, the projection and potential changes, the opinion, whether the impact of trade liberalization would be beneficial or adverse to the Indian livestock industry is sharply divided. Little effort has been made so far to assess the performance of livestock industry in the liberal and global framework.

Objectives

Thus keeping in view the above the study covers the following objectives:

- To compare the production and performance of livestock and livestock product industry in the pre and post-WTO agreement period, and
- To assess the competitiveness of Indian livestock and livestock products in a global framework.

Data Collection

This study is based on the secondary data. The required data have been collected from various government records/ publications and also from various Websites. It is a time series data and the relevant data have been collected from the period of 1984-85 to 2004-05.

Analytical Tools

The data collected, tabulated was subjected to statistical analysis as per the objectives of the study. Tabular analysis and quantitative techniques have been used for analysis of data.

Results and Discussion

Comparison of production and performance of Indian livestock products in pre-AOA and post-AOA period

A comparison of the production and performance of Indian livestock products in pre-AOA and post-AOA period, the average production and coefficient of variation of various products was ascertained and presented in Table 1.

Growth Rates of Production of livestock products in India in pre-AOA and post-AOA period.

TABLE I

A Comparison of Production of Indian Livestock Products in Pre-AOA and Post-AOA Period

(000 Tonnes)

Products	*Pre-AOA (1984-85 to 1994-95)*		*Post-AOA (1995-96 to 2004-05)*		*Quantity Gap (%)*
	AVG	*CV*	*AVG*	*CV*	
Milk (MT)	50.63	12.47	81.06	14.31	60.10
Eggs (Million No.)	19484.9	16.19	35659.84	21.93	83.01
Wool (Million Kg.)	40.35	2.57	46.18	6.41	14.44
Beef and Veal	801.5	67.55	1424.8	3.09	77.76
Buffalo Meat	775.1	65.17	1412.8	3.15	82.27
Mutton and Lamb	166.8	12.61	227.4	3.51	36.33
Goat Meat	408	9.41	464.2	1.71	13.77
Poultry Meat	327.4	46.26	1090.4	38.80	233.04
Pig Meat	303.4	52.00	484.3	3.24	59.62
Total Meat	3098.8	41.90	5241.1	10.13	69.13

To have a comparison of growth rate of production of various livestock products produced in India in the pre-AOA and post-AOA period, annual Compound Growth Rate was ascertained and presented in Table 2.

It could be observed from the Table 2 that the annual growth rate of production were low in the post-AOA period as compared to the pre-AOA period for most of the products except egg and wool, which is but natural since with the start of various development projects the increase in production is very high in the initial stages but in the subsequent years though it increased but the increase was comparatively lower. Rather, it could be said that the production becomes more or less stagnant. This is in the case of all the biological products. The heat is being felt in the production of Wheat and Paddy, which increased at a very high rate with the onset of Green Revolution but now the production of wheat and paddy too become stagnant or the increase is very little. In the case of wool, the compound growth rate is slightly higher because of the late take-off period. In case of negative growth rate, the percentage rate of change in the pre-

TABLE 2

Annual Compound Growth Rate of Production of Livestock Products in India in Pre-AOA and Post-AOA Period

(000 Tonnes)

Products	*Pre-AOA (19984-85 to 1994-95)*	*Post-AOA (1995-96 to 2002-05)*	*% Change*
Milk (MT)	4.19	3.76	-10.26
Eggs (Million No.)	5.59	5.70	1.96
Wool (Million Kg)	0.12	1.01	741.66
Beef and Veal	33.96	1.02	-96.99
Buffalo Meat	32.86	1.02	-96.89
Mutton of Lamb	3.73	1.15	-69.16
Goat Meat	1.03	0.55	-46.60
Poultry Meat	15.96	13.53	-15.22
Pig Meat	23.98	0.04	-99.83
Total Meat	17.53	3.29	-81.23

AOA and post-AOA period varied between 10 to 100 percent while in case of eggs and wool the growth rate was positive and varied from 2 percent to 742 percent.

II Growth trends in production of livestock and livestock products: India and the world.

To ascertain the progress made by India in the pre-AOA and post-AOA period in the world trade, India's share in the production of various livestock products was ascertained in the pre-AOA and post-AOA period. The coefficient of variation too were worked out and presented in Table 3.

It could be observed from the Table 3 that the production in India increased at a much faster rate as compared to that of total production in the World. The coefficient of variation was low in the post-AOA period both for India and the World except for eggs in case of India. Because of the increase in production, India's share in the total world export also increased substantially. India's share in the pre-AOA period was only 9 percent for milk which increased to 14 percent in the post-AOA period showing an increase of over 59 percent in the post-AOA

TABLE 3

Production of Livestock and Livestock Products in India and the World in pre-AOA and post-AOA Period

(000 MT)

Production		*India*		*World*		*India's in Production*		
		(1984-85 to 1994-95)	*(19996 to 2004-05)*					
		Pre-AOA	*Post-AOA*	*Pre-AOA*	*Post-AOA*	*Pre-AOA*	*Post-AOA*	*% Change*
Milk	Avg.	44820.33	81847.25	508259.70	583751.80	8.81	14.02	59.14%
		CV	22.18	12.20	6.66	4.17		
Eggs	Avg.	920	1568.25	31740	51895.70	2.89	3.02	4.5%
		CV	33.39	60.74	15.37	8.96		
Beef veal	Avg.	1013.33	1445.25	50941.67	56935	1.98	2.53	27.78%
		CV	18.83	3.80	9.77	3.24		
Poultry meat	Avg.	220	565.75	34672	69312.5	0.63	0.81	28.57%
		CV	56.77	10.22	22.77	12.63		
Mutton Lamb	Avg.	172.33	228	6395	7557.50	2.69	3.01	11.90%
		CV	7.55	3.03	10.06	5.27		
Total Meat	Avg.	3290.33	5081.25	160860.70	231313	2.04	2.19	7.35%
		CV	20.01	11.78	13.92	7.22		

period. India's share in the world production of beef and veal and poultry meat also registered an increase of over 28 percent. In case of mutton too, the percentage increase was found to be 12 percent. Considering all type of meat, the increase in the post-AOA period was found to be more than 7 percent. Eggs were only commodity where the increase was found to be about 4.5 percent. This lead to conclude that WTO had a positive impact on India and its share in the total exports increased tremendously for almost all the products. This could be attributed to the reduction in subsidies granted by various governments on the various products exported by them since

India doesn't subsidize export so it became competitive which is further ascertained and presented in Table 4. To ascertain this, NPC of various livestock products in the pre-AOA and post-AOA period was ascertained.

Nominal Protection Coefficient (NPC)

The estimates of NPC, as defined by the Indian export to World export price ratio, are presented in Table 4.

TABLE 4

Nominal Protection Coefficients of Livestock Products in Pre-AOA and Post-AOA Period

Year	*Bovines*	*Meat (fresh, chilled or frozen)*	*Meat offal fresh*	*Cheese and Curd*
Pre-AOA				
1984-85	10.83	0.89	1.06	-
1986-87	1.00	0.78	1.12	-
1988-89	0.58	0.50	0.57	0.16
1990-91	0.62	0.41	-	0.17
1992-93	0.50	0.42	-	0.84
1993-94	0.50	0.43	-	-
AVG.	2.33	0.57	1.09	0.39
Post-AOA				
1995-96	0.07	0.47	-	0.48
1997-98	-	0.53	1.18	0.50
1999-2000	-	0.59	0	0.79
2001-02	-	0.61	0.60	0.71
2003-04	0.15	0.53	0.38	0.41
AVG.	0.11	0.54	0.72	0.57

It could be observed from the Table 4 that the NPC for bovines was more than unity (2.33) in the pre-AOA period. Hence, it is not competitive. In the post-AOA period, NPC was reduced to 0.11 which made the product very competitive in the world export. Similarly, in case of meat offal fresh, NPC in pre-AOA period was more than unity (1.09) and hence not competitive. In the post-AOA period, the values of NPC were less than unity and hence became competitive product.

CONCLUSION AND SUGGESTIONS

Finally, it is observed that the average production in the post-AOA period was much higher as compared to the pre AOA period showing that there is a positive impact of WTO. However, the annual growth rate of production was low in the post-AOA period as compared to the pre AOA period for most of the products except egg and wool. Further, the study reveals that livestock production in India increased at a much faster rate as compared to that of production in the world. NPC was more than unit pre-AOA period for bovines and meat offal fresh but was less than unity in post-AOA period. They were not competitive in pre AOA period but become competitive in post-AOA period showing positive impact of WTO. Thus, it may be concluded that India is not yet a major player in the World livestock and livestock product market. It is imperative to improve by enhancing India's trade competitiveness and achieving the status of net exporter of those products in which India has a comparative advantage. The following suggestions are made:

- India is very rich in terms of livestock resources. Since the production and productivity of the available cattle and buffalo breeds is very low. There is therefore, a great need to develop cost effective new technologies in the area of animal breeding, fodder and feed resources and animal disease control. Though India has become the highest producer of milk, but the livestock strength is also highest.
- Cost effective processing and packaging technologies should be developed for dairy and meat industry and an attempt should be made to develop packaging technologies for enhancing the shelf life and keeping qualities of various processed products.
- IPR should be registered for production and export of various indigenous products like lassi, milk-based indigenous sweets like barfi, rassogullah, gulabjamun, rabri, etc.
- In all the spheres of production of the various value

added livestock products, cost reduction measures should be used to reduce the cost so as to compete with the other countries of world in the global market.

Finally, it may be concluded that the combined effects of both macroeconomic reforms and WTO commitments have entered into the new environment in which the livestock industry is operating. The Livestock industry is showing structural changes in the trade pattern. This development at the domestic and global level indicates that Indian livestock industry has to compete and face the world market. It is hoped that findings of this study will certainly help the Indian livestock sector to be more competitive and compatible in the new regime of WTO.

Index